GENDER INEQUALITY

A Comparative Study
of Discrimination and Participation

SAGE STUDIES
IN INTERNATIONAL SOCIOLOGY

Editorial Board

GENDER INEQUALITY

A Comparative Study of
Discrimination and Participation

Mino Vianello ● Renata Siemienska

Natalia Damian ● Eugen Lupri

Renato Coppi ● Enzo D'Arcangelo ● Sergio Bolasco

Foreword by Cynthia Fuchs Epstein

 SAGE Studies in International Sociology 39
sponsored by the International Sociological Association/ISA

SAGE Publications Ltd
28 Banner Street
London EC1Y 8QE

SAGE Publications Inc
2111 West Hillcrest Drive
Newbury Park, California 91320

SAGE Publications India Pvt Ltd
32, M-Block Market
Greater Kailash - I
New Delhi 110 048

British Library Cataloguing in Publication data available

Library of Congress catalog card number 90-60195

Typeset by Centro Interdipartimentale per il Calcolo Scientificio dell'Università di Roma "La Sapienza"
Printed in Great Britain by Billing and Sons Ltd, Worcester

CONTENTS

GENERAL APPENDICES 251

SPECIFIC APPENDICES 338

References 347

Index of Names 357

THE AUTHORS

Sergio Bolasco,   Associate Professor, Dept. of Sociology and Political Science, University of Salerno.

Renato Coppi,   Professor, Dept. of Statistics, University of Rome.

Natalia Damian,   Former Associate Professor at the University of Bucharest, now Assistant to the Research Division, Ministry of Immigrants' Absorption, Jerusalem.

Enzo D'Arcangelo,   Associate Professor, Dept. of Statistics, University of Rome.

Eugen Lupri,   Professor, Institute of Sociology, University of Calgary.

Renata Siemienska,   Associate Professor, Institute of Sociology, University of Warsaw.

Mino Vianello,   Professor, Interdisciplinary Group for Social Research, Faculty of Statistics, University of Rome.

Pur mo venian li tuoi pensieri tra i miei
con simile atto e con simile faccia,
sì che d'entrambi un sol consiglio fei.

Dante, *Inferno*, XXIII, 28-30

PREFACE

This book is the product of solid empirical research. It is an *experimental* study --- and we emphasize this feature from the outset --- which is designed to answer crucial questions such as: what are the factors that favour or hinder the access of women to power? Is the current opinion that equates public with male and private with female still tenable? Do women in a socialist system fare better than women in a capitalist system; if so, in what ways? The answers to such questions show that the evolution towards gender equality is affecting all spheres of life. It is undoubtedly one of the greatest transformations since the dawn of human history. We are not concerned with countries, utopias and ideological mumbling, nor do we refrain from lengthy analyses: we are interested in facts and their relevance at the theoretical level --- and we strive hard to that end. The readers of this book will need to be patient but the words of the Talmud may be of comfort to them: "Patience needs a long time, because it yields fruits that last for a long time."

* * *

This is a jointly authored work, conceived in a unitary way, and not an edited collection of papers. Authorship is as follows:

The Introduction was prepared by Mino Vianello.

Chapter 1, *The Context of the Research,* was jointly authored by Natalia Damian, Eugen Lupri, Renata Siemienska and Mino Vianello.

Chapter 2, *Gender Differences and Values*, and chapter 4, *At Work*, were written by Renata Siemienska.

Chapter 3, *In the Family*, was written by Mino Vianello and was later submitted to Eugen Lupri, a specialist in the field of Family Sociology, for his advice; note 10 is his.

Chapter 5, *Public Participation*, was written by Mino Vianello.

The Conclusion was prepared by Renata Siemienska (first part); by Sergio Bolasco, Renato Coppi and Enzo D'Arcangelo (second part); and by Mino Vianello (third part).

Appendix A, *Basic Information Concerning Women in the Four Countries*, was prepared: for Canada by Eugen Lupri, for Italy by Mino Vianello, for Poland by Renata Siemienska, and for Romania by Natalia Damian.

Appendix B, *Multivariate Statistical Analysis of the Determinants of Men's and Women's Public Participation*, was jointly authored by Sergio Bolasco, Enzo D'Arcangelo and Renato Coppi.

Appendix C, *The Sample Demographic Structure*, was written by Renata Siemienska.

The Specific Appendices were prepared by Mino Vianello.

The final draft of the entire book was done by Mino Vianello in co-operation with Renata Siemienska.

Mino Vianello

Rome

ACKNOWLEDGEMENTS

The obligations incurred in carrying out this research are many and varied. We are indebted above all to the many scholars, mostly women, who have long been working on gender problems. We have drawn largely upon the body of knowledge built up through their efforts. This book has also benefited decisively from the stimulating work in the area of participation carried out with exceptional vigour over many years by Sidney Verba. He has generously contributed helpful critical comments on some of the chapters.

We are grateful to Prof. Judith Buber Agassi of J.W. Goethe Universität, West Germany; Prof. Colin Campbell of Georgetown University, Prof. Theodore Caplow of the University of Virginia, Prof. Carol Christy of the University of Ohio, Prof. Beverly Cook of the University of Wisconsin, Prof. Jean Bethke Elshtain of Vanderbilt University, Prof. Cynthia Fuchs Epstein of the City University of New York, Prof. Jane Jacquette of the Occidental College, all USA; Prof. Janine Mossuz-Lavau of the Centre d'Etude de la Vie Politique Française Contemporaine of the Centre Nationale des Recherches Scientifiques (CNRS) in Paris; Prof. Carole Pateman of Sydney University, Australia; Prof. Gregory Smith of the American University in Rome; Prof. György Széll of the University of Osnabrück, West Germany; and Prof. Susan Welch of the University of Nebraska, USA. All of them kindly read the whole manuscript and made valuable suggestions.

We are also grateful to Dr. Anna Birindelli of the University of Rome, Prof. Andrée Michel of the Study Group on Sex Roles of the CNRS in Paris, Prof. Menachem Rosner of Haifa University, Israel and Prof. Giovanni Sgritta of the University of Rome, all of whose criticisms helped to improve chapter 3, on gender differences in the family. To them, and to many others who go unnamed, we are deeply grateful.

We are especially indebted to Nathan Glazer for his gift of time and knowledge, and the support he gave us in several ways.

The Consiglio Nazionale delle Ricerche deserves thanks for the financial assistance it has given us, as well as the University of Rome which repeatedly came to our aid with substantial grants.

The demanding work at the computer was done promptly and competently by Silvano Salvatore and Marcello Stazi.

Our warmest thanks go to Dr. Letizia Caddeo and Dr. Gianna Sbordoni who assisted us with such perseverance in the various phases of the research.

The English-language draft was first revised by Prof. Sarah Griffith and later carefully edited by Dr. Siba Kumar Das.

We should like to thank in particular Dr. Massimo Carlucci for his continuous assistance in the preparation of the manuscript and Dr. Francesco Bianchi as well as Dr. Marco Congia for their expertise in following all the stages in the preparation of the type-setting.

ABBREVIATIONS

The following abbreviations are used throughout the tables and figures:

BCW   Blue-collar workers
DM   Decision-makers
FBCW   Female blue-collar workers
FDM   Female decision-makers
FT   Female teachers
FWCW   Female white-collar workers
HW   Housewives
MBCW   Male blue-collar workers
MDM   Male decision-makers
MOW   Men out of work
MT   Male teachers
MWCW   Male white-collar workers
POW   People out of work
T   Teachers
WCW   White-collar workers

The following abbreviations are used for methods of statistical analysis, especially in the appendices:

CoA   Correspondence Analysis
MCA   Multiple Classification Analysis
MCoA   Multiple Correspondence Analysis
PCA   Principal Component Analysis
SCoA   Simple Correspondence Analysis

HISTORY OF THE RESEARCH

In 1972, at the Annual Congress of the Yugoslavian Sociological Association in Portorose, Mino Vianello proposed to some sociologists from different countries a comparative research project on women's participation in decision-making. A conference was duly organized near Zagreb in 1973, thanks to a grant from the Consiglio Nazionale delle Ricerche, which also generously financed the successive phases concerning the international co-ordination of the research as well as the collection of data in Italy (the collection of data in each country was covered financially by local sources). The conference was attended by Sheila Allen (UK), Berit Ås (Norway), Tinye Backus (Netherlands), Margarethe Brothun (Federal Republic of Germany), Caroline Dexter (USA), Tamara Dobrin (Romania), Cornelia Flora (USA), Barbara Lodbozinska (Poland), Elina Haavio-Mannila (Finland), Miro Mihovilovic (Yugoslavia), Lazslo Molnar (Hungary), and Mino Vianello (Italy).

After a further extensive exchange of ideas with other colleagues throughout the world, Vianello organized in 1976 a meeting in Assisi of those people who proved to be actively interested in carrying out empirical research. The following participated in this meeting: Riitta Auvinen (Finland), Hedy D'Ancona (Netherlands), Tamara Dobrin (Romania), Margrit Eichler (Canada), Miro Mihovilovic (Yugoslavia), Olive Robinson (UK), Renata Siemienska (Poland), and Mino Vianello (Italy).

Unfortunately, no scholar among those contacted from countries that it would have been extremely interesting to have in the sample (such as France, the two Germanies, Hungary, the Scandinavian commonwealth, the UK, and the USA) proved to have the time or the facilities to participate in such complex research.

Two further meetings (1978 and 1980) in Ariccia, near Rome, were attended by Natalia Damian (Romania, first meeting), Tamara Dobrin (Romania, second meeting), Hedy D'Ancona (Netherlands, first meeting), Margrit Eichler (Canada), Renata Siemienska (Poland), Mino Vianello (Italy). During the first of these meetings, the results of the pre-test (in 1976, of about 100 cases in each country) were discussed and a questionnaire prepared; during the second, a plan of analysis of the data --- collected in the meantime in Canada, Italy, Poland and Romania --- was elaborated.

Another meeting, which had been held in Kalisz, Poland, in 1979, was attended by Margrit Eichler, Renata Siemienska and Mino Vianello.

Thanks to a grant from the Consiglio Nazionale delle Ricerche, Renata Siemienska could meet the cost of staying several times in Rome to work with Mino Vianello, while the travelling expenses were financed as part of Polish National Project III.2. In 1982 Tamara Dobrin and Margrit Eichler could no longer participate in the research and their places were respectively taken for Appendix A by Natalia Damian and Eugen Lupri, while the analysis carried out in the text was redistributed between Renata Siemienska and Mino Vianello.

FOREWORD

In the last two decades, inquiry into the basis for gender inequality has evoked interest in the theoretical framework for interpreting distinctions between the sexes, and has spurred research activity. No subject evokes more debate than analysis of gender distinctions. It has challenged the very roots of scientific inquiry in the social and biological sciences. The problems of bias have been of concern on every level of analysis, yet there is little agreement even about what constitutes bias. Ideology has infused the discussion and debates about gender bias within the scientific community have been politicized.

Cultural assumptions about the inevitability of differences between the sexes have persuaded observers, both within and outside the scientific community, that a person's sex status accounts for his or her behaviour and attitudes. This is usually true whether the interpretation of sex differences is "positive" or "negative", in the sense that one sex is viewed as deficient in attributes accorded to the other sex.

Dedication to the notion of immutable or entrenched sex differences may be found in many contemporary studies as well as those of the past. Indeed, many feminist writers adhere to the difference model, specifying distinct attributes for each sex, in attitudes and behaviour and in emotion and cognition. They claim that women, in contrast to men, are more "caring"; more attuned to personal relationships; less concerned about success; more oriented to the home. Many of the scholars claim that women have different values and even a different culture.

These assumptions are not new; they have been part of conventional wisdom for many eras and they have appeared and reappeared in various theoretical frameworks: human capital theory in economics, evolution theory in sociobiology, and psychoanalytic theory. All of these assume basic and universal differences between the sexes.

However, such assumptions, although they persist, are being challenged. New techniques (meta-analysis, for example) permit review and re-assessment of many past studies. Some of this work (see Feingold, 1988 for a review) shows that cognitive differences between men and women are disappearing. The traditional theories have also been investigated and questioned with regard to their logic and inner consistency. In an investigation of many disciplines and subfields within them, I have found that most distinctions believed to be peculiar to either sex are deceptive (Epstein, 1988). When subjected to rigorous analysis they often prove to be entirely ephemeral or superficial, to be products of labelling or of symbolic separateness. Many distinctions that can be measured are not universal but are specific situations which change as social circumstances change. Some distinctions seem to hold over time because considerable social effort is exerted to insure that they do not diminish. The social controls of law, social policy, etiquette and convention act as powerful mechanisms by which gender distinctions conform to cultural expectations.

The analysis on which these conclusions rest is drawn from a body of scholarship of which this current volume is an important example. This scholarship addresses the basic question asked by the social science enterprise: "Is reality so?"

In this important effort, Mino Vianello and his associates, Sergio Bolasco, Renato Coppi, Natalia Damian, Enzo D'Arcangelo, Eugen Lupri and Renata Siemienska, grapple with questions of differences that lead to social equality, attempting to find out what is so, and what is not. Their inquiry is ambitious, multi-dimensional and cross-national, which is necessary if one is responsibly to address questions of universality. Thus, this inquiry is a pleasing antidote to the overgeneralized conclusions of social scientists who depend on local subjects, often children or college students in experimental social psychology laboratories, to provide evidence for grand theories of gender distinctiveness.

Vianello and his colleagues seek to compare and contrast women and men in countries chosen for their political and ideological differences, their exposure to women's movement activism, and their secular or religious orientation. Within each country they compare women and men at different levels of the economic and political hierarchy, from workers to decision-makers.

The findings of these studies are often surprising and run contrary to popular wisdom. The reader will find much to consider. Although it is important to locate these findings in the rich detail of the study, I shall point to certain themes in an overture to the main discussion.

Social class, religion, and the presence of a women's movement are important factors affecting people's attitudes towards gender equality, women's access to work and political life, and women's responsibilities to the family. For example, although

Socialist doctrine in Poland and Romania specifies egalitarian ideology, respondents in these countries are more conservative on many issues than are those in Italy and 'Canada, where feminist issues have become a matter of public debate. Furthermore, in Communist Poland, the impact of Catholic Church doctrine may be seen in the conservative views of Poles towards women's roles in society, and similarly in Italy, although there women's movement ideology competes to a certain extent with Catholic doctrine. It is not surprising to find that blue collar workers in all countries tend to express the most traditional points of view regarding the sex division of labour in the home; tolerance of deviance from traditional customs and ideas seems to rise with education and social class position generally (McClosky and Brill, 1983).

But when one moves from normative views about customs and social arrangements, the studies show that men and women share similar motivations about such basic activities as work. In all countries, women and men find satisfaction in work and say they would continue to work even if their financial situation made it no longer necessary. This viewpoint does decline slightly for those whose work is probably the most taxing, namely blue-collar workers in Canada and Italy. Romanian and Polish workers are less negative on this matter, which may have to do with ideology and a work environment different from that of capitalist societies.

In all countries, women and men accept or reject promotions at work for similar reasons. Family considerations are named by men as well as women as reasons for refusing promotions; in socialist countries, workers are concerned with being criticized by co-workers for advancing before them. Yet, in a few areas, not only do men and women show differing outlooks, but they also differ in ways that run counter to the stereotypes. For example, more men than women turn down promotions because they are concerned that they cannot handle new responsibilities.

In all countries, a vast majority of the people interviewed claim to support equal opportunities for women, but there is ambivalence about how this view should be accomplished. In all four countries, for example, most people are ready to fire women from jobs when the choice is between a man and a woman.

Other research indicates that in many societies women's access to positions of power has less to do with either their traditional duties in the home (although the burden falls heavily on women with little assistance from men) or their lack of interest in political or public affairs than with the barriers that they face in the tracking system (see Epstein and Coser, 1981). Women can surmount these barriers if they are members of the Communist Party in Eastern Europe and some Third World countries, or if, in capitalist countries, they can muster political patronage and support and can raise money for campaigns. Everywhere they are helped by prior training or preparation considered traditional for public office: for example if they have attended particular schools and universities, achieved a law degree, campaigned for candidates, or been members of a resistance movement that comes to power. Nevertheless, continuing stereotypes about women's cognitive and emotional characteristics play a role in excluding them from the pools of eligible candidates for political and economic positions.

It is only in the past decade that stereotypes about women's interest in public life have begun to be dispelled. There has not been much scholarship devoted to the social factors that engage women in or reject them from the political process. With this book, and the work of Stacey and Price in the UK (1981), Haavio-Mannila et al. in Scandinavia (1985), Klein in the USA (1985), and that of Epstein and Coser (1981) and a few other social scientists, we are seeing breakthroughs in theoretical frameworks and the attendant consequences for public policy.

This book provides both the theoretical background and the hard facts which, one hopes, will contribute to the reasoned perception that will result in a reduction of gender inequality.

Cynthia Fuchs Epstein

Graduate Centre, City University of New York

INTRODUCTION

1 The Object of the Research

This is a book about gender (in)equality in different areas of social life: values, family, work, and public affairs.

The "in" is in parentheses to highlight an emerging reality that our study has tended to confirm, namely, that today it is possible in several respects to speak of gender equality and not just of gender inequality. While important disparities still survive, the world of women and the world of men are much less separate and distinct realities than before.

However, there still is a barrier between the two worlds which concerns two crucial and emblematic phenomena: the divisions of domestic chores and the exercise of public power. Paradoxically, the ancient dichotomy between public life and domestic life has been eroded everywhere except in these two areas of central importance.

A major purpose of this study is to argue that a fundamental step towards full gender equality lies in the re-socialization of men to tasks that are vital for family life (together with the development of professionalized services made possible by technological advances). However, without in any way implying that public power is more important than domestic chores, the study will concentrate more on participation in public life and, in particular, on the wielding of public power. Changes that have taken place in this area, almost unnoticed so far, are of exceptional interest.

2 The Research Design

2.1 *The Sample*

This study is based on data collected systematically in four countries: Canada, Italy, Poland and Romania. We think that the four are a good sample, not only because they represent two globally different socio-economic-political systems but also because of the differences between countries within each system. Canada, for instance, is a country more exposed than Italy to modernizing patterns of life. This is because of its proximity to the United States, the influence of Protestantism, and the lack of a feudal past. Italy is a more traditional, partly backward, and somewhat rigidly stratified society; largely as a consequence of the temporal influence of Catholicism, but also for other far distant historical reasons, the emphasis on hierarchy is strong, in spite of an anarchistic bent in everyday life. Poland is a country in which a strong cultural and political influence is exercised by the Catholic Church. This was already partly exposed to a process of modernization prior to World War II. Romania, on the other hand, has a predominant religion (Greek Orthodox) which does not have any direct political influence and the cultural impact of which is less favourable to modernization. In both Poland and Romania the standard of living and the level of industrialization are lower than in the other two countries. In Romania the power of the Communist Party in all aspects of life is overwhelming. This is much less true in Poland, where a free trade-union movement could develop, albeit for a short time: something that cannot be dreamt of in Romania.

At the same time, in all four countries, official ideology and political and social forces (1) affirm gender equality. In none of them are there legal restrictions to that goal. Besides, they all belong, broadly speaking, to the same cultural background: the Judaic-Christian tradition, with the same basic values, the same kind of family structure and conception. In each country, divorce exists, and birth control and abortion are legal. All are also industrialized countries with similar educational systems (2). Thus, it should be possible to extrapolate from them specific cultural and institutional patterns that bear directly on the problem under investigation.

We used these four countries as "test-tubes" embodying different conceptions, from each of which we drew a certain number of respondents. *What we have, therefore, is not a representative but a purposive sample.* This must be underlined. It is merely for convenience that we speak of "Canadian blue-collar workers", "Polish teachers", "Romanian housewives", and so on. *We are not interested* in generalizing our results to the whole country nor to the four cities where the majority of the sample comes from nor to the political elite. Ours is a *causal analysis*, and for this we needed a purposive sample.

In each country, we have 1,100 respondents, subdivided as shown in Table 1. All respondents were between 20 and 60 years of age, except office-holders for whom there was no age limit.

In other words, we decided to include 600 people *of both sexes* (5) in each country who have an extra-domestic job. These respondents are grouped in three categories to permit reasonable

Table 1 Subdivision of Respondents in All Four Countries

Category	Males	Females
Blue-collar workers	100	100
White-collar workers	100	100
Primary school teachers	100	100
People out of work	100 (3)	100
Decision-makers	150	150 (4)

inter-country comparisons: blue-collar workers, white-collar workers, and teachers. The following are the reasons for our focus on these categories. First, it is possible to determine a social status ranking among them (a ranking which is difficult to achieve for other categories, given the differences between the four countries). Second, blue-collar workers represent in all countries a crucial economic, social and political force. Third, white-collar workers are or tend to become the largest stratum in contemporary society. Finally, primary school teaching (in all four countries a highly feminized profession) represents the first important public socialization agency for the newer generations. We also decided to include 200 people *of both sexes* in each country who are characterized by being out of work outside the home. Lastly, 300 people, again of both sexes, in each country were included to contrast with the rest of the sample in that they are decision-makers.

This kind of purposive sample permits cross-national comparisons of the interrelationship of gender and class in a much finer way than a comparison of the absolute magnitudes of the sex differences, such as would be permitted by a representative sample. We decided, therefore, to have 400 male and 400 female respondents in each of the non-power-holding categories (with the exception of men out of work, 300 in number, because that category has been excluded in Poland on the ground that it would have been made up mostly of handicapped persons or people who do not want to work) and 600 male and 600 female respondents who hold power, selected in a way that will shortly be illustrated.

Thus, we have in total 800 blue-collar workers, 800 white-collar workers, 800 teachers, 700 people out of work, and 1,200 office-holders.

Let us describe our sample. Blue-collar workers are manual workers without subordinates. They have been randomly selected in factories, likewise randomly selected, with at least 100 employees, each belonging to one of the following sectors represented by a number of plants in all four chosen cities: textile, chemical and pharmaceutical, food, and electronics industries. Factories having typically good or bad working conditions (e.g. recent strong labour troubles or especially good fringe benefits) have been excluded.

White-collar workers are non-manual workers, without subordinates, who perform basically routine tasks. They have been selected randomly in the same factories as blue-collar workers. They are the indoor counterparts of the latter.

Primary school teachers are teachers in the public system without administrative duties. They have been randomly selected from official lists of public teachers supplied by local authorities.

Housewives are women who live steadily with a man or alone and do not work at all for pay, not even part-time. They have been randomly selected from a working or low middle-class background. It is only for brevity's sake that they are included in the category "people out of work" (a label which uses the term "work" in the sense of "extra-domestic work").

Men out of work are men without paying jobs, whether unemployed or unable to work. They have been randomly selected on the basis of lists supplied by the relevant local agencies.

All respondents from the above-mentioned categories live in: Canadian sample, Toronto; Italian sample, Rome; Polish sample, Warsaw; Romanian sample, Bucharest. We wanted to have respondents with comparable experience in environments that offer the best opportunities for the forms of participation we are interested in. From this point of view, the big city represents the most congenial environment. In order to keep this factor under control, we restricted our sample (or better, a part of it) to these four cities.

The procedure for the office-holders is different. We selected 150 women *in each country* (not city), starting with women in the most important positions and moving down progressively until the desired number of respondents was reached. The order of importance of the positions is as follows:

1 members of the national cabinet;
2 representatives in the national parliament or senate;

3 members of intermediate (state, regional or provincial) governments;
4 mayors and members of local city governments;
5 representatives of intermediate assemblies;
6 representatives of local city councils;
7 high officials in public administration, such as directors and
vice-directors of departments and chief aides of ministers;
8 members of central committees of political parties;
9 members of central committees of trade unions;
10 top managers in industrial plants;
11 top managers in commercial firms;
12 top people in socio-cultural institutions, such as universities,
hospitals, scientific or professional associations.

Once the list of the 150 office-holding women had been
prepared and the interviews completed, an equal number of men
from the same organizations and at the same level was randomly
selected. For example, if we found three women in category 1, we
then randomly selected three male cabinet members.

In this way we actually selected *two samples*: one of
non-office-holders, belonging to some specific categories, and
another of office-holders. The first sample was made up of working
people (blue-collar workers, white-collar workers, primary school
teachers) and of people out of extra-domestic work; in the second
sample, men were matched with the most important women in the
country (not in the city: this is the reason why we call the
respondents by the name of the nation, not of the city).

Some might wonder why these categories of working people
were selected, and not others. One reason has been given above:
namely, that they can easily be ranked in terms of socio-economic
opportunities. Of course, other categories might have been
included, had our budget allowed it (6).

Any attempt to specify to what extent this kind of sample
represents the demographic reality of the populations of the four
cities or the four nations would be too complicated. Indeed, since
for our purposes it is not necessary, we did not try to determine
how far off the mark each sample might be. A description of the
four countries, as a background for our samples, is provided in
chapter 1 of this book.

As a consequence of this sampling procedure, the following
comparisons are feasible and operative, while others (such as
between a category of one sex in one country and a different

category of the other sex in another country) are in general meaningless:

1 between the sexes within the same category by country (example: Canadian male blue-collar workers v. Canadian female blue-collar workers);
2 between categories by sex within the same country (examples: Canadian male blue-collar workers v. Canadian male white-collar workers, Canadian male blue-collar workers v. Canadian male teachers);
3 between the same category by sex and by country (example: Canadian male blue-collar workers v. Italian male blue-collar workers);
4 between the set of differences existing within the same country among categories by sex (example: comparison between differences existing among male categories and those among female categories in Canada, i.e. how much a variable discriminates among the categories by sex in each country);
5 between the set of differences existing among categories by sex in each country (example: comparison between differences existing among male categories in Canada and those among male categories in Italy, i.e. how much a variable discriminates among the categories of the same sex in one country and how much in another).

This means that it is possible to examine by country (and across countries) the interaction of any variable with the categories in the sample by sex. In fact, for *each* variable we have tested the differences (means or percentages) for all these five possible comparisons. *Every time we report a difference, therefore, it must be understood that it is a statistically significant one*, although the coefficient and the correspondent probability level will be cited only rarely. *It is implicit that, when we do not mention an inter-sex difference (the first comparison in the list), no significant difference was found.*

2.2 *The Tools of the Research*

The advantages and disadvantages of the survey technique are too well known and so there is no need to illustrate them here.

On the basis of a pre-test, in 1976, of about 100 cases in each country, we prepared a questionnaire of a little less than one hour's duration. (The length of time varies, of course, with the level of education in the different categories of the sample.) The original questionnaire was in English. In order to be sure that translation errors were kept to a minimum, in Italy, Poland and Romania, a control set of English-speaking people not connected with the research were asked to re-translate the questionnaire into English. Comparisons were then made between the different translations in each language. Thus, the final questionnaire in each language is reasonably identical to the English prototype.

Questionnaires were filled in by each respondent with the assistance, when needed, of an interviewer. No mention was made, in approaching the respondent, either of the international character of the research or of the specific topic (gender differences) under investigation. The object of the research was presented as an academic study on work, family, beliefs, and public participation.

At the same time, we collected in each country aggregate data *referring to the year in which the questionnaire was administered* (1979-80) and we looked into the findings of relevant studies carried out in the recent past. The collection was done in a systematic way, covering the same areas in each country. A general treatment of these data is provided in chapter 1.

The usefulness of such a framework is obvious. To give just one example, the significance of women of a certain category having 13 years of schooling is much greater in a country where the average for a woman is 8 years than in another where it is 11 years. It is this framework that will allow a real understanding of the correlates of participation which result from the analysis of the micro-level data collected through the questionnaire. We would therefore urge the reader to become acquainted with the framework.

2.3 *Measurement Techniques*

We generally used traditional measurement techniques. They will be described in detail when necessary in the text and in the appendices.

3 The Structure of the Book

Social systems are assumed in this research to be the independent variables. Even if we know that socialism (as it exists) has not produced total gender parity, it nevertheless seems reasonable to think that to live in a social system where the emphasis is on egalitarianism, where no large private fortunes are allowed, where production is geared not to profit but largely to the satisfaction of collective needs, and where the vast majority of women work outside the home, should make a basic difference.

Chapter 1 of this book, which describes the conditions for women in four countries, highlights the macroscopic differences that depend on the social systems.

The next three chapters concern respectively the intervening variables that are vital for an understanding of gender differences in public participation: values, family, and work. If an egalitarian transformation does not take place in these areas, it is impossible to think of gender egalitarianism in political participation.

Women live in a world which from time immemorial has been shaped by men. The culture that surrounds them is masculine. Women's patterns of behaviour are oriented by values that assign them a subordinate place in public life. We wanted to find out where traditional habits of mind about the role of women in society and their relation to work and sex have changed more. Many factors are necessary to allow women access to power, but one prerequisite is that women think that it is proper for them to participate in public life to the same extent as men think that it is.

Women not only have limitations on access to power but fail even to desire power, since they are socialized to become primarily wives and mothers. The institution which sanctions this is the family. Many changes have occurred in the last twenty years in the way the family operates. We wanted to find out whether more gender parity now exists in the family, where the rebuttal of the traditional division of chores is stronger, and how these tendencies correlate with participation in public life.

Another prerequisite is participation in the labour force. The image that a working woman holds of herself changes, her self-reliance heightens, and isolation in the home increasingly appears to her to be a nonsense. If women are exposed to trade-union activities, they may develop an interest in broad issues of an economic and a political nature and, at the same time, they may learn the skills necessary for successful political mobilization. In any event, collectively organized activities no longer appear to be a distant world. They may even appear to be necessary tools.

Other aspects of work that make it a step to public participation are the style of leadership in the workplace and the level of internal democracy. White and Lippit (1960) were among the first to demonstrate that workers in democratic situations are more likely to be socialized into the skills and attitudes necessary for political participation.

Chapter 5 presents an attempt to explain gender differences in political participation. It tests the apathy or barrier hypothesis, especially as far as party and public offices are concerned. A multivariate analysis, described in Appendix B, links all the above-mentioned variables in an attempt to explain their impact on participation and power.

4 A Warning for the Reader

Although the main goal of this research is to offer an explanation of gender differences in public life, with special reference to power, a large part of the book is of a descriptive nature. No research is purely explanatory. This is more true the more the data are exciting in themselves and the more original is the topic (Baxter and Lansing, 1983: 221-222). The data presented in this study are of unique interest, and not only because of the subject. It is indeed very rare that original data from the East European countries on topics of political relevance, gathered with the same questionnaire and consequently comparable, are analysed on a centralized basis together with data from Western countries.

Description, however, is not an end in itself. We lingered, as a rule, on those findings that are useful from an interpretative viewpoint and that familiarize the reader with our sample.

A final note: for brevity's sake, we often use expressions which are not precise. When we speak of a Canadian sample, for example, we should say "the blue-collar workers, the white-collar workers, the teachers, and the people out of work who live in Toronto as well as the decision-makers on a national scale in Canada" (but even that would not be accurate, because the decision-makers do not make up a representative sample). When we speak of "people out of work" and include housewives among them, we use a label that might be interpreted as implying that housewives are inactive. It is merely as shorthand that we use the term "work" in the sense of "extra-domestic work". The same applies to the expressions "working mothers" v. "non-working mothers".

Another example concerns the use of the attributes "capitalist" and "socialist". While the first label is clear enough, the second lends itself to ambiguous interpretations. Here we use "socialism" for regimes which consider themselves on the road to communism.

In reality, we are aware that not only does the ideal of socialism, to which we refer often, diverge from its implementation, but also that there are deep differences between the countries which adopted such a system --- in our case between Poland and Romania (see ch. 1). Still, at times, for brevity's sake, we lump them together under the same label of "socialist".

Notes

1 One exception (although not the only one) may be the Catholic Church. The fact that it is strong in two countries belonging to two different modes of production is a fortunate co-incidence that will allow us to measure its impact in deeply different contexts. Yet, although the traditional philosophy of the Church is that the family must have priority for women (Pius XI, 1930: par. 10 and especially 27; 1937: par. 11), there is less opposition on the part of the Church today to women being concerned with public life. Since traditional habits of mind, which are typical of the Catholic Church, are much more diffused in the countryside than in the urban environment, we accordingly restricted our research to cities.

2 The latter characteristics make for a crucial difference between the countries in our sample and those in the sample of Verba et al.'s study (1978).

3 Unemployed men by definition are not supposed to exist in Poland and Romania. This is the reason why this category does not appear in the Polish sample. In the Romanian sample it does appear, but it comprises almost only disabled people. This inconsistency arises from the different approaches taken respectively by the Polish and Romanian authors.

4 In Romania only 65 women in positions of power were found who would accept being interviewed. Consequently, the number of male decision-makers in that country is also below 150.

5 An important characteristic of the present work, which oddly is almost never found in women's research, is to compare systematically male and female findings (Rogers 1978: 155).

6 Another reason for selecting teachers is that their educational level, the kind of function they perform, and the time they have available predispose them to political activity. From the point of view of political participation, they are midway between, on the one hand, the other two categories of working people and, on the other, the decision-makers. In some countries, being a teacher is one of the channels for entering a political career. Thus, for instance, in Poland we find a high level of participation by female teachers (Siemienska, 1983a).

1 THE CONTEXT OF THE RESEARCH

1 The Chosen Parameters

The aim of this chapter is to help the reader to understand better the findings presented in the book.

We have already stressed that our sample is not representative. In order to minimize demographic, economic and social differences among the four countries and to focus on an advanced area in each of them, the respondents, with the exception of decision-makers, were selected from a metropolitan centre of paramount importance in each country. It would have been more accurate to describe the four cities' demographic, economic and social structures too, and then to proceed to an evaluation of the gap between them and the respective countries as a whole. However, this would have meant at least doubling the length of the present chapter. It might also have not been feasible since it would have entailed additional studies that would be hard to carry out. On the other hand, the merely hypothetical alternative of describing only the four cities' structure was discarded as reductive: even if the respondents live in a context which in many respects is different from the rest of the country, it is nevertheless the latter's structure that influences their lives to a significant degree. Since the data were collected in 1979-80, this short description of the plight of women in the four countries concentrates on the period around those years. Important subsequent facts are ignored.

1.1 *Contrasting Models*

The most significant contrast in our sample is that between a free enterprise model and a socialist model. It is superfluous to explore the details of this contrast. Their ideology, economic organization, and political structure are at odds with one another.

But it must be emphasized that, notwithstanding some basic similarities at the institutional level, the countries belonging to each model differ widely from each other.

Poland is a country with a stronger cultural tradition than Romania; its ruling party is ostensibly limited by the influence of the Catholic Church, while in Romania the party has unrestrained power. Poland has a greater intellectual potential than Romania.

From an economic point of view, this shows in the fact that Poland appears among the ten top countries in the world in terms of the percentage of scientists and engineers who are engaged in research and development (1980: 2,622 per 1 million inhabitants).

Romania, in contrast, though less developed than Poland, shows one of the highest rates of industrial production, ranking 6th among the ten top countries: (1975 = 100) 1980: Romania, 138; Poland, 101 (the first of the ten bottom countries); Italy, 111; Canada, 106. All Romania's resources have been drastically mobilized for it to become an industrial society, to the point that from time to time the government has adopted pro-natalist measures. However, this is a goal which Romania has in common with the other Eastern European countries, Poland included. In spite of the fact that, at the time of our research, the more advanced Poland was going through a period of turmoil which accentuated the industrial setback of the late 1970s, it was still considered the 11th strongest industrial power in the world, ranking 8th in industry's share of the Gross National Product (GNP).

Remarkable differences also exist between Canada and Italy. Canada belongs largely to the Anglo-Saxon Protestant tradition, and reflects the American pattern of life, while Italy is a country in the Catholic tradition, imbued with the anarchistic approach to life typical of Mediterranean culture and with feudal remnants that tend to preserve a somewhat rigid stratification. Canada is richer (Physical Quality of Life Index, 1981: Canada, 9th among the ten top countries, Italy, 15th; Per Capita Consumption Index (1970 = 100) 1980: Canada, 29th, 133.5; Italy, 72nd, 114.1). Canada is better organized (Index of Net Social Progress 1979-80: Canada, 11th; Italy 21st). Canada has the world's second largest contribution by services to GNP (1982: Canada, 63%; Italy, 51%). Regarding education, Canada is second in the world for people with post-secondary training (1980: Canada, 30.9%; Italy, 2.6%; even granted that, because of differing criteria in defining post-secondary training, the data are not strictly comparable, the gap is impressive). If we turn to politics, Canada is, from an institutional point of view, a democracy which is solidly anchored to the British tradition, while Italy falls in line with the French tradition, with all its weaknesses and pitfalls but also its liveliness. In spite of deep changes, the influence of the Catholic Church at the political level is still more relevant in Italy than in Canada. In this respect, as well as in others, Italy resembles Poland.

Table 1 compares all four countries on the basis of some crucial dimensions. Canada emerges as an advanced society, followed by Italy, with Romania at the bottom but trying hard to bridge the gap.

Table 1 Rank Order of the Four Countries along Basic Dimensions (1980)

General Fertility Rate	Romania	Poland	Canada	Italy
	76.6	75.6	58.6	48.9
Modernization (1970-80)	Canada	Italy	Poland	Romania
	39.0	33.5	15.7	9.7
Urbanization	Canada	Italy	Poland	Romania
	80.0	69.0	57.0	50.0
GNP per capita ($)	Canada	Italy	Poland	Romania
	10,130	6,480	3,900	2,340
Annual growth rate of	Romania	Poland	Canada	Italy
GNP per capita (1970-79)	9.2	5.2	2.9	2.2
Industrial share of GNP	Poland	Romania	Italy	Canada
	64	64	43	33
Industrial production	Romania	Italy	Canada	Poland
(1975-80) (1975 = 100)	138	111	106	101
Physical Quality of	Canada	Italy	Poland	Romania
Life Index	96	95	93	91
Index of Net Social	Canada	Italy	Poland	Romania
Progress (1979-80)	174	163	158	152
People with post-	Canada	Poland	Romania	Italy
secondary school training (%)	30.9	5.7	4.6	2.6
Post-secondary	Canada	Italy	Poland	Romania
enrolment per 100,000	3,539	1,937	1,723	873
Political liveliness	Italy	Canada	Poland	Romania
(1970-79)	38.4	24.4	0.6	0.5
Universal suffrage for	Poland	Italy	Romania	Canada
women (year gained)	1919	1945	1946	1948

Sources: *UN Statistical Yearbook*; World Bank, *World Development Report*; R.J. Estes (1983) *The Social Progress of Nations*, Praeger. These references, and especially the latter, supply also the explanation of the criteria used in the construction of the indices.

2 Matters Relevant to Women

The following paragraphs look at single areas or institutions which are particularly relevant from the point of view of women.

2.1 *Family Structure*

The multi-family household has been in sharp decline since the end of the war in all countries, although less markedly in Romania and in Poland, particularly in the countryside. At the same time, the numbers of non-family households and single-parent families have increased conspicuously.

In Canada and Italy the numbers of widowed and divorced women have kept growing while the number of married women has decreased to a much larger extent than in Poland and Romania.

In Canada and Italy the fertility rate has been steadily decreasing at a rate slightly faster than in Poland. In Romania it has undergone wide fluctuations owing to the changing demographic policies of the government.

In general, the number of day-care centres for children under 3 is inadequate, in spite of the fact that the largest increase in the labour force has taken place among mothers, including young mothers.

Contraception and abortion are legal in all countries, but are difficult to obtain in Romania.

Divorce exists in all countries, but in Romania only by default.

2.2 *Matrimonial Property*

A husband and wife may choose to keep their properties legally separate, otherwise the assumption is that they have a joint property. Professional and personal assets are excluded from it. In Canada and Italy these non-family assets often concern a business which in the overwhelming majority of cases, belongs to the husband. In this sense, in the matter of separation or divorce, a woman is disadvantaged even if there is a tendency to recognize her contribution as a housewife to the husband's business.

2.3 *Custody of Children and Child Support*

In the case of separation and divorce, custody is awarded in consideration of the best interests of the child. In the vast majority of cases, it is awarded to the mother (Canada, 1969-79: 85.6%; Italy, 1978-80: 88%; Poland, 1949-66: 89%; no data for Romania). Since fathers usually earn more than mothers, the onus of supporting children financially falls mainly on the former. In all countries, however, the allowance that should be transferred monthly from father to mother is rather low; in Italy and especially in Canada it is not rarely defaulted upon (Eichler, 1983: 297-8).

2.4 *Rape*

The dimension of the phenomenon is not known, because only a fraction of the cases is reported to the police. Yet, it seems to be a tangible reality. It is punishable by imprisonment everywhere, but there is no judicial unanimity as to what rape means. In Italy, for instance, the Supreme Court ruled that the insistence "which is necessary to win a woman's natural reluctance and coyness is not violence".

In Canada and Italy the spouse can be condemned for rape of the partner, but such sentencing is very rare. In the latter country, the only cases of incrimination concerned violent sodomy.

In Italy and Romania, if reparatory marriage takes place, "the affair" is considered closed.

The reform of the rape law has been one of the goals most strongly --- and successfully --- pursued by the feminist movement in Canada and especially in Italy.

2.5 *Prostitution*

Prostitution is a crime in Poland and Romania. In Canada and Italy, while to solicit anyone in a public place is an offence, prostitution in itself is not.

The phenomenon is more common in the latter countries, although its relevance has decreased in comparison with the prewar period. In Italy, prostitution in authorized brothels was suppressed in 1951.

Panderism is a crime, but is difficult to prosecute because of silence.

2.6 Public Support Systems

The law provides income protection, health care and a so-cial-service system for those citizens who need them. In all of the countries, family allowances, old age pensions, income supplements, and unemployment insurance fall far short of the monthly costs that the families actually incur.

National health systems are highly developed in all four countries. The differences in per capita investment, however, are impressive. Canada ranks first by far, Italy second, Romania last. Yet, in Canada and especially Italy, investments are mostly absorbed by infrastructural and administrative costs and are translated into benefits for those in need to a much lesser degree than in Poland and Romania. Everywhere the assistance to the elderly is scanty.

2.7 Education

Canada has by far the highest rate in school, followed by Poland. Great progress has been achieved in this area by Romania. Italy ranks last.

In the high school system, the number of girls and boys is about the same. At university level, about one-third of students are female, except in Poland, where there are slightly more women registered than men.

Yet, in all countries (save Poland, where there is a sizeable number of women in Medicine), women concentrate in the "expressive faculties" and the caring professions.

Educational materials as well as the mass-media keep portraying the traditional image of women.

2.8 Labour

All four countries have witnessed an impressive growth in the numbers of employed women (except, as far as Italy is concerned, in the agricultural sector). In Poland, by 1935 women already made up 33.5% of the workforce. What is new about this process is the fact that female employment now embraces young women (below 25) and young mothers, even with small children, especially in the age group 25-44 (in Italy, though, there is a contraction at about 30). This is true not only in Poland and Romania, where public policy prescribes full employment, but also in Canada and Italy.

In Canada, Italy and Poland women's employment is particularly accentuated in the tertiary sector, and in Romania in the primary sector.

Unemployment, especially in Canada and Italy, is more marked for women than men.

But what characterizes women's work conditions in all countries is the fact that they concentrate in jobs of poor prestige and low self-realization. Practically all managers are men. In Italy, above two million women are in the "black economy".

Men's wages are higher and consequently pensions and fringe benefits are higher for them than for women. Part-time jobs in Canada and Italy are more common among women than men.

In no country do pensions cover women's contributions to the household.

2.9 *Protective Labour Legislation*

Gender discrimination is prohibited by law as to both hiring and pay. Legislation also ensures job security for female employees before and after childbirth.

2.10 *Public Structures*

About one-third of the public administration in each of the four countries is made up of women, but they are found mainly in the support occupations.

In Canada and Italy the number of women in trade unions is growing faster than the number of men, but very few of the women are at the top. This is true also in Poland (of course, we refer to the pre-1980 period) and in Romania, where (especially in the latter country) the vast majority of women is affiliated to a union.

In general, with the partial exception of Italy, women are poorly represented in politics, and very few of them are found in leadership positions.

The feminist movement --- rather a mosaic of movements --- exists only in Canada and Italy, being closer to politics in the latter than in the former. In Italy there are feminine organizations in each party. In Poland and Romania feminine organizations are committed to follow the ruling party line. In Canada and Italy the feminist movement has played an especially important role in the campaigns for divorce and abortion.

3 Conclusion

The tendency towards gender egalitarianism appears to be slowly at work everywhere in many important respects, although its complete achievement is still far away.

At the macro level, few truly *radical* differences emerge among the four countries. The question is whether micro-level data, such as those presented in the coming chapters, can put significant differences and interrelationships into relief. As we stressed already, the design of our research uses these four countries as if they were test-tubes from which observations might be drawn for an experiment. This kind of analysis, studying the interconnections among the crucial variables that have been chosen, might produce evidence of processes that are not discernible at the global level and might throw light on the dynamics of such a tendency.

2 GENDER DIFFERENCES AND VALUES

1 Questioning Attitudes, Values and Expectations

Most scientists and observers of social life do not hesitate to state that women are less interested than men in politics or, broadly speaking, the sphere of public life. This difference is considered by some as natural, and as being congruent to the different roles played by men and women in society.

This view is strongly attacked by feminists, who consider it more a justification of the existing inequality than a valid reason for the unequal involvement of men and women in public life (Deckard, 1983; Chafe, 1972). The idea of *natural* differences between the interests of men and women is rejected by feminists, who claim that it is not based on serious biological research. Rather, they attribute the lack of women's interest in public life to differences in socialization, which prepares girls for submissive roles and boys for dominant roles in all spheres of life.

Such socialization is responsible for the internalization not only of different conceptions of female and male roles by girls and boys respectively but also of the very conceptions of femininity and masculinity. Results of many studies show that the views which women themselves entertain about their skills and role in society are often limited by what is considered "feminine". Moreover, women defend the idea that their roles are complementary to and thus not competitive with those played by men.

A number of researchers have shown the differences in the socialization of girls and boys, in the way that they are treated by parents, starting from birth. Analyses of interaction between kindergarten teachers and their pupils of both sexes, and later between school teachers and their students in primary and high schools, have reached similar conclusions (Maccoby and Jacklin, 1974; Fischer and Cheyne, 1978). Content analysis of textbooks used in schools in many countries has also demonstrated that the manner of portraying women and men is similar in all of them. In these texts women appear as centred on the family and/or have jobs that are considered fit for a woman, while men devote themselves to professional activity, the arts, politics, etc. From the beginning women are brought up to keep away from politics, or at least to become involved in public life only to the extent to which it is congruent with the performance of their traditional roles. Therefore, women are ready to follow men rather than to play an active role on their own behalf.

The last twenty years have brought about a re-interpretation of established ways of thinking about what is proper for men and for women with respect to their roles in society. In the West, feminists made attempts to shake women's traditional values, attitudes and aspirations (Chafetz, 1984; Friedan, 1982; Lorber et al., 1981; Roszak and Roszak, 1969). Politicians and ideologists of the socialist countries of Eastern Europe proclaimed, just after World War II, that men and women are equal in all respects, that they possess equal abilities and that they should have equal chances to participate in cultural, social, economic and political life.

In spite of the still existing inequality of men and women and the persistence of traditional values and attitudes with regard to gender equality, some changes have indeed taken place in the last decades. Women work outside the household more often than before. They are also more educated and more active in political life. We want to know to what extent these changes, found in all the countries included in our study, correspond to changes in values and attitudes with regard to gender equality.

Three kinds of orientation are possible:

1 traditional : it supports a strict division of gender roles in society, based on the belief that men's and women's predispositions are different and that men are superior;

2 egalitarian : it claims that the division of roles is based not on gender differences but on individual abilities which in reality diversify people;

3 radical extremists : it maintains that it is necessary to reverse the traditional division of roles, giving, even if temporarily, more power to women than to men.

It is reasonable to assume that the traditional and the egalitarian types are paramount among our respondents, the latter being more common in the category of decision-makers and in the socialist countries for the obvious reason of their egalitarian ideology.

We also assume that attitudes, values and expectations may not be congruent, although several authors point out that there is "evidence that attitudes toward gender roles are related to political and religious views" (Deaux and Kite, 1987). Respondents may share egalitarian beliefs more easily about occupational activities than about the division of roles in the household or participation in public life. This differentiation of attitudes, values and expectations reflects women's real involvement in different types of activities. Rapid political and economic change brings in new pressures and demands, ideas and institutions which prompt, to some extent, changes in individual behaviour despite the personal hierarchy of values.

In this chapter we shall present attitudes towards the position of women and men in society, obligations to the family, professional careers and participation in public life. We often asked respondents to give answers to "symmetric" questions: one related to women's obligations, the other to men's. This approach has the logic of avoiding the prejudice that women are obviously different from men, that women's and men's worlds of values are *essentially* separate.

2 Attitudes towards "Natural" Differences between Female and Male Propensities

The previously discussed question of whether differences between men and women have biological or rather social roots was the reason for including in our questionnaire four statements that allow us to ascertain, from the respondents' reaction to these, the degree to which the belief in "female nature" is accepted by respondents from different categories in the four countries.

These are the four statements:

(a) "A woman is by nature much more ready to obey than a man is."
(b) "It is more natural for a woman than for a man to remain a virgin."
(c) "It is more important for a woman than for a man to know how to attract a person of the opposite sex."
(d) "Boys and girls have different tasks in life and should, therefore, be brought up differently."

In general, the findings point towards a continued prevalence of a traditional outlook in Poland and Romania. About two-thirds of the respondents in these countries accept completely or partially the first three statements, while in Canada and Italy about one-third do. The fourth statement elicits a positive answer among one-third of the respondents in Poland and Romania, in Canada and Italy among a quarter. The prejudice embedded in this statement is, of course, the easiest to overcome.

Contrary to what one might have expected, women tend to agree more than men about the second item. While a detailed discussion of this finding is likely to lead us into areas going beyond the scope of the study, it is interesting to note the persistence in women of a restrictive approach to such a vital factor affecting personal growth.

Not only white-collar workers, men out of work and housewives accept the first statement more often than other categories but also blue-collar workers: this is even so in the two socialist countries.

Also, it is only with regard to this first statement that we find in Canada and Italy a high proportion of female teachers and decision-makers who reject it completely or partially.

Male decision-makers are no more liberal than other men. As a matter of fact, when we come to the third item, in Poland and Romania their attitude is even more traditional than that of the males in the other categories.

* * *

Once again, contrary to what one might have thought, it seems that neither religion nor a socio-political system is an important factor in determining beliefs about the nature and status of men and women. Rather, the results suggest that there is a close relationship between a rejection of the traditional point of view and the presence of feminist ideology. In Canada and Italy, where feminist movements were strong in the 1960s and 1970s, respondents reject the traditional point of view more often than in Poland and Romania. In the two socialist countries a traditional outlook persists because the socialist ideology emphasizes the equality of men and women mainly in economic and social terms, paying less attention to the roots of gender inequality. Indeed, the correlation matrix among the four items discussed above (Table 1) evidences that the acceptance of both traditional and non-traditional points of view is more consistent in Canada and Italy than in Poland and Romania.

This means that, in countries where the traditional approach to the women's issue has been systematically attacked by feminists, the question of the traditional or non-traditional point of view has been brought to a conscious level, while in the other countries the more general emphasis on equality in official ideology has not had much effect in changing long-standing traditional viewpoints.

Table 1 Intercorrelations among Attitudes towards "Natural" Differences between Female and Male Propensities †

	Canada			Italy			Poland			Romania		
	1	2	3	1	2	3	1	2	3	1	2	3
2	.44			.49			.26			.22		
3	.25	.36		.30	.32		.09	.21		.21	.11	
4	.37	.47	.43	.36	.39	.45	.13	.20	.30	.21	.27	.30

† All coefficients are highly significant (p < .01).
1 To attract opposite sex more important for a woman
2 To remain virgin more natural for a woman
3 To raise boys and girls differently
4 Women more ready to obey

* * *

To demonstrate better and in a more synthetic way the differences among the countries, we had recourse to the index described in Appendix 24.

As shown in Fig.1, egalitarian attitudes prevail in Canada, in Romania and especially in Poland. But the surprising result is that the people who share a traditional outlook are more numerous in Poland and especially Romania than in the other two countries where, on the contrary, the respondents who adopt a radical extremist view are sizeable groups.

3 Ideal Handling of Domestic Chores

It seems reasonable to assume that the attitudes towards the topics that we examined in the previous paragraph influence various areas of women's life (Bernard, 1975; Elkin and Handel, 1984). One such area is the performance of domestic chores (Eichler, 1983; Siemienska, 1983b).

Respondents were asked: "Who should cook the family's meals? do the dishes? do the everyday family shopping? do the laundry? clean the house? look after the children?"

We shall touch upon this issue again in chapter 3, par. 4.2, but our interest there will be to stress the differences between the real and the ideal distribution of domestic chores and to correlate

Fig. 1 Attitudes towards "Natural" Differences between Female and Male Propensities †

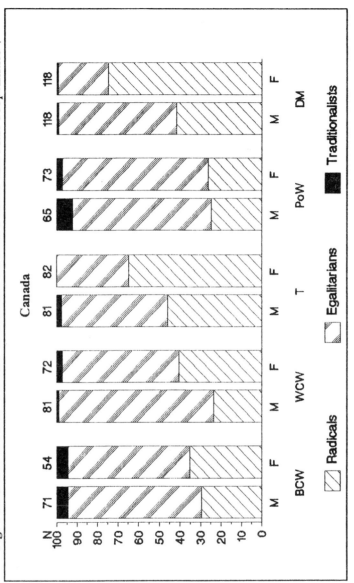

† The figure reports only pure types. This is the reason why the Ns here are lower than in the sample.
See abbreviation list for explanations of categories.

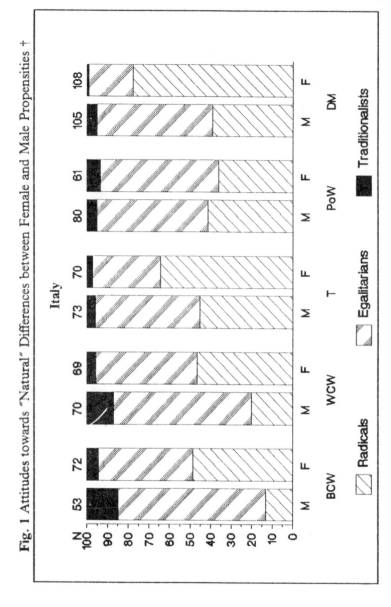

Fig. 1 Attitudes towards "Natural" Differences between Female and Male Propensities †

† The figure reports only pure types. This is the reason why the Ns here are lower than in the sample.
See abbreviation list for explanations of categories.

Fig. 1 Attitudes towards "Natural" Differences between Female and Male Propensities †

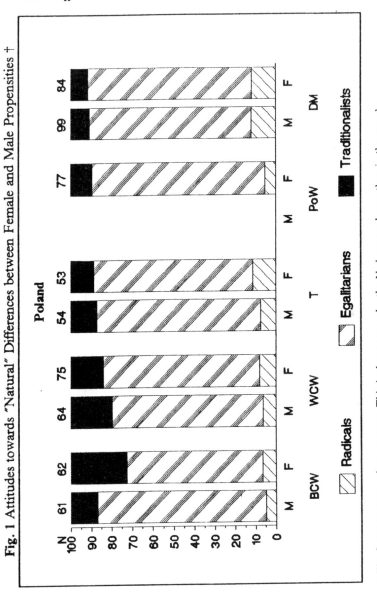

† The figure reports only pure types. This is the reason why the Ns here are lower than in the sample. See abbreviation list for explanations of categories.

Fig. 1 Attitudes towards "Natural" Differences between Female and Male Propensities †

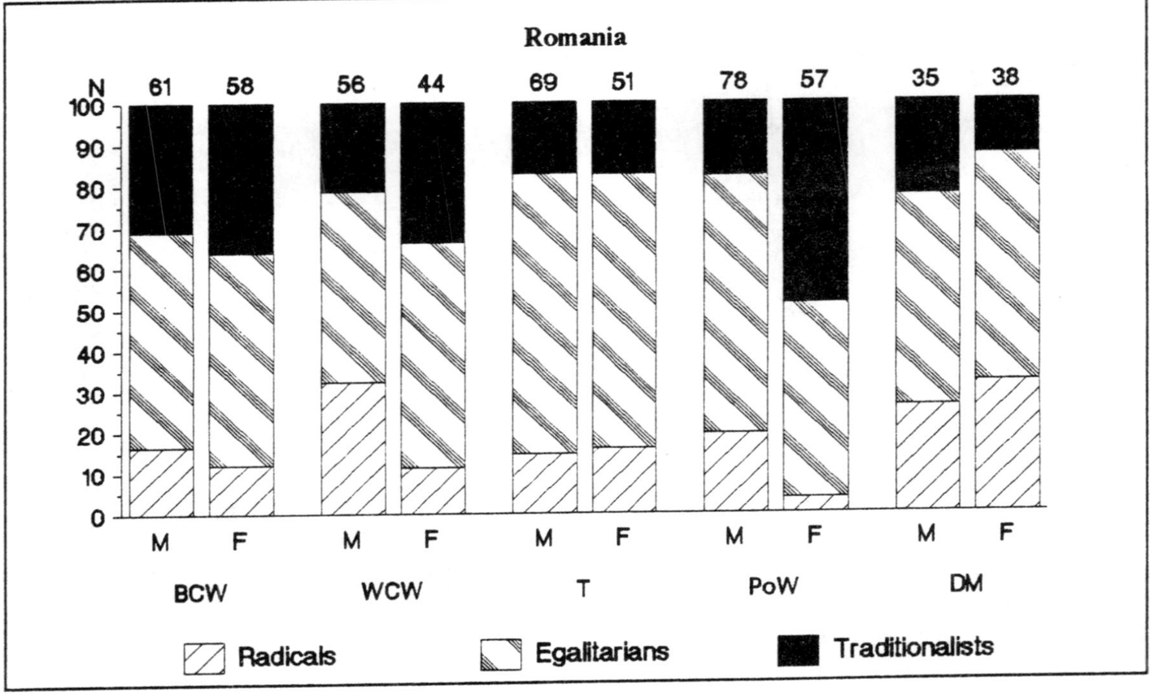

† The figure reports only pure types. This is the reason why the Ns here are lower than in the sample.
See abbreviation list for explanations of categories.

them with other variables. Here we give a short description of the phenomenon.

In Canada and Italy over 60%, in Poland over 50%, but in Romania only one-third of the respondents maintain that everyday cooking should be equally shared by men and women. Such an opinion is expressed by an even higher percentage in all countries about dish-washing (from 76% in Canada to 50% in Romania) and especially about child care (80% in Canada and Italy, 70% in Poland and Romania).

On the other hand, the traditional point of view prevails in all countries, and especially among women, as far as house-cleaning and laundry are concerned.

It is interesting that in Romania a sizeable number of people (about 37%) state that shopping should be done always or mainly by husbands, while in the other countries it is considered a chore to be done either by women or by both spouses. We do not know whether such a "progressive" pattern, which deviates from the generally traditional picture that characterizes Romania, results from a conscious transformation of attitudes or else, as sounds reasonable, from the fact that obtaining food supplies in a condition of permanent scarcity becomes such a time-consuming activity that women, overburdened by a double role, cannot afford to do it.

In general, the situation for women appears less discriminatory than the traditional model prescribes. The results are presented in Table 2 (under column I, the Ideal) in chapter 3. However, they are rather striking in the light of what one might expect nowadays, because they prove unequivocally that, in spite of some differences across the four countries and with the exceptions of child care, and of shopping in Romania, both men and women tend to allot the performance of domestic chores to wives. At times, women are even more conservative than men! This is the case for Romanian white-collar workers and teachers and for Canadian blue-collar workers.

The picture looks different for child care. For this activity, the general attitude is that fathers should contribute about as much as mothers.

Although a conservative attitude prevails in Romania more than in the other countries, our data show that such an attitude is not typical of socialist countries (as some writers claim: Lapidus, 1978; Karchev and Yasmaya, 1982), because Italy, not Poland, comes next to Romania in terms of conservatism. This means that attitudes towards the performance of domestic chores are shaped not by the system's ideologies but by a combination of cultural and economic factors.

Of course, this traditional attitude may also be explained by the fact that the status of housewife still looms large in our patterns of culture as the ideal one for women (Bose, 1980; Nilson, 1978). As expected, housewives in all countries believe that wives, even working wives, should perform more domestic chores than men. Yet, the differences between the attitudes of housewives and those of the females in the other categories are almost all significant. This is a clear sign that things are changing. The conspicuous exception is represented by blue-collar workers in all countries, who show an even more traditional leaning on many items than housewives do!

By contrast, female decision-makers everywhere state to a lesser extent than the females in the other categories that wives should perform domestic chores. However, not all differences, especially in Romania, are significant. We shall discover in the next pages that, while having responsibilities in public life has an impact on perceptions concerning day-to-day aspects of family life, female decision-makers with higher education and status tend also, in many respects, to defend the traditional outlook.

Since this question was addressed to unmarried as well as to married people, one might surmise that the answers of married people would be different. An inspection of the data shows that this is not so.

* * *

To give a global picture of the gender differences, we used an index built on the above described items (see App. 25). But, before examining the results, we wish to note (Table 2) that the items do not interrelate homogeneously in all countries.

The idea of what should be done by whom is least consistent in Romania, followed by Poland and Canada, and is the most consistent in Italy.

The picture that emerges (Fig. 2) shows that everywhere there are very few respondents upholding a radical extremist attitude (they do not even appear in the Canadian sample), while those sharing an egalitarian orientation are the majority in all countries, especially in Canada. However, the traditional attitudes appear to survive to a sizeable extent, especially in Romania and Italy.

If we cross the data presented in this table with those of Fig. 1, we find that the traditional attitudes towards "natural" differences

Table 2 Intercorrelations among Attitudes towards the Division of Domestic Chores†

	Canada					Italy					Poland					Romania			
	1	2	3	4	5	1	2	3	4	5	1	2	3	4	5	1	2	3	4	5
2	.27					.73					.30					.46			
3	.35	.29				.60	.62				.32	.31				.02	.18		
4	.48	.37	.26			.60	.71	.55			.30	.39	.23			.44	.45	.02	
5	.39	.42	.32	.56		.61	.72	.60	.74		.27	.46	.31	.39		.28	.37	.23	.38
6	.29	.33	.30	.29	.38	.48	.44	.51	.35	.48	.37	.32	.22	.20	.28	.27	.28	.14	.30	.36

† All coefficients are highly significant (p ≤ .01), except two cases in Romania.
Who should:
1 cook; 2 do dishes; 3 shop; 4 do laundry; 5 clean; 6 look after children

between men and women are matched by traditional attitudes towards the division of domestic chores.

4 Attitudes Related to Work

There are many deeply entrenched beliefs concerning women's attitudes towards work. All of them, directly or indirectly, are connected with the persuasion that for women the fulfilment of feminine drives has precedence over other things, and that men approach work quite differently from women. Is this so or is it a stereotype?

4.1 *Work and family duties*

We formulated the hypothesis that at a time of rapid educational advancement for women and the massive entry of women into the labour force, women will be more likely than men to support the principle of not subordinating the career to family duties. This should occur more in socialist than in non-socialist countries. To assess current attitudes on this point, respondents were asked to accept or reject these two statements:

(a) "If to pursue her career a woman has to stay away from home for long periods of time, she should give up her career".
(b) "If to pursue his career a man has to stay away from home for long periods of time, he should give up his career".

Fig. 2 Attitudes towards the Division of Household Chores †

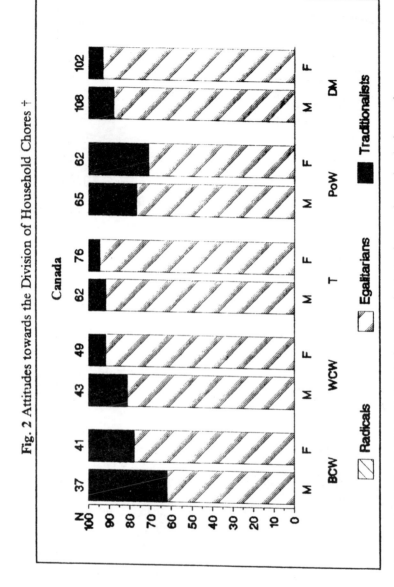

† The figure reports only pure types. This is the reason why the Ns here are lower than in the sample.
See abbreviation list for explanations of categories.

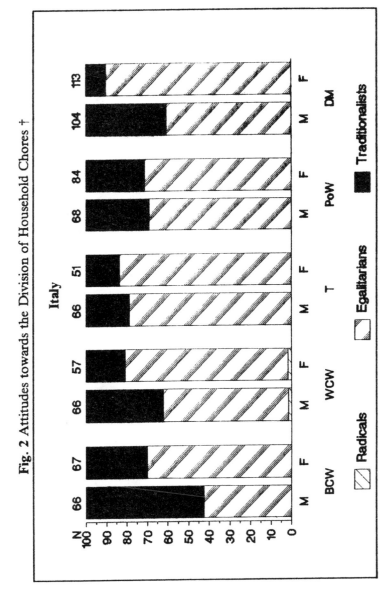

Fig. 2 Attitudes towards the Division of Household Chores †

† The figure reports only pure types. This is the reason why the Ns here are lower than in the sample. See abbreviation list for explanations of categories.

Fig. 2 Attitudes towards the Division of Household Chores †

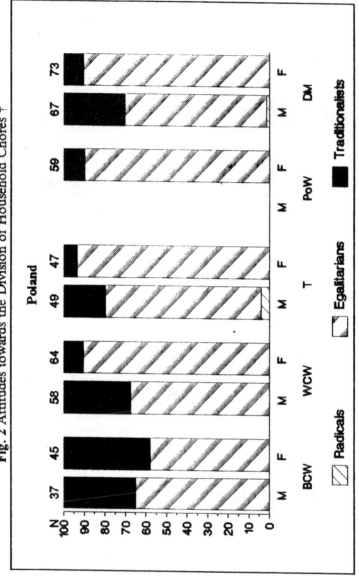

† The figure reports only pure types. This is the reason why the Ns here are lower than in the sample. See abbreviation list for explanations of categories.

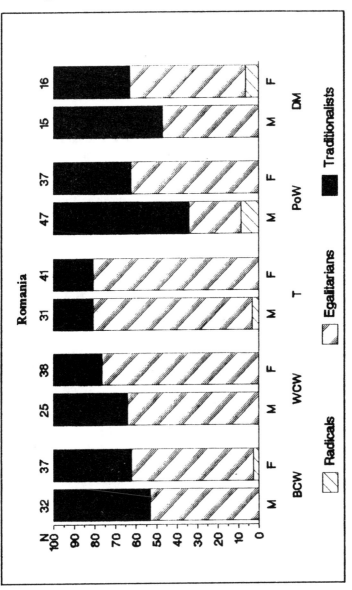

Fig. 2 Attitudes towards the Division of Household Chores †

† The figure reports only pure types. This is the reason why the Ns here are lower than in the sample. See abbreviation list for explanations of categories.

4.1.1 *For women*

Both Romanian men and women reject the view that a married woman should give up her career if it involves spending much of her time out of the house. In the other three countries, this view is rejected only by female decision-makers.

As expected, although the differences are not significant, except in Italy, more men than women believe that women should give up their careers. Romanian males in all categories and Canadian white-collar workers, teachers and decision-makers are the exception to this. Also, less educated people hold this view more than those with advanced education.

In all countries, except Poland, housewives support the traditional point of view more than other women, a fact that can be easily interpreted as a rationalization of their condition.

4.1.2 *For men*

The study was designed, among other things, to ascertain to what extent the expectations for men and women are symmetrical. The second statement was included for this reason. The pattern of replies reveals, as might have been expected, a much more benevolent attitude to men's careers. In comparison with the first statement, more men and, above all, more women (except in Poland) reject the view that family-life requirements should prevent men from accepting a job. The only exception was found not among women but among men: Italian blue- and white-collar workers.

Within each category, these differences between women and men are seldom significant, except in Italy where men in all categories agree with this statement more than women.

Differences are found to exist between people of the same sex from various categories, but in general they are not significant. As expected, significantly more male and female decision-makers than people of the same sex in other categories see no reason why men should give up their jobs if they conflict with family life.

* * *

All in all, the differences in the distribution of answers to both questions lead us to the conclusion that, with some exceptions, both women and men favour the view that for women the family has higher priority, and for men work. However, acceptance of such disparity declines everywhere, and especially in Romania, with growing education, and depends, above all, on the roles performed by the respondents: both male and female decision-makers strongly oppose letting one's family-life requirements take precedence over work.

In general, Italy and Poland appear to be the most conservative countries in both cases. This can be reasonably attributed to their Catholic background. Romania, on the other hand, seems to have undergone a deep revolution, putting her ahead of even Protestant Canada. But the general pattern that emerges is uniform: for the first statement, the countries, except Romania, fall within a general range of agreement; for the second, there is considerable disagreement.

4.2 "To Work or not to Work" if it is not a Financial Necessity

Historical research has shown that, at the early stage of women's entry into the labour market, women generally accepted conditions of work which correlated strongly with their lack of technical or vocational skills; they also displayed little ambition, which was reflected by, among other things, little interest in promotion (Bursche, 1973; Klein, 1965; Sarapata, 1977). In our times, women's work roles should have a less marginal position in their lives, although it is reasonable to assume that this attitudinal change does not happen uniformly in society as a whole and is more pronounced among better educated women.

Accordingly, we set out to check what is still commonly believed: that women are more likely than men to give up their jobs if they can afford to, since they go out to work mainly to support their families with an additional wage (Bardwick, 1971: 146 and ch.11; Vroom, 1964; Waluk, 1965; Wieruszewski, 1975). Feminists, naturally, oppose this point of view, calling it a male approach to the problem (Feldberg and Glenn, 1979; Hunt, 1984; Purcell, 1984).

Our data confirm what other research had already shown (Powell, 1988), i.e. that in all countries most women and men wish to continue (or, in the case of people out of work, to start) working, even if their financial situation does not make it necessary to do so. Men are not much more strongly oriented to work than women.

More specifically, the smallest proportion of respondents who want to continue working even without financial pressure is found among Italian blue-collar workers of both sexes, Italian and Romanian men out of work, and, particularly, among housewives.

Once again, Romanians stand out iń showing a stronger orientation to work. They, more than Poles and very much more than Canadians and Italians, want to continue working even if earning a living is not a financial necessity.

In general, more men than women within each category declare this intention, though only rarely is the difference significant (and never in the case of decision-makers).

Decision-makers in all countries are more willing to continue working. Comparisons yielded significant differences (p. < .01) between male and female decision-makers and the other categories of the same sex.

4.3 *Reasons for Continuing and Giving up Work*

4.3.1 *Reasons for Continuing Work*

Among the reasons given in Canada, Italy and Poland for continuing to work are, above all, the desire to be among people, to develop one's skills, to do something useful for society, to be independent, and, finally, to have more money (the exact ranking of this last reason depends on the respondent's category). The financial motive seems to play a less important role, once people are not under economic stress, compared with the others.

In Romania, somewhat different reasons are given: the most important being the wish to do something useful for society and, second, to have more money. The desire to be among people, so strongly emphasized by the respondents in the other countries, comes fourth in Romania.

Even though the financial motive is not the major reason for women to go beyond the traditional housekeeping duties, it might play a stronger role for them than for men. However, a comparison between men and women belonging to the same categories yields a result that runs against such stereotyping. In most cases, respondents of either sex are guided by exactly the same reasons in their hypothetical decision to keep working. Only the desire to be among people appears to be slightly more of a motivating factor for women, and only slightly because the significant differences are few.

The wish to develop one's skills is prevalent among men, except in Canada where the impact is felt of the feminist movement in perceptions concerning the importance for women also to realize their personalities. As expected, we find this reason more frequently cited by decision-makers and teachers.

The desire to be useful to society varies strongly in extent by category, and is selected, as we might have expected, most often by decision-makers and teachers, and least often by housewives. In fact, decision-makers and teachers by definition perform activities which have to do with social reality, while housewives are confined to a micro-group. No gender differences appear in this respect.

The need for independence is mentioned more by decision-makers than by other categories.

In general, Italians and Poles are more alike in their answers than with respectively either the Canadians or the Romanians. This proves once more that the ideology of a regime is not related to basic differences.

* * *

All in all, categories, more than gender, differentiate our respondents (Powell, 1988).

4.3.2 *Reasons for Giving up Work*

The study also tackled another issue, perhaps even more interesting than the one discussed above, namely, the reasons why respondents would stop working if the economic necessity to earn a living were eliminated. It is generally thought that men and women have different reasons for doing this. Our findings, however, show few significant differences between men and women from the same categories (none in Poland).

The main reasons for men in Italy and Romania are the need for independence, hobbies, and the wish to develop one's skills. In Poland there is also, even more, the preference for non-paid work and the need for contacts with other people; in Romania health problems play a significant role.

The main reasons for women are the same but, above all, in all four countries, family commitments rank first. The gender difference concerning family commitments is impressive in all countries, especially in Canada and Poland where about 23% of the men and 76% of the women responded that family needs would cause them to give up working.

It is interesting to point out that housewives, who mention family and health reasons more often than other women, do not consider staying at home and looking after the family as an opportunity for self-realization and independence.

Women more than men also cite a preference for non-paid work, except in Italy; health reasons in Poland and Romania; and the spouse's hostility. For all other reasons, men outrank women.

4.4 *Who Would Accept Promotion and What Kind ?*

According to belief, which is already disproved by our findings, women would work only to support their families and, consequently, would consider work to be marginal in their lives. In this view, they are not too interested in promotion. In order to find out whether this is true, we asked this question:

"Imagine you were offered the following possibilities in your work place, would you accept them or not?
1 To move to a higher level position that has considerably more obligations and responsibilities for you.
2 To move to a higher level position that requires a training that entails many sacrifices on your part.
3 To move to a higher level position where you may be frequently criticized.
4 To move to a higher level position in which you would have a group of 'problem' employees working for you.
5 To move to a higher level position in which there are more worries connected with your work than you now have.
6 To move to a higher level position even though it will make difficulties for your family."

As shown in Fig. 3, respondents everywhere are eager to accept promotions which are connected with more responsibility and which require additional training. Poles are less discouraged than others by problem employees; Romanians, likewise, are less discouraged by having more worries, in comparison with the necessity to undergo additional training. In all countries promotions which interfere with family life are the least acceptable. Poles appear to be the least ready to accept them. As shown by the analysis of the reasons for turning down a promotion (see Fig. 1 in ch. 4), Poles more than the others mention family reasons.

We find a common pattern of responses, with some deviations, for all countries. The only difference is that the respondents from the socialist countries tend less often to accept positions in

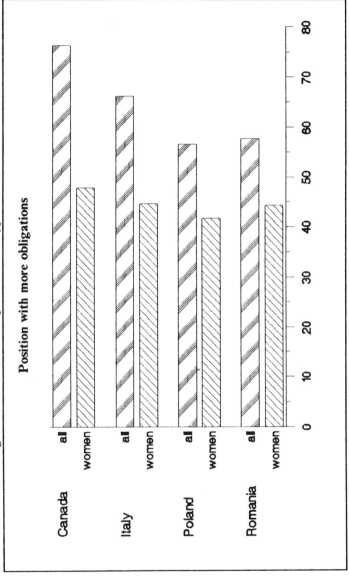

Fig. 3 Readiness to Accept Different Types of Promotion †

Position with more obligations

† Percentage of women out of the total number of respondents who would accept such a type of promotion.

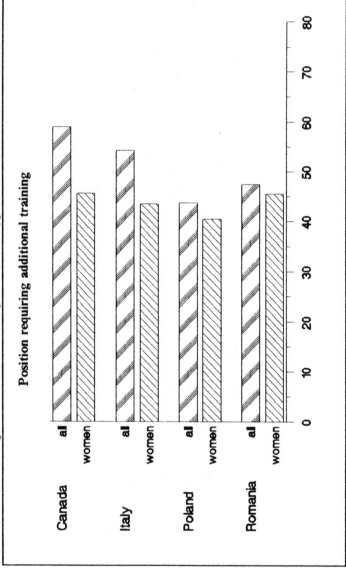

Fig. 3 Readiness to Accept Different Types of Promotion †

† Percentage of women out of the total number of respondents who would accept such a type of promotion.

Fig. 3 Readiness to Accept Different Types of Promotion †

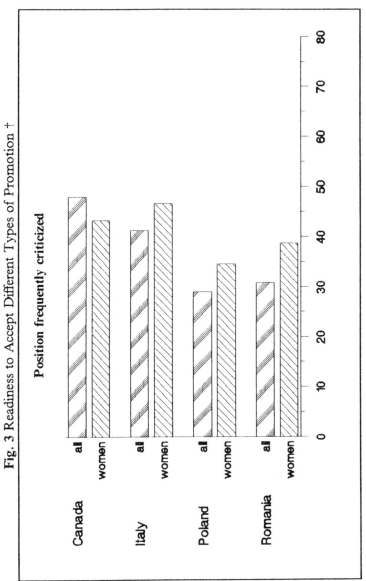

† Percentage of women out of the total number of respondents who would accept such a type of promotion.

Fig. 3 Readiness to Accept Different Types of Promotion †

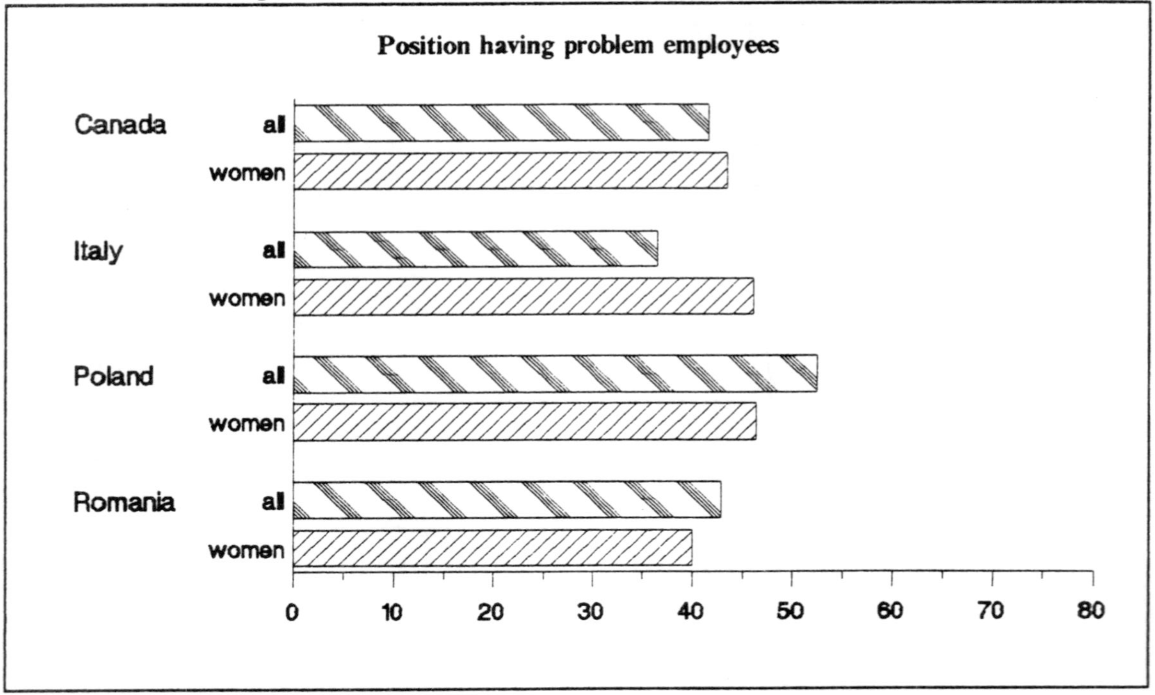

† Percentage of women out of the total number of respondents who would accept such a type of promotion.

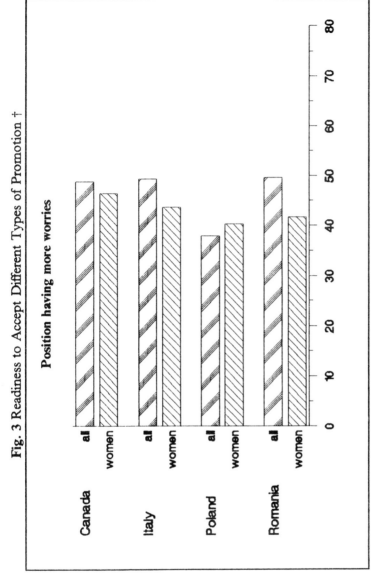

Fig. 3 Readiness to Accept Different Types of Promotion †

† Percentage of women out of the total number of respondents who would accept such a type of promotion.

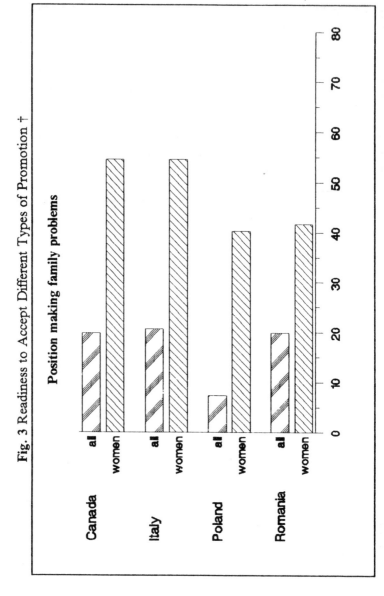

Fig. 3 Readiness to Accept Different Types of Promotion †

† Percentage of women out of the total number of respondents who would accept such a type of promotion.

which they would be frequently criticized. Maybe this reflects the ideological principle that socialist societies are not split by any major conflict and, as a consequence, life in them is built on social harmony and mutual understanding.

As we expected on the basis of our previous findings, the differences between men and women do not correspond to a stereotypical dychotomic picture. With few exceptions, women usually make up only a little less than a half of the respondents who would accept promotions. In other words, they are not basically uninterested in career advancement, even if in all categories men outnumber them in their readiness to move to a higher position.

Even the largely diffused opinion that women, more often than men, tend to reject promotions entailing family problems is not supported by our data. As a matter of fact, in Canada and Italy women accept such promotions more than men do.

4.5 *Preferred Types of Protest*

It is commonly held that women are less eager than men to protest against unfavourable working conditions. To prove this, we asked the following question:

"If a decision concerning your work was made with which you totally disagree, what would you do?"

The replies to this question allow us not only to validate the frequent belief about women's passivity (Knowles, 1952) but also to find out what kind of methods of protest that respondents of both sexes are ready to use. We formulated the hypothesis that women who protest prefer to choose ways that are restricted to their own workplace, while men are more often ready to turn to organizations outside of it.

As shown in Table 3, the number of respondents who would not react at all is small everywhere (from 4.5% in Canada to 13.5% in Romania). Comparing the answers of men and women belonging to the same categories, we find variations from country to country. In Canada almost no differences are found. In Italy, men more often than women declare their passivity, while in Poland the opposite is true in all categories, with the exception of decision-makers. In Romania the proportion of men and women varies from one category to another.

Table 3 Expression of Different Types of Protest†

	BCW M	BCW F	WCW M	WCW F	T M	T F	PoW M	PoW F	DM M	DM F	Total
Canada											
1	4.0	5.1	3.0	3.0	3.0	2.0	13.0	9.4	2.0	2.7	4.5
2	78.0	84.8	90.0	93.0	90.0	93.0	70.0	85.4	72.1	75.8	82.4
3	37.0	27.3	30.0	38.0	57.0	67.0	48.0	44.8	53.1	57.7	46.8
4	52.0	34.3	21.0	10.0	31.0	31.0	50.0	27.1	12.2	24.2	28.3
5	13.0	9.1	6.0	5.0	21.0	8.0	13.0	15.6	11.6	19.5	12.4
6	62.6	50.0	73.5	65.0	73.7	66.0	52.5	35.2	87.2	89.9	67.9
Italy											
1	14.0	6.1	5.9	3.0	6.0	5.1	3.1	11.1	5.6	2.7	6.1
2	69.0	59.8	77.2	84.0	80.8	87.0	79.6	50.5	76.6	82.6	75.2
3	43.0	49.5	58.4	46.0	50.5	55.0	70.4	30.3	51.0	63.8	52.3
4	42.0	29.2	32.0	27.0	32.3	21.0	50.0	44.4	14.6	29.1	31.3
5	6.0	6.2	4.0	9.0	20.2	11.0	22.4	0.0	7.6	16.1	10.4
6	82.0	74.5	78.2	86.0	80.0	70.7	68.4	39.8	86.9	90.6	77.6
Poland											
1	8.2	13.1	10.0	12.5	6.1	12.0		10.0	4.6	3.4	8.4
2	81.6	83.8	85.0	88.5	84.7	84.0		82.0	90.7	93.1	86.5
3	48.0	36.4	36.0	28.8	41.8	23.0		54.0	44.4	29.7	37.9
4	29.6	26.5	33.0	20.2	20.4	20.0		37.0	46.4	39.3	31.5
5	58.2	46.9	44.0	34.6	24.5	41.0		60.0	20.5	22.1	37.9
6	43.2	24.5	52.0	45.2	61.9	56.1		28.7	82.7	73.8	55.2
Romania											
1	8.1	11.0	16.2	11.1	16.0	17.7	11.5	21.9	10.2	8.3	13.5
2	88.9	88.0	71.7	75.8	71.0	66.7	78.1	70.8	66.1	76.7	75.8
3	54.5	45.0	46.5	33.3	37.0	31.3	60.4	37.5	43.1	35.0	42.6
4	53.5	45.0	40.4	34.3	41.0	32.3	55.2	27.1	44.1	31.7	40.7
5	25.3	12.0	11.1	12.1	23.0	9.4	26.0	6.3	8.5	5.0	14.5
6	33.7	26.0	42.0	39.2	56.0	36.7	57.3	22.5	66.7	66.1	43.4

† The table gives the percentage saying "yes" to each method of protest
1 Nothing
2 Complaint to supervisor
3 Complaint to head of workplace
4 Go to a party or union
5 Contact mass-media
6 Other

The rank order of different kinds of protest is the same in all countries, save partially in Poland: complaint to the immediate superior, complaint to the head of the workplace, turning to a political party or union, contacting the mass-media. In Poland the mass-media are mentioned more often than turning to a party or the union.

We have to be aware that turning to a political party or union may have different meanings. In the socialist countries, it might mean looking for help in the local party cell within the workplace or contacting a higher level in the party hierarchy outside one's workplace. Our questionnaire does not allow us to identify the levels of those organizations to which our respondents would appeal.

The analysis reveals a common pattern for all countries. Women outnumber men in almost all categories as far as turning to the immediate superior is concerned, except in Romania where the picture varies from category to category. Complaining to the head of one's workplace tends to be mentioned more often by Canadian and Italian women, less often by Polish and Romanian women in comparison to their male counterparts. The two other ways of protest, i.e. turning to a political party or a union and contacting the mass-media, are found to be more "masculine" than "feminine". The gap between men and women ranges from a few percentage points to about 15%. But in this respect Canadian and Italian female decision-makers are exceptions: they turn to parties or unions more often than their male counterparts. As far as the mass-media are concerned, all female decision-makers, Italian and Romanian white-collar workers and Polish teachers are more willing than their male counterparts to have recourse to them.

The results partially validate our hypothesis. It is not true that women are just passive. The differences between them and men are merely differences of degree. But it is true that some ways of protest are more congenial to men than to women. Women are readier than men to limit their protest to what can be done without too much noise, although again it would be highly incorrect to say that women choose only quiet methods.

4.6 *Passive v. Active Orientation to Work*

The index of passive-active orientation to work has been constructed on a basis of three questions dealing with the wish for vertical mobility, the readiness to protest, and the willingness to continue working (see App. 19). Fig. 4 shows the results obtained with it.

In Canada, Poland and Romania the active orientation to work is tendentially high, while in Italy tendentially low. In all countries men show a higher orientation than women, but, if we examine the picture in more detail, category by category, we realize

Fig. 4 Passive-Active Orientation towards Work †

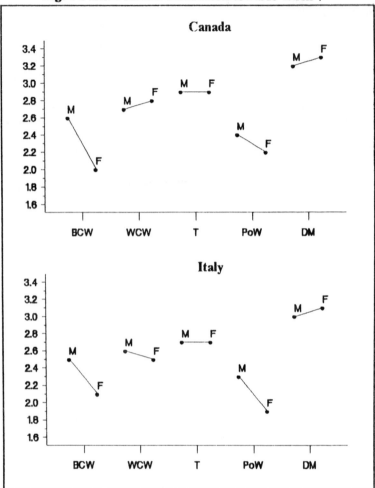

† A high score means an active orientation.

Fig. 4 Passive-Active Orientation towards Work †

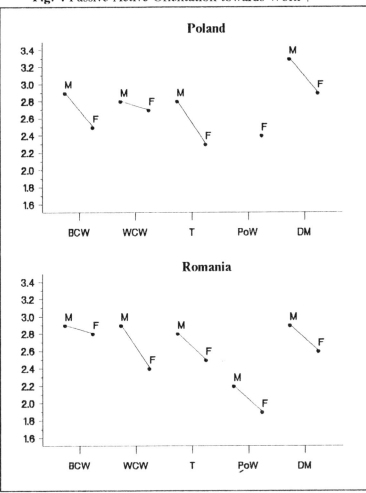

† A high score means an active orientation.

that the significant difference is limited to blue-collar workers, except in Romania; to teachers, except in Canada and Italy; and to decision-makers in Poland and Romania. Table 4 shows the results of a multiple classification analysis (MCA).

Table 4 Predictors of Passive-Active Orientation to Work (MCA)

Factors	Rank	Beta	More active respondents
Category in the sample	1	.2070	Decision-makers
Age	2	.1430	40-59 years
Alienation	3	.1148	Not or little alienated
Education	4	.1133	Highly educated
Sex	5	.0918	Men
Control over work conditions	6	.0886	Who perceives having more control
Years of residence in the neighbourhood	7	.0820	No clear pattern
Country	8	.0806	Canadians and Poles
Father's occupation	9	.0617	Professionals, high and middle level managers, teachers
Religious practice	10	.0582	Not practising
Work seniority	11	.0571	6-10 years
Mother's occupation	12	.0542	Professionals, teachers, middle level managers
Work satisfaction	13	.0516	More satisfied
Performance of govt and unions as to gender equality	14	.0197	No clear pattern

R^2 = .16.

This analysis clearly demonstrates that gender is not the most important factor differentiating passive-active orientation. The respondent's occupation, age, degree of political alienation, and education are more important in this respect. These predictors are also more important than type of country, personal experience in the workplace, social origin, and appraisal of the performance of the political system with regard to ensuring equal rights for men and women, which we expected to play a more decisive role (see ch. 4, par. 5).

The first subjective predictor is political alienation. Active orientation is higher among people who are not alienated from the system, who consider themselves as part of it and who do not feel hopeless (see par. 6 below). These results are congruent with many other studies which show that the feeling of alienation is matched by apathy. Historical experience teaches us that the feelings of alienation and apathy may turn into an explosion of dissatisfaction aimed at introducing radical changes.

We can conclude that women are more passive than men but, simultaneously, that sex *per se* is a less important factor in this respect than other factors of a social nature.

4.7 *Should Women and Men be Treated Equally?*

4.7.1 *Normative Equality as to Vocational Training*

Everywhere a clear majority of respondents (between 87.3% and 89.2%) believe that women and men should have the same opportunities to receive vocational training. The few people who opt for more favourable conditions for either men or women are almost equally divided in all countries.

A comparison of women's and men's replies within each category shows that slightly more women than men hold the opinion that women should be favoured. In Canada and Italy more women than men believe that both sexes should enjoy equal chances in this respect. The differences rarely exceed 10%. In Poland they almost do not exist. In Romania a reverse pattern is observed: more men than women consider that opportunities to vocational training should be equal. In all countries differences among categories are small. Only blue-collar workers express less often the need for equal chances: this is true also in the socialist countries.

4.7.2 *Normative Equality as to Job Opportunities*

The distribution of answers concerning the respondents' attitude towards women's and men's opportunities to a job is, to a large extent, the same in all countries. As in the case of vocational training, about the same percentages in all countries (83.3% to 88.7%) opt for gender parity. Also, in this instance, slightly more women than men are ready to accept equal, or more favourable, conditions for women. Again, as in the previous case, more male than female Romanians express the wish to privilege women. Blue-collars workers tend slightly less often to opt for an improvement of women's opportunities in having access to jobs: once more, this is true also in the socialist countries.

4.7.3 *Normative Equality as to being Fired*

The respondents' opinions differ significantly when they come to the question concerning who should be fired first. Relatively fewer people, although still the majority (except in Poland), opt for equal treatment in firing (from 43.5% in Poland to 71% in Canada and Romania). The gender difference on this issue is striking: in all countries, especially Italy and Poland, women outnumber men in each category.

In general, everywhere less educated respondents appear more often to support discriminatory practices against women. This is especially noticeable among men, although the same tendency appears among women.

* * *

The index of "sex inequality" has been described in Appendix 23. It offers an overall picture on the issues just examined.

In general, Romanians and Canadians are more in favour of sex equality (over 70%) than Italians (54.3%) and Poles (44.8%).

As shown in Fig. 5, the differences between men and women from the same categories are significant in all countries, with the exception of Romania. Everywhere, however, women much more often than men (usually 20% and in Italy even more) state that men should not be privileged at all.

In Canada and Italy, the more educated respondents (white-collar workers, teachers and decision-makers) opt more often for the elimination of any discrimination against women. In Romania, however, all categories of respondents support this. In Poland the findings are also different; surprisingly, teachers of both sexes, housewives, and decision-makers (especially men) take a stand against any type of inequality less often than the other categories.

A comparison of the indices of perceived inequality and expected inequality shows that in all countries, except for Polish female blue- and white-collar workers and teachers, the respondents expect an increase in the equality of opportunity for both sexes in the next five years. The improvement is especially marked in Romania. However, they think that inequality will still persist. Men are more optimistic than women with regard to future equality, with the exception of Italians, among whom the expectation is reversed.

It is interesting to note that in all countries decision-makers, especially females, while they are not so optimistic about changes

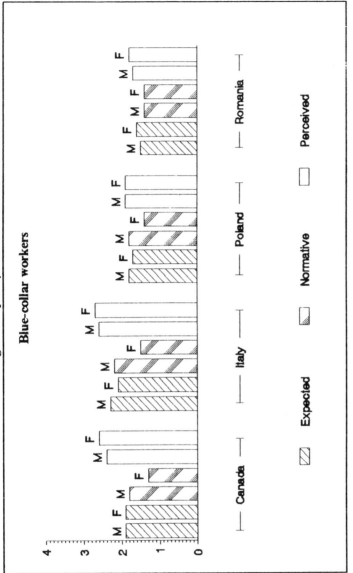

Fig. 5 Inequality in Work †

† A high score indicates inequality.

Fig. 5 Inequality in Work †

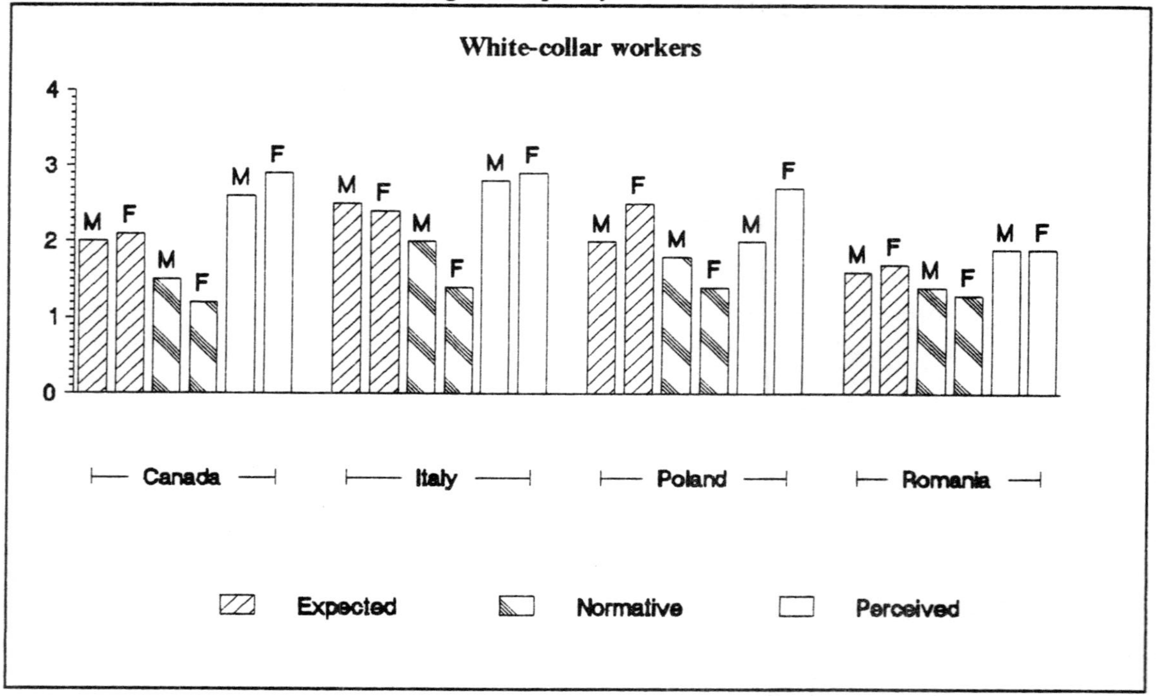

White-collar workers

† A high score indicates inequality.

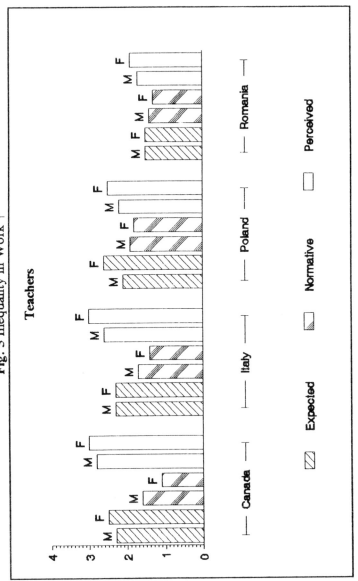

Fig. 5 Inequality in Work †

† A high score indicates inequality.

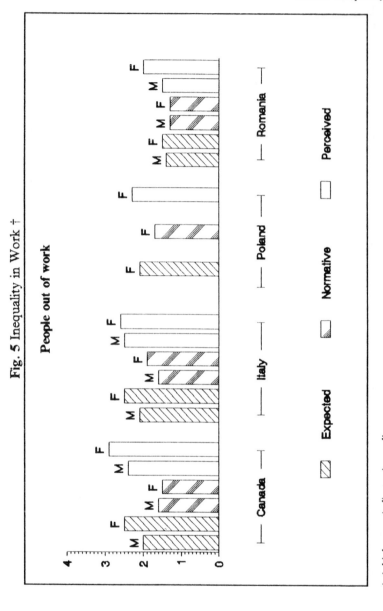

Fig. 5 Inequality in Work †

† A high score indicates inequality.

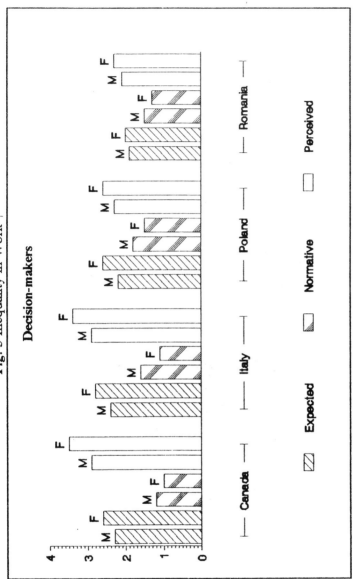

Fig. 5 Inequality in Work †

† A high score indicates inequality.

in the near future, constitute a group of people who, more than others, emphasize a need to eliminate discrimination against women. It is reasonable to assume that they are, at least, sensitive to the problem, if not ready to give it priority. Polish decision-makers, though, are an exception: they are more pessimistic when they talk about future opportunities but are less in favour of normative equality than both decision-makers in the other countries and members of other categories in Poland. Therefore, one may assume that they will not be too much interested in this issue.

5 Attitudes towards Women in Leadership Positions

Women's access to the labour force has not been followed by an equivalent increase in their participation in power. Although, as we have shown, careers for women have become more and more acceptable to women themselves and to men, leadership positions, especially the top ones, are still held almost exclusively by men. The prevalent opinion is that this is so because women are not interested in such positions, inasmuch as they focus their attention on family affairs which are *naturally* connected with their roles in society. Different studies carried out in many countries support this view.

In spite of a large number of respondents having had female supervisors, it is surprising that, of the many women and men expressing a positive opinion about women's predispositions to hold leadership positions, few state that they would prefer to have a female supervisor. Their number does not exceed 5% in any country, with the exception of Romania where they reach 13.5%. Canadians and Italians are very close to each other in their preferences: about a quarter of the respondents prefer a male supervisor, while in Romania the percentage is higher (35.2%) and in Poland the highest (50.8%). The other respondents say that the sex of the supervisor does not make a difference. These findings show that it is not respondents from the socialist countries, but rather respondents from countries with developed feminist movements, who tend to be more egalitarian in this respect. It is worth stressing that the tendency to prefer a male supervisor is equally expressed by women and men, though female decision-makers and teachers represent an exception.

In Canada and Italy, also, the more educated female respondents tend to prefer a male supervisor less. This correlation does not exist in the case of men in any country.

To probe this issue, we asked the following question:

"Should women, in your opinion, have the same chances as men have to hold a position of leadership?"

Polish respondents are the most traditional in this respect: only 2.1% state that women should be preferred. They are followed in sequence by the Italians, Canadians and Romanians (7.2% of the latter). The number of people who consider that men should be preferred ranges from 24.6% in Poland to 10.6% in Canada. In other words, the majority of our respondents (between 72.5% and 83.2%) share the opinion that women should have equal access to leadership positions. It is also true that such an opinion is more often expressed by women than men in all countries and categories (with the exception of Canadian male blue-collar workers and decision-makers). In most categories, the number of women opting for equal access is higher than the number of men by 10% to 30%. The smallest intra-category differences are found among Romanian respondents.

We also tested the respondents' opinions concerning different abilities considered to be components of leadership roles with the following questions:

"Do you think that women are as good as, better than, worse than men in the workplace with respect to:
(a) Solving conflicts among people?
(b) Motivating others to do what they have to do?
(c) Understanding the needs of people?
(d) Grasping people's thoughts?
(e) Defending their own ideas even if people oppose them?
(f) Rewarding and punishing?"

All in all, the tendency is to consider women equal to men, but this is by no means the rule (Table 5). For instance, women are considered better than men in understanding the needs of people and their thoughts. It depends on the item in question, the category of the respondent and the country. A high percentage of male decision-makers, for example, especially in Poland, express a negative opinion as far as the first, second, and last items are con-

Table 5 Women's Ability on the Job in Comparison with Men's with regard to certain Capacities

	Canada M	Canada F	Italy M	Italy F	Poland M	Poland F	Romania M	Romania F
(a) Solving conflicts among people								
Blue-collar workers	2.1	2.0	1.9	1.8	2.0	1.8	2.1	1.9
White-collar workers	2.2	2.0	2.0	1.7	2.2	1.9	2.0	1.7
Teachers	2.2	1.9	2.1	1.8	2.2	2.2	2.2	1.8
People out of work	1.8	1.8	2.0	1.7		2.0	2.2	1.7
Decision-makers	2.1	1.8	2.1	1.6	2.6	2.1	1.8	1.7
(b) Motivating others to do what they have to do								
Blue-collar workers	2.2	2.0	2.0	1.8	2.0	2.0	2.1	1.7
White-collar workers	2.3	2.0	2.0	1.9	2.2	1.8	2.1	1.7
Teachers	2.2	2.0	2.0	1.9	2.0	1.8	2.0	1.8
People out of work	1.8	1.8	1.8	1.7		1.9	2.4	1.7
Decision-makers	2.1	2.0	2.0	1.8	2.3	2.0	2.3	1.7
(c) Understanding the needs of people								
Blue-collar workers	1.8	1.6	1.7	1.6	1.7	1.6	1.8	1.5
White-collar workers	1.9	1.5	1.8	1.3	1.7	1.5	1.7	1.4
Teachers	1.9	1.5	1.8	1.4	1.6	1.4	1.6	1.5
People out of work	1.6	1.5	1.5	1.6		1.6	1.8	1.2
Decision-makers	1.7	1.5	1.6	1.4	1.6	1.2	1.5	1.2
(d) Grasping people's thoughts								
Blue-collar workers	2.1	1.9	1.8	1.7	1.6	1.6	2.0	1.4
White-collar workers	2.2	1.9	1.8	1.4	1.7	1.5	1.7	1.4
Teachers	2.2	2.0	1.8	1.5	1.4	1.3	1.7	1.5
People out of work	2.0	1.5	1.6	1.5		1.5	1.9	1.3
Decision-makers	2.1	1.9	1.7	1.4	1.8	1.3	1.6	1.4
(e) Defending their own ideas even if people oppose them								
Blue-collar workers	2.2	2.0	1.9	1.8	2.1	2.0	2.2	2.0
White-collar workers	2.3	1.9	1.8	1.8	2.2	2.2	2.1	1.8
Teachers	2.2	2.3	2.1	1.9	2.1	2.2	2.2	2.1
People out of work	2.1	2.1	2.1	1.7		1.8	2.3	2.1
Decision-makers	2.1	2.3	2.0	1.9	2.2	2.4	2.2	2.2
(f) Rewarding and punishing								
Blue-collar workers	2.1	2.4	2.1	2.0	2.2	2.1	1.8	2.1
White-collar workers	2.2	2.2	2.1	2.0	2.4	2.2	2.2	2.0
Teachers	2.2	1.9	2.2	2.0	2.6	2.2	2.2	2.2
People out of work	2.0	2.0	2.3	1.8		2.2	2.3	2.1
Decision-makers	2.2	2.1	2.3	2.0	2.6	2.2	2.3	1.9

1 = women are better; 3 = women are worse.

cerned. This may result from their limited experience with situations where women are called on to solve conflicts and to motivate or reward people. It may also be because of their fear of having women as competitors.

We find in general that in Romania, and even more so in Poland, higher percentages of respondents state that women are not as good as men. (Compared with Canada and Italy, about one-third v. one-fifth as to the first and second items, more as to the last two items.) This shows that the perception of women's abilities is more congruent with the attitudes toward female and male propensities than with other values examined in this chapter.

Women are not always more in favour of women than men are. A surprising view, for example, is the very strong negative evaluation delivered by female decision-makers in Canada and Poland as to the second item: they surpass not only all other female categories in that country and the female decision-makers in the other countries but also their male counterparts, who, as we have just seen, give a very negative evaluation of women!

Finally, we tried to measure the ability of women to see reality with a different eye from men. We asked our respondents to express agreement or disagreement with the following statement:

"Women always fare better than men in political leadership positions."

This was based on the experience that women, whenever and wherever they have had positions of political leadership, have fared better than men. A moment of reflection will persuade that this is not an odd idea. However, disagreement is general and is even rather strong in Canada, followed by Italy. Women disagree less than men, it is true, but the differences are not always significant. Decision-makers, followed by teachers, is the category that disagrees most and this holds true also as far as female decison-makers are concerned! The correlation between education and rejection of the statement proves that male dominance has shaped values to the point that women lose trust in themselves even against evidence, and their way of looking at reality becomes masculine.

* * *

The correlations (not shown here) among the items concerning these abilities, are rather high in all countries, with a few exceptions regarding men especially.

On the other hand, the appraisal of women's abilities and the belief that women should be favoured in obtaining leadership positions are seldom correlated, save for Canadian men and Italian women. This lack of consistency reflects a dramatic situation: when the respondents are asked to evaluate some aspects of leadership, without mentioning that they are talking about leadership functions, they feel "free" to respond on the basis of their *experience*, but, when they are asked about their *attitude* towards women in leadership positions, they find themselves entangled in the old stereotypes.

We formulated the hypothesis that people whose social micro-environment (procreation family, actual milieu) is characterized by political activism are more free from these stereotypes, since they have had the opportunity to appraise individual performances (see App. 4 and 5).

Our hypothesis was only very partially validated, with the exception of Italy. Italian women whose social milieu was or is relatively more involved in politics have a tendency to accept the idea that women should be favoured in leadership positions (correlations range from .11 to .26, p = .01 to .001; more educated categories show stronger coefficients). In this respect, Italian women deviate from all other respondents. In the other cases, significant correlations are rare.

Also fairly rare are significant correlations between the political involvement of the respondents' social milieu and the appraisal of women's performance in different leadership functions. Their number ranges from 4 for Canadian women to 14 for Polish women (maximum 42). Correlations are not more frequent for women than men. Previous researchers have shown that women are more influenced by their social milieu than men, but our study supports the view that this is only very modestly true and only as far as the Italian and Polish samples are concerned.

5.1 *Attitudes towards Women in Power*

The answers to the questions described above were used for the construction of the overall index "Attitudes towards women in power" (see App. 21). Figure 6 shows the results obtained with it.

Everywhere the majority of the respondents does not share the view that women are less capable than men in a leadership position. Such a traditional point of view is more often expressed in Poland and Romania than in Canada and Italy; however, in all countries, those who uphold it represent a small minority.

Our assumption that the existence of a feminist movement promotes the growth of a relatively large group of radical extrem-

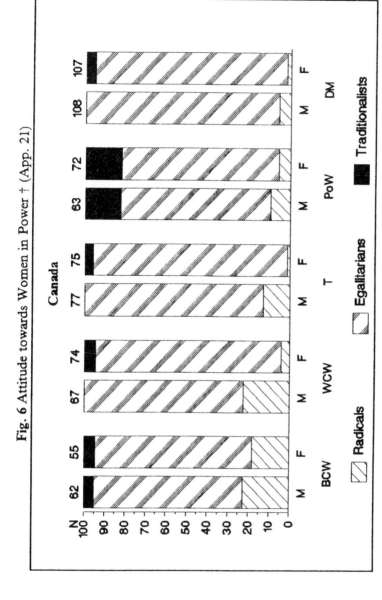

Fig. 6 Attitude towards Women in Power † (App. 21)

† The figure reports only pure types. This is the reason why the Ns here are lower than in the sample.
See abbreviation list for explanations of categories.

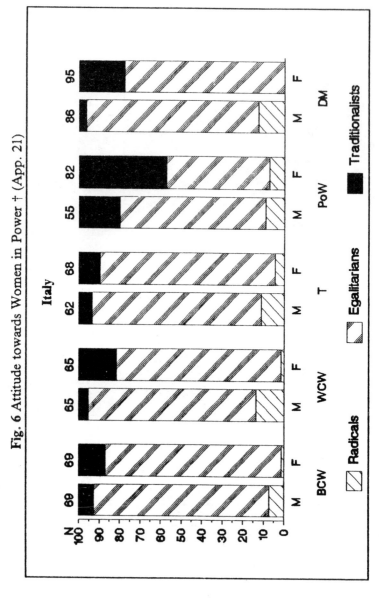

Fig. 6 Attitude towards Women in Power † (App. 21)

† The figure reports only pure types. This is the reason why the Ns here are lower than in the sample.
See abbreviation list for explanations of categories.

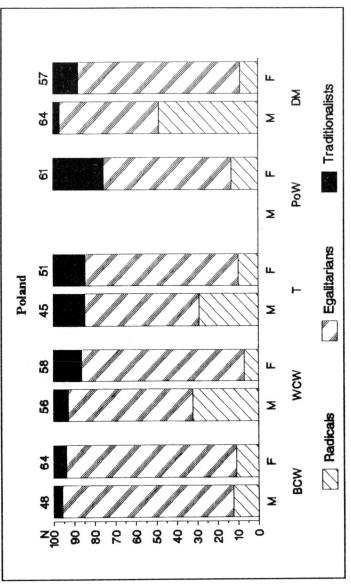

Fig. 6 Attitude towards Women in Power † (App. 21)

† The figure reports only pure types. This is the reason why the Ns here are lower than in the sample.
See abbreviation list for explanations of categories.

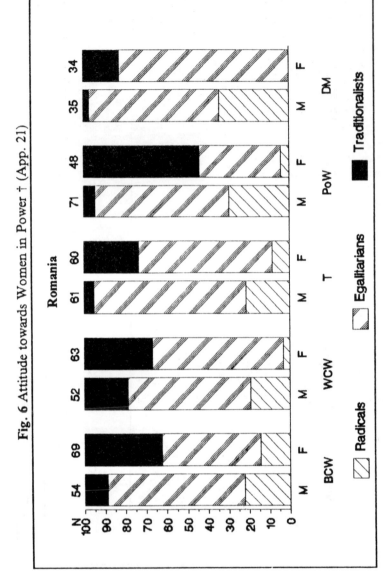

Fig. 6 Attitude towards Women in Power † (App. 21)

† The figure reports only pure types. This is the reason why the Ns here are lower than in the sample.
See abbreviation list for explanations of categories.

ists was not upheld. Their number is the highest in Poland and Romania, where there is no feminist movement at all.

In all countries, and especially in Canada, the egalitarian approach prevails.

Decision-makers differ from the respondents of other categories. In Canada and Italy they express more often an egalitarian attitude. In Poland and Romania, on the contrary, male decision-makers tend to be traditional.

A multiple classification analysis (Table 6) shows that the significance of the factors influencing the attitudes towards the presence of women in leadership positions is different from the pattern that emerged in the case of the passive-active orientation towards work (see Fig. 5).

Table 6 Predictors of Attitudes towards Women in Positions of Power (MCA)

Factors	Rank	Beta	Respondents more positively oriented
Orientation to women's extra-domestic work	1	.1977	Favourable to women's work
Country	2	.1352	Italians and Romanians
Sex	3	.1295	Women
Length of residence in the neighbourhood	4	.1218	11-15 years, 21-25 years
Category in the sample	5	.0976	Housewives
Education	6	.0969	Less educated
Father's occupation	7	.0900	Unskilled blue-collar workers
Mother's occupation	8	.0891	Small business, farmers
Ideal division of domestic chores	9	.0734	Opting for non-traditional version of household chores
Religious practice	10	.0406	Practising
Political alienation	11	.0367	Less alienated
Age	12	.0364	50-59 years
Traditional v. non-traditional female propensities	13	.0129	No relationship

$R^2 = .11$.

We assumed that non-traditional attitudes about division of household chores and female propensities would influence strongly the respondents' attitude to women as leaders. Our findings proved the hypothesis false. Non-traditional orientation towards the access of women to extra-domestic work is the only factor found to play a decisive role. Country and sex, although less important, also play a significant role in shaping attitudes about women's access to power positions. The political system does not appear to be a factor of paramount importance, contrary to what might have been expected: in fact, Italians and Romanians are more positively oriented than Poles and Canadians.

6 Alienation

The term "alienation" has been used in a variety of ways (Gamson, 1961; Neal and Seeman, 1964; Olsen, 1969; Israel, 1971). This has led at times to its being confused with other concepts which have an autonomy of their own (e.g. anomia: Srole, 1956; McClosky and Schaar, 1965).

Alienation is defined here as a sensation of powerlessness in political matters; a lack of meaning and clarity about what one is supposed to believe; a disorder and confusion in moral norms.

Alienation is considered to be one of the important factors influencing people's involvement in public life. It is a rather common belief that women are more alienated than men.

The questions which were used to test this variable refer to the above-mentioned dimensions. They were taken from earlier studies, and have been the subject of methodological discussions which we shall not repeat here. The respondents were asked to choose among answers ranging from "totally disagree" to "totally agree" in respect of the following three statements:

(a) "Sometimes politics and government seem so complicated that a person like me cannot really understand what is going on".
(b) "A person like me cannot try to influence the course of the events".
(c) "Life is nowadays so confused that one does not know how to distinguish right from wrong".

The picture that emerges is rather complex. Only in the case of the last item is there in all countries a clear tendency to disagreement, although there is a variation from 76% in Canada and Romania to 58.5% in Italy. As for the first item, the agreement fluctuates around 40%, but there are strong differences as far as total disagreement is concerned (from 43% in Romania to 25.1% in Poland). Opinions vary sharply about the second item, which is the most rich in meaning of the three: in Poland the feeling of powerlessness is shared by 61% of our respondents, in Italy by 50%, in Romania by 39.3%, in Canada by 28.7%.

Men, in general, tend to disagree with the statements, especially the first two, more than women, but the difference is not too great (at most by 15%, with a few exceptions above that percentage in Poland and Romania).

Decision-makers, especially female ones, as expected, show a lower feeling of powerlessness. In all four countries, blue-collar workers look more at a loss than any other category for all three items.

* * *

The index of alienation, constructed on the basis of these three questions, gives the picture shown in Figure 7.

Italians and Poles share a higher level of alienation than the respondents in the other two countries. Decision-makers are significantly less alienated than all other respondents. This finding is congruent with the results of many other studies (Siemienska, 1983c; Tannenbaum et al. 1974). Blue-collar workers show a higher level of alienation than the majority of the other categories, except in Poland and Romania. A high degree of alienation, as expected, is also characteristic of housewives, especially in Italy. The exception is Canadian housewives.

The frequently expressed opinion (Robinson et al., 1973) that women are more alienated than men is supported by the findings of our study but, although the differences between men and women are almost all significant, there is no such dichotomy between non-alienated men and *essentially* alienated women.

There are exceptions even to this pattern. Female decision-makers in Canada and Italy and Italian female blue-collar workers are less alienated than their male counterparts.

7 Conclusion

In this chapter we have presented an analysis of different types of values, attitudes and expectations, some concerning the "private" sphere and others the "public". We have shown that this distinction, as a dividing line between women and men, does not hold.

Fig. 7 Alienation †

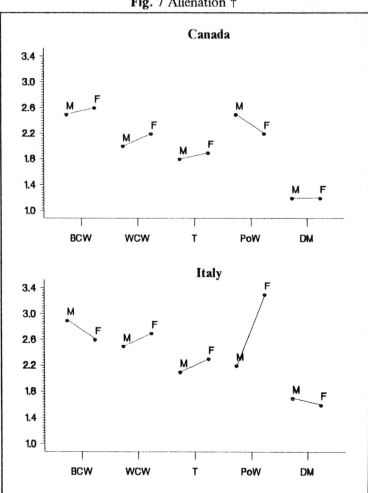

† A high score means alienation.

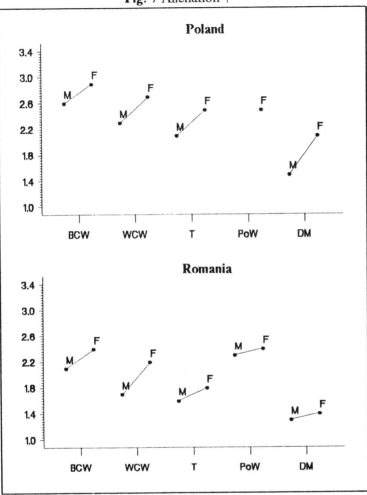

Fig. 7 Alienation †

† A high score means alienation.

Socio-political systems differentiate values, attitudes and expectations only to some degree and in a very specific way. Poles and Romanians of both sexes are in many respects more traditionally minded than Canadians and Italians. This finding suggests that the presence of a strong feminist movement has a definite impact. It is interesting that in Canada and Italy the egalitarian tendency (neither pro-feminine nor pro-masculine) is more common than in Poland and Romania, where often a mixture of traditionalists and radical extremists prevails. Respondents from the latter countries display a more traditional attitude as far as female propensities and ideal division of household chores are concerned, but they express a more pro-work orientation and a more egalitarian approach in regard to access to education and extra-domestic work. We assume that this has to do with the different models of women's mobilization in the labour force (see ch. 4). Women in socialist countries have been persuaded to begin work as equal co-workers with men without any consideration for a "female nature", while in the West the feminist movement developed a multilevel analysis of women's position in society.

Our results do not support current beliefs about basic gender differences in values, attitudes and expectations. This is the more startling inasmuch as we find a wide gap between men and women in terms of power. Obviously, as the analysis that is carried out in chapter 5 and Appendix B of this book shows, gender differences in values, attitudes and expectations do not explain much of the lack of parity in that area.

3 IN THE FAMILY

1 The Question of Gender Parity at Home

The reader may wonder why we tackle the issue of gender parity in the family, which is traditionally portrayed as the core of private life, while this research concerns more public life.

Aside from our rejection of the idea that the family belongs exclusively to the private sphere, the reason why we explore this area of social life is our belief that without gender parity in the family no parity can be achieved in general.

The family is a crucial institution in any society, which depends on it for survival and progress, and it represents a unique existential experience for men and women alike. However, while for men it does not appear as an obstacle to participation in public life, it may do so for women. It is a question not only of the time and energy that women have to devote to the family, but also, today above all, of habits of mind. If men do not share equally with their partners domestic chores and child care and do not adopt an open attitude towards women's relations with the outer world, the traditional exclusion of women from public life will be perpetuated (Sapiro, 1984: 174-180).

We cannot deal here with the various explanations of gender inequality in the family that are given by different sociological theories (1). The reader, however, will easily catch the implications of our findings from that point of view.

It is a tenet of Marxism that gender equality can be achieved only in a society where women work outside the home on a footing of equality with men in the framework of a system where the family is relieved of its main function, i.e. the reproduction of labour power, and where production is geared to the satisfaction of general needs in an egalitarian context (Vajda and Heller, 1971; Larguia and Dumoulin, 1976; Beechey, 1978; Molyneux, 1979; Hartmann, 1981b; Holmstrom, 1981; Young, et al., 1984) (2). Unquestionably, in the socialist countries deep changes have indeed affected the family structure (Szalai et al., 1972; Jancar, 1974; Lapidus, 1978; Heitlinger, 1979; Sas, 1981; Karchev and Yasmaya, 1982; Siemienska, 1983b). We have here an opportunity to test whether, from the specific point of view of gender parity within the couple, countries inspired by socialist philosophy present a more favourable picture for women than countries that have developed along liberal-democratic lines, replete as they are with limits and contradictions which weigh heavily on women in spite of efforts to mitigate them.

2 Income

As Fig. 1 shows, in all countries and in all categories of our sample, men state that they earn more than their wives and women state that they earn less than their husbands. All differences are statistically significant. Unfortunately there are no couples in our sample and so our respondents' answers cannot be matched, but nevertheless the uniformity in all countries is striking.

Female decision-makers everywhere show a higher earning capacity in relation to their husbands than do women in other categories. This important but not unexpected finding indicates that access to decision-making in the public sphere is associated with a certain degree of economic autonomy. In all countries housewives' scores are lower than all other female categories. The pattern for men is less clear (3).

3 Child Care

We are aware that the measure which we used is very rough. It does not reflect the quality of child care and represents a subjective evaluation of the time given to it (Table 1).

The gender contrast is striking. In all four countries men answer that their wives take care of the children "often", while women state that their husbands do it only "at times" or even (as in Canada) "almost never". The difference is statistically significant within each category in all countries.

However, in Poland, and especially in Romania, women (with the exception of decision-makers) say that their husbands take care of the children to some extent, although always less than they themselves.

This sharp diversity in the answers of men and women may be owing to the fact that, at least in Canada and Italy, the male respondents' spouses are mostly housewives. In Canada, housewives make up 86% of the wives of those respondents who answer that the wife "always" takes care of the children, and 62% of those who answer "often"; in Italy the percentages are respectively 72% and 53%. The scores also show, however, that working mothers

Fig. 1 Income Parity †

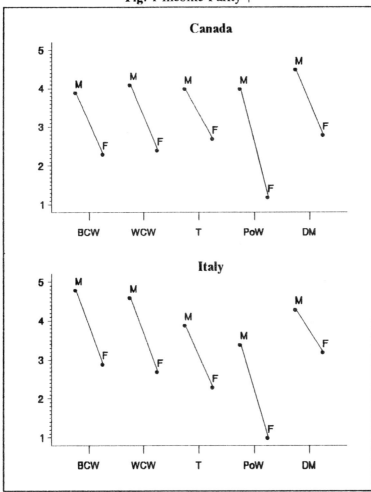

† All differences are significant at a p ≤ .01.
The question asked was the following:
'Who earns more: you or your spouse?'

    1 = Only my spouse earns;
    2 = My spouse earns more than I;
    3 = We earn about the same;
    4 = I earn more than my spouse;
    5 = Only I earn.

Fig. 1 Income Parity †

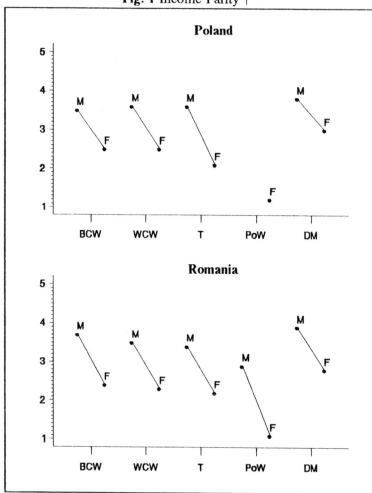

† All differences are significant at a p ≤ .01.
The question asked was the following:
'Who earns more: you or your spouse?'

    1 = Only my spouse earns;
    2 = My spouse earns more than I;
    3 = We earn about the same;
    4 = I earn more than my spouse;
    5 = Only I earn.

Table 1 Rank Order for Child Care (first three and last items)

The question asked was the following: "If there are children who live with you, who takes care of them after school and how often?" For each of the following answers--nobody; my spouse; the school; a relative; a domestic help; a neighbour; one of the children; another person; myself--the scores were: 1 = "always"; 2 = "often"; 3 = "at times"; 4 = "never or almost never".

Rank	Canada	Italy	Poland	Romania
			Male blue-collar workers	
I	Spouse* (2.4) <	Spouse* (1.3) <	Spouse* (2.0) <	Spouse* (1.6) <
II	Myself (3.3) >	Myself (3.3) >	Myself (2.2) <	Myself* (2.1) >
III	Relative (3.4) >	Relative* (3.8) >	Relative (3.4) =	School (3.4) =
Last	Domestic help (4.0) =	All others (4.0), except Nobody (3.9) >	Domestic help***(4.0) >	Neighbour (4.0) >
			Female blue-collar workers	
I	Relative (3.1) <	Relative*, Myself (2.9) <	Myself (2.4) >	Myself* (1.4) <
II	Myself (3.2) <	Spouse* (3.3) >	Spouse* (2.8) >	Spouse* (1.7) >
III	One of the children (3.3) <	School* (3.4) <	Nobody, School (3.3) <	Relative <, School = (3.4)
Last	Domestic help (4.0) =	Domestic help (4.0) =	Neighbour (4.0) >	Domestic help>, Another person >, One of the children (4.0) >

The asterisks indicate the level of significance of the gender difference within the same category:
*p ≤ .01;   ** .05 > p > .01;   *** .10 > p > .05
The signs >, < or = indicate the sense of the differences: for instance, the sign > indicates that the score is higher for the category in question than for the same category of the other sex.

Table 1 Rank Order for Child Care (first three and last items)

Rank	Canada	Italy	Poland	Romania
Male white-collar workers				
I	Spouse* (1.8) <	Spouse* (2.0) <	Spouse*** (2.1) <	Myself (1.7) >
II	Myself (2.9) >	Myself (2.6) >	Myself (2.4) =	Spouse* (1.8) <
III	Relative (3.5) >	Relative* (3.6) <	School*** (3.4) <	Relative (3.3) =
Last	Domestic help (4.0) >	Domestic help*** >, Another person (4.0) =	One of the children <, Neighbour (3.9) >	Domestic help >, Another person (4.0) =
Female white-collar workers				
I	Myself (2.5) <	Myself (2.2) <	Myself (2.4) =	Myself (1.6) <
II	Neighbour (3.2) <	Relative* (3.0) <	Spouse*** (2.6) >	Spouse* (2.3) >
III	Relative (3.3) <	Spouse* (3.4) >	School*** (3.5) >	Relative (3.3) =
Last	School (4.0) >	Neighbour >, Another person (4.0) =	Neighbour >, One of the children (4.0) >	Neighbour >, Another person (4.0) =
Male teachers				
I	Myself (2.8) >	Spouse* (1.9) <	Spouse* (1.7) <	Spouse* (1.6) <
II	Spouse* (2.9) <	Myself* (2.4) >	Myself* (2.5) >	Myself (1.7) =
III	Neighbour (3.5) >	Relative*** (3.6) >	Relative (3.3) <	School, Relative (3.7) >
Last	Domestic help* (4.0) >	All others (4.0), except School (3.9) >	Domestic help (4.0) >	Neighbour (4.0) =
Female teachers				
I	Myself (2.5) <	Myself* (1.4) <	Myself* (1.9) <	Myself (1.7) =
II	Spouse* (3.1) >	Spouse* (2.9) >	Spouse* (2.7) >	Spouse* (2.6) >
III	Neighbour (3.2) <	Relative*** (3.4) <	Relative (3.5) >	Relative (3.4) >
Last	Domestic help* (3.8) <	Neighbour (4.0) =	All others (3.9), except School and Nobody (3.6) <	Neighbour (4.0) =

Men out of work

Rank			
I	Spouse* (2.0) <	Spouse* (1.6) <	Myself (2.5) >
II	Myself* (2.9) >	Myself* (2.8) >	Spouse** (2.6) <
III	Relative (3.5) <	School* (2.9) <	School* (2.8) <
Last	Nobody, One of children (4.0) >	Domestic help (4.0) =	Another person (4.0) >

Housewives

Rank				
I	Myself* (1.8) <	Myself* (1.3) >	Myself (1.2)	Myself* (1.2) <
II	Spouse* (3.4) >	Spouse* (3.7) >	Spouse (2.4)	Spouse** (2.8) >
III	Relative (3.8) >	Nobody*, School*, Relative*, One of the children* (3.9) >	Nobody, School, Relative, Neighbour, One of the children (3.8)	School* (3.6) >
Last	Domestic help (4.0) =	Domestic help =, Neighbour*** (4.0) >	Another person (4.0)	Nobody (4.0) >

Male decision-makers

Rank			
I	Spouse* (2.1) <	Spouse* (1.8) <	Spouse* (1.8) <
II	Myself* (3.2) >	Myself (2.5) <	Myself* (2.3) =
III	One of the children*** (3.4) <	School, Relative (3.5) =	Relative*** (3.2) <
Last	School* (3.9) >	One of the children (.0)	All others (3.8), except School > * (3.4) and Domestic help (3.6) <
	Nobody =, Neighbour = , Another person** (3.9) >		

Female decision-makers

Rank			
I	Domestic help* (2.7) <	Myself (2.6) >	Myself (2.3) =
II	School* (2.9) <	Spouse** (2.7) >	Spouse* (3.1) >
III	Myself* (3.1) <	Nobody** (3.3) <	Nobody (3.5) <
Last	Nobody >, One of the children*** (3.8) >	Domestic help >, Neighbour = , One of the children (3.9) <	School* >, Neighbour >, One of the children (4.0) >
	Nobody =, One of the children (3.9) >		

are extensively involved in child care. In Poland the percentages of husbands who answer that their spouses are housewives and "always" or "often" take care of the children are 16% and 6%; in Romania, 16% and 3%: massive extra-domestic employment obviously makes a difference. What about the attitude towards this issue from an ideal point of view?

As Fig. 2 shows, respondents in all countries and categories say that husbands should be involved in child care only fractionally less than wives. On this issue there is general agreement between males and females belonging to the same category. However, male decision-makers in all countries except Poland (where, in any case, decision-makers of both sexes tend to be conservative), along with male white-collar workers in Canada and Italy, support significantly more than their female counterparts the traditional view that children should be nurtured mainly by mothers (although, even for these categories, the tendency is not in favour of a strong asymmetry in child care). The cross-country comparisons show that the traditional outlook prevails most of all among males and females in Romania, followed by Poland and then Canada and Italy. Surprisingly, traditional habits of mind survive to a great extent in those countries where husbands tend to be more cooperative than in the others. It is legitimate to think that this tendency results not from ideological persuasion nor new custom but from impending economic difficulties or social constraints.

The few significant intracategory correlations between these two variables --- actual and ideal child care --- indicate (at first sight, paradoxically) that women whose husbands tend never to take care of children say that the mothers should always do it, while men whose wives tend to be little absorbed by child care do not refrain from saying that the mothers should always do it. In reality, this paradox reflects the asymmetry that characterizes gender roles. Whether or not their wives take care of children, men do not change their outlook: they believe that it is always the mother's job. By contrast, women think that they should take care of the children, if their husbands do not. This result is confirmed by what we found when we disregarded categories. Correlating the two variables by sex in each country, we found a significant, although not strong, correlation for women (except in Romania), confirming the above-mentioned paradox, while for men we found no correlation. Thus it seems plausible to argue that one of the reasons why women take care of their children is that they are afraid that hus-

Fig. 2 Ideal Distribution of Tasks concerning Child Care

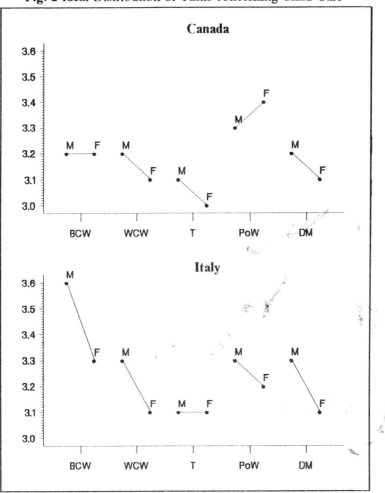

In Canada the differences are significant for WCW and DM; in Italy for the same categories and BCW.

The question asked was the following:

'If in a family both parents work, who in your opinion should take care of the children?'

1 = Always the husband;
2 = The husband more than the wife;
3 = Husband and wife to the same extent;
4 = The wife more than the husband;
5 = Always the wife.

Fig. 2 Ideal Distribution of Tasks concerning Child Care

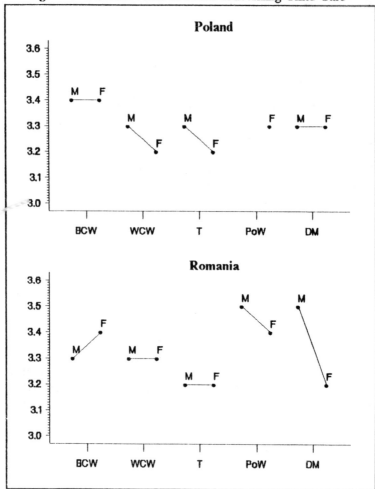

No differences are statistically relevant.
The question asked was the following:
'If in a family both parents work, who in your opinion should take care of the children?'

    1 = Always the husband;
    2 = The husband more than the wife;
    3 = Husband and wife to the same extent;
    4 = The wife more than the husband;
    5 = Always the wife.

bands would not bother to do so, even at the expense of children being neglected to some extent.

When we contrast this picture with the findings about the respondents as providers of child care (Table 1), persons of both sexes everywhere seem quite committed. In some categories, especially in Poland and Romania, it is not rare for fathers and mothers to state that they take active care of the children and, at the same time, that their partners are also active in it (4).

As regards other forms of child care (Table 1), our findings show that infrastructures, such as full-time schools or kindergarten, are more widely available in Italy, Poland and Romania than in Canada. As far as gender diversity is concerned, within each category the significant differences are few, although women tend to have recourse to these infrastructures more often than men. The conspicuous exception is represented by Romanian male decision-makers, who turn to these infrastructures significantly more often than female decision-makers. It is worth pointing out that female blue-collar workers in all four countries use these infrastructures to about the same extent, that is, relatively seldom.

As for the other forms of child care, relatives appear to be a kind of help that still exists everywhere, but only to a limited extent. Domestic help for child care, especially in Poland and Romania, is rarely available. The highest scores are found for Canadian and Italian female decision-makers, and for Italian teachers and female white-collar workers. When we compare categories of the same sex within each country, the same pattern emerges everywhere: decision-makers of both sexes have more recourse to domestic help than any other category.

In all countries, other traditional forms of child care, such as a neighbour or another child, have largely vanished, with the partial exception of Canada.

* * *

If we look at the rank order of the possible providers of help, we see (Kendall's W., data not shown here) that, for each category, the child care situation is very similar in the four countries. The coefficients are all highly significant.

Almost everywhere, men mention the wife as the person who mainly takes care of children, but rank themselves immediately afterwards. This is a momentous transformation in family life, clearly distinguishing the present situation from the past, when child care was essentially the task of women (Nash, 1965; Droppleman and Schaefer, 1963; Benson, 1968; Lynn, 1974; Ariès, 1960; Gokalp and Leridon, 1983; Sgritta and Saporiti, 1982). This tendency towards an "ideal" symmetry is not surprising, if one considers the structural changes that have taken place in the family since World War II. In the four countries, these changes have been different but highly significant (5).

In general, however, irrespective of the socio-political system, the burden of child care still falls mainly on mothers although the situation seems slightly better in Poland and Romania. The waning of the traditional forms of help has made the mother's task more difficult, but a certain egalitarianism regarding male parental roles seems to be in the making (6).

4 Domestic Chores

4.1 *Actual Distribution of Domestic Chores between the Couple*

The chores studied were cooking, dish-washing, shopping, laundry and house-cleaning. Although we cannot describe these results item by item, the reader will discover them from column A in Table 2. Because these five tasks are performed mainly by wives, women's scores refer to themselves, men's to their wives. We remind the reader that our respondents' wives in Canada and Italy are largely housewives.

All chores fall unequivocally in the woman's domain whether she works or not (Watt, 1980), with the partial exception of shopping. This duty implies the use of money, contact with the outer world, and a certain freedom of decision (plus perhaps, in Poland and Romania, more time having to be spent on it than in the Western countries). Both women and men acknowledge this. In the socialist countries the situation for women is not much better than in the capitalist countries: indeed, if Italy is the most traditional country, Canada --- not Poland or Romania --- is the least.

Even so, differences exist among the tasks. Doing the laundry, for example, appears to be a more female activity in all countries than washing the dishes. Abhorrence of anything connected with clothes seems to be a male trait everywhere (Talmon, 1983).

Husbands cooperate little, except slightly in Poland. They cooperate least of all in Italy.

Interestingly enough, besides housewives, the women most exploited in this respect are, on one side, blue-collar workers and,

Table 2 Actual and Ideal Distribution of Domestic Chores

The questions asked were the following:
A = actual
   "How much do you and your spouse share the following domestic chores?"
I = ideal
   "If in a family both parents work, who in your opinion should do the following domestic chores?"

1 = "always the husband"; 2 = "the husband more than the wife"; 3 = "husband and wife to the same extent";
4 = "the wife more than the husband"; 5 = "always the wife"

	Canada				Italy				Poland				Romania			
	A	d†	I	d†	A	d†	I	d†	A	d†	I	d†	A	d†	I	d†
								Cooking								
M. blue-collar workers	4.0	.1	3.5	0	4.8	.7*	3.7	.1	3.8	-.4**	3.6	0	4.4	0	4.0	0
F. blue-collar workers	3.9		3.5		4.1		3.6		4.2		3.6		4.4		4.0	
M. white-collar workers	4.0	-.1	3.6	.1	4.5	.3**	3.6	.3*	3.8	-.1	3.6	.3**	4.3	-.2***	4.0	.1
F. white-collar workers	4.1		3.5		4.2		3.3		3.9		3.3		4.5		3.9	
M. teachers	4.0	.1	3.3	.1	4.3	0	3.4	0	3.8	-.2**	3.5	.2	4.3	-.1	3.7	0
F. teachers	3.9		3.2		4.3		3.4		4.0		3.3		4.4		3.7	
Men out of work	3.8	-.6*	3.4	0	4.5	-.4*	3.6	.2**	---		---		4.1	-.6*	3.9	0
Housewives	4.4		3.4		4.9		3.4		4.3		3.3		4.7		3.9	
M. decision-makers	4.2	.5*	3.3	.1*	4.5	.4*	3.6	.4*	4.2	.1	3.7	.2**	4.4	.1	3.9	0
F. decision-makers	3.7		3.2		4.1		3.2		4.1		3.5		4.3		3.9	

†d means difference. The levels of confidence are indicated as follows: p = * ≤ .01; ** .05 > p > .01; *** 10 > p > .05

Table 2 Actual and Ideal Distribution of Domestic Chores

	Canada				Italy				Poland				Romania			
	A	d†	I	d†	A	d†	I	d†	A	d†	I	d†	A	d†	I	d†
							Dish-washing									
M. blue-collar workers	3.8		3.3		4.8		3.8		3.6		3.1		4.2		3.6	
F. blue-collar workers	3.9	-.1	3.2	.1	4.5	.3**	3.6	.2***	4.2	-.6*	3.5	-.4	4.2	0	3.8	-.2
M. white-collar workers	3.8		3.1		4.6		3.6		3.8		3.3		3.7		3.3	
F. white-collar workers	4.0	-.2	3.0	.1	4.5	.1	3.4	.2***	3.8	0	3.2	.1	4.4	-.7*	3.7	-.4*
M. teachers	3.6		3.1		4.2		3.4		3.4		3.3		3.9		3.3	
F. teachers	3.5	.1	3.1	0	4.5	-.3*	3.5	-.1	3.8	-.4*	3.2	.1	4.2	-.3***	3.5	-.3***
Men out of work	3.9		3.3		4.2		3.5		---		---		4.2		3.9	
Housewives	4.3	-.4*	3.3	0	4.9	-.7*	3.5	0	4.2		3.2		4.6	-.4**	3.7	.2
M. decision-makers	3.8		3.1		4.6		3.6		3.9		3.2		4.1		3.4	
F. decision-makers	3.4	.4*	3.0	.1	4.1	.5*	3.2	.4*	3.8	.1	3.1	.1***	4.1	0	3.4	0

Table 2 Actual and Ideal Distribution of Domestic Chores

Shopping

	Canada				Italy				Poland				Romania			
	A	d†	I	d†	A	d†	I	d†	A	d†	I	d†	A	d†	I	d†
M. blue-collar workers	3.1		3.2		4.6		3.7		3.5		3.3		3.2		2.8	
F. blue-collar workers	3.6	-.5*	3.4	-.2***	3.9	.7*	3.4	.3**	4.1	-.6*	3.4	-.1	3.4	-.2	2.7	.1
M. white-collar workers	3.5		3.2		4.3		4.1		3.5		3.3		2.8		2.6	
F. white-collar workers	3.7	-.2	3.3	-.1	3.9	.4**	3.3	.8**	3.7	-.2	3.1	.2*	3.6	-.8*	2.6	0
M. teachers	3.3		3.1		3.7		3.3		3.5		3.2		2.7		2.6	
F. teachers	3.6	-.3	3.2	-.1	3.8	-.1	3.2	.1	4.0	-.5*	3.2	0	3.3	-.5*	2.7	-.1
Men out of work	3.6		3.4		4.1		3.4		—		—		3.0		2.9	
Housewives	3.9	-.3	3.3	.1	4.7	-.6*	3.4	0	4.0		3.3		3.7	-.7*	2.8	.1
M. decision-makers	4.0		3.2		4.3		3.4		3.9		3.2		3.1		2.4	
F. decision-makers	3.5	.5*	3.1	.1	3.4	.9*	3.1	.3*	3.6	.3***	3.1	.1**	2.8	.3	2.2	.2

Table 2 Actual and Ideal Distribution of Domestic Chores

Laundry

	Canada				Italy				Poland				Romania			
	A	d†	I	d†	A	d†	I	d†	A	d†	I	d†	A	d†	I	d†
M. blue-collar workers	4.5		4.0		5.0		4.2		3.9		3.7		4.8		4.3	
F. blue-collar workers	4.6	-.1	4.0	0	4.8	.2***	3.9	.3**	4.2	-.3	3.7	0	4.6	.2	4.2	.1
M. white-collar workers	4.6		3.8		4.9		4.1		4.0		3.6		4.3		4.1	
F. white-collar workers	4.3	.3	3.7	.1	4.8	.1	3.8	.3**	4.1	-.1	3.5	.1	4.7	-.4**	3.8	.3**
M. teachers	4.1		3.5		4.7		3.7		3.9		3.5		4.4		3.8	
F. teachers	4.2	-.1	3.2	.3**	4.8	-.1	3.8	-.1	4.2	-.3***	3.4	.1***	4.6	-.2	3.9	-.1
Men out of work	4.2		3.7		4.8		3.8		---		---		4.3		4.0	
Housewives	4.7	-.5*	3.8	-.1	4.9	-.1	3.7	.1	4.3		3.6		4.8	-.5*	4.1	-.1
M. decision-makers	4.6		3.3		4.8		3.7		4.2		3.6		4.5		3.9	
F. decision-makers	4.0	.6*	3.2	.1**	4.6	.2**	3.3	.4*	4.1	.1	3.3	.3*	4.3	.2	3.9	0

Table 2 Actual and Ideal Distribution of Domestic Chores

	Canada				Italy				Poland				Romania			
	A	d†	I	d†	A	d†	I	d†	A	d†	I	d†	A	d†	I	d†
								House-cleaning								
M. blue-collar workers	4.0		3.6		4.8		4.0		3.5		3.3		3.7		3.3	
F. blue-collar workers	4.2	-.2	3.5	.1	4.5	.3*	3.7	.3*	3.9	-.4***	3.4	.1	3.9	-.2	3.5	-.2
M. white-collar workers	4.1		3.3		4.5		3.6		3.5		3.2		3.5		3.3	
F. white-collar workers	4.0	.1	3.3	0	4.4	.1	3.5	.1	3.8	-.3**	3.2	0	4.1	-.6*	3.3	0
M. teachers	3.7		3.2		4.4		3.5		3.4		3.1		3.6		3.2	
F. teachers	3.6	.1	3.1	.1	4.5	-.1	3.5	0	3.8	-.4*	3.2	-.1	4.1	-.5*	3.4	-.2
Men out of work	4.0		3.4		4.4		3.6		---		---		3.9		3.6	
Housewives	4.5	-.5*	3.6	-.2	4.8	-.4*	3.5	.1	4.3		3.2		4.3	-.4*	3.3	.3**
M. decision-makers	4.3		3.0		4.6		3.6		3.9		3.3		4.1		3.3	
F. decision-makers	3.8	.5*	3.2	-.2	4.3	.3*	3.3	.3*	3.5	.4*	3.0	.3*	4.0	.1	3.2	.1

on the other, wives of decision-makers. It looks as if the two extremes have something in common. This is true in all countries.

Canadian female decision-makers appear to be the only feminine group that breaks away from a condition of almost complete subjugation, although female decision-makers are advantaged to some extent everywhere.

4.1.1 *Some Hypotheses*

We wondered whether age, education and social class (see App. 1) affect the actual condition of women in domestic work. The answer is in general affirmative although, especially for age, there are exceptions among the categories. Younger women tend to have a slightly more egalitarian arrangement with their husbands, particularly as to cooking, doing the laundry and cleaning the house. Education and social class clearly exert a strong influence in the same direction for all five activities.

4.2 *Ideal Distribution of Chores between the Couple*

The main findings were presented in chapter 2, par. 3, where we saw that, in spite of some differences across the four countries, both men and women tend to assign the performance of domestic chores to wives and that, as a matter of fact, women are even more conservative than men. To what extent does the ideal distribution of chores in the family differ from reality? The differences between the means of the two sets of scores show that, in all countries and for all categories, the opinion of both men and women is that wives do more than they should.

Two remarks are appropriate at this point.

The first concerns male decision-makers. We saw that they enjoy a privileged condition in the actual performance of domestic chores. Interestingly enough, this category also shows in all countries the largest gap for all male categories between the real situation and the ideal one. Is this gap the result of a feeling of guilt, a demagogic move, a stereotype? The correlations with the actual performance of domestic chores show that the gap increases the more the wives perform these tasks (7). Men moralize, in other words, but continue to act as before.

Second, it is also demonstrated that housewives in all countries show the largest gap among the female categories. Thus, it is not decision-makers, a small fraction of women, who suffer most from this situation but housewives: a very large segment of the female population. In terms of potential for change, this is an important finding.

In general, the gap between the ideal and the real distribution of domestic chores, as far as male categories are concerned, is greatest in Italy and smallest in Poland and Romania; for female categories, the gap is greatest in Italy (again) and smallest in Canada. Italy clearly appears as the country most strongly marked by discrepancy in this area, and also --- like Romania --- more traditional in reality.

4.2.1 *Some Hypotheses*

Age

Younger age groups attenuate the traditional attitude but only modestly in Poland, Romania, and Canada. Only in Italy is the impact impressive: younger women tend to refuse the traditional approach. Of course, Italy is also the country, second only to Romania, where the actual performance of chores falls most heavily on women's shoulders.

The items are not discriminated equally by age. Washing the dishes and child care are less affected in general.

Age has even less effect on men's attitudes, except again in Italy where younger men show more egalitarian leanings. The impact of age is especially weak in Romania, and even more so in Poland. But in Poland a certain parity tends to exist both in reality and in the ideal model, while this is not the case in Romania, where men of all ages accept in reality and support ideally the traditional division of tasks to just about the same degree.

Education

The hypothesis that education attenuates the traditional orientation is fully proved only for Italian and Polish blue-collar workers and Canadian teachers and housewives; in the other cases we find only a tendency in this direction. It is dramatic to note that it does not hold true for decision-makers, except in Romania for both genders and in Canada for men. As a matter of fact, in Poland and particularly in Italy, the more highly educated the decision-makers (*especially female*), the more strongly do they hold the view that wives more than husbands should take care of domestic chores.

The chores are not discriminated equally by education. Shopping and cleaning the house, for example, are less affected in general.

Among men, the tendency towards a correlation between education and a decrease in the performance of domestic chores by women is evident in Poland and especially in Italy, with the exception of decision-makers in both countries; in Canada the tendency exists almost only for male decision-makers. In Romania the tendency is nearly always irrelevant statistically (8).

Social Class

The hypothesis is validated in general at the category level, although much more consistently in Italy than in the other three countries, especially Romania. In all countries, however, there is a remarkable exception: the higher the class from which come the decision-makers, both male and *especially female*, the more they support the traditional viewpoint that domestic chores should fall to the wife.

The various chores are discriminated differently. It is interesting to observe a general reluctance to assign laundry to husbands.

5 Frustration and Domestic Work

The asymmetric distribution of domestic chores is a tangible symptom of inferiority for women (Peattie and Rein, 1983: chapter 3 and pp. 70-74). It would be strange if we did not find that they generally agree with the statement: "Women are inevitably sacrificed within the traditional family."

Indeed, women in all four countries largely agree with this statement. Men also tend to agree, especially in Italy and Poland. The agreement is far stronger for both sexes in these countries than in Romania and Canada, especially the latter. This result for Canada is bewildering, because one would have expected to find a greater degree of agreement with such a statement owing to the existence of a substantial militant feminist movement in that country.

It is unreasonable, however, to expect a correlation between this agreement and the actual performance of domestic chores by wives more than husbands. The sacrifice of women in the family depends on many factors, of which the performance of domestic chores is but one. In fact, a significant correlation with all five items exists only in Italy (for female teachers) and in Romania (for female white-collar workers) and in all cases the coefficients are positive, even if not significant.

At the global level, only in Romania do we find a consistent set of strong correlations for all five. In other words, apart from Romania, some women who agree with the statement indicated above do not do much more housework than their husbands, while others do. It is clearly the condition of the wife which is felt as a limitation in itself, because of the powers of all kinds that still inhere to husbands. Significantly enough, even men who agree with the statement do not necessarily affirm that their wives take care of domestic chores much more than they. In Canada, in fact, the opposite is true, at least at the global level.

As for the ideal distribution of domestic chores, we find few women or men in the various categories who agree with the statement and at the same time share the view that domestic chores should be done equally by both spouses or more by husbands. This happens only among male decision-makers in Romania and Italy as well as among Italian men out of work, Italian male teachers, and Italian female blue-collar workers. In some cases, as a matter of fact, especially in Poland, people agree with this statement, but at the same time affirm that this or that chore should be performed more by wives than husbands. Obviously, in the present context, even if women and men agree that wives are sacrificed within the traditional family, they either do not consider a genuine egalitarian distribution of domestic chores to be a realistic possibility or have not actually reached a level of consciousness that allows them to accept a different behaviour pattern for women. This is certainly the case with female blue-collar workers and male decision-makers in Romania and with male white-collar workers, teachers of both sexes, and male decision-makers in Poland. Italy is the only country where in each category there is a stronger tendency in this sense: people who feel that wives are sacrificed within the traditional family also actively desire a more egalitarian distribution of domestic chores. As previously stated, it seems reasonable to assume that it is the condition of wifehood as such which, consciously or unconsciously, is felt to be the main limiting factor. As we saw in chapter 2 (par. 4.1), it is the norm for women to give priority to family, and this norm is also shared by men --- indeed, more strongly than by women. Since the culture that surrounds women is masculine, it seems reasonable to formulate the hypothesis that even as women tend to accept this norm, they feel that they are sacrificed within the traditional family. In fact, a positive correlation between the

two exists in all categories and, in many instances, especially in
Poland and Romania, at a significant level (9). At the global level
the correlation is very strong for both sexes in all countries, with
the exception of Italy, where traditional family attachment contin-
ues to have strong roots.

6 Perception of Influence on the Spouse

Our concern here is not the problem of power or the
decision-making process in the family. We are limiting ourselves
rather to men's and women's perceptions of their own influence
on their respective partners. Perception, of course, does not
necessarily reflect reality. Even so, people's behaviour is largely a
product of their perceptions; therefore, if we know how people
perceive a reality, we can predict, to a certain extent, what they will
do.

We must emphasize that we are refraining from stating
anything about the couple. We know nothing of the tensions that
exist within couples, of the importance for each partner of the areas
of influence that we selected or of the level of communication
between the partners. We wish to discover only the gender
differences concerning perceptions of influence on the spouse in
areas of general importance.

The questions dealt with:
(a) problems concerning work (e.g. whether to leave a job and take
another one);
(b) problems concerning political and trade-union participation;
(c) the use of free time.

These three areas differ widely. The first concerns the link
between the family and the economy, from which the family
members draw their means of subsistence; the second the world of
power in its many aspects; the third a reality that is connected
closely with family life. Following a diffuse stereotype, we initially
thought that, particularly for the first two issues, there would be a
difference between husbands and wives.

However, a certain symmetry prevails between the sexes in
all countries (Fig. 3). Only in Romania do men feel they have a
stronger influence regarding work and politics. In the other countries there are also cases in which women feel they exert more influence on their spouses than do men of the corresponding
category. Patriarchy seems to have largely waned, but the assump-

Fig. 3 Perception of Influence on the Spouse
Problems concerning work

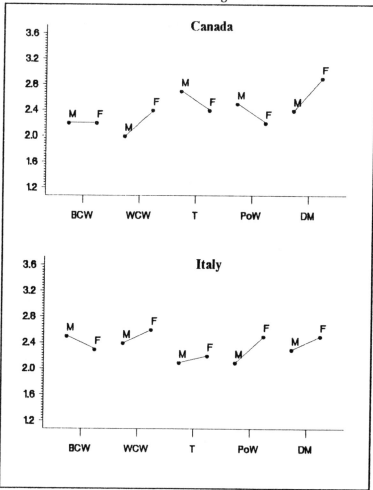

In Canada the differences are significant for WCW, PoW and DM; in Italy only
for PoW.

The question asked was the following:
'How much do you think you influence your spouse about the following
problems?'

   1 = Not at all;
   2 = Little;
   3 = Quite a bit;
   4 = Much.

Fig. 3 Perception of Influence on the Spouse
Problems concerning work

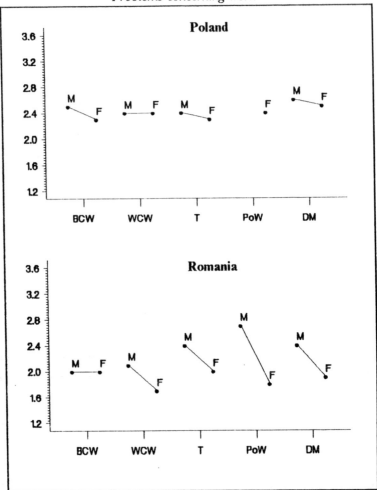

No difference is significant in Poland; all are in Romania, except for BCW.
The question asked was the following:
'How much do you think you influence your spouse about the following problems?
    1 = Not at all;
    2 = Little;
    3 = Quite a bit;
    4 = Much.

Fig. 3 Perception of Influence on the Spouse
Problems of political and trade union participation

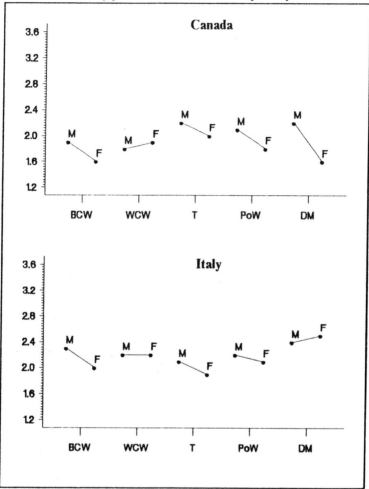

In Canada there are two suggestive differences, for BCW and PoW, and a significant one for DM; in Italy only for BCW.

The question asked was the following:
'How much do you think you influence your spouse about the following problems?'

- 1 = Not at all;
- 2 = Little;
- 3 = Quite a bit;
- 4 = Much.

Fig. 3 Perception of Influence on the Spouse
Problems of political and trade union participation

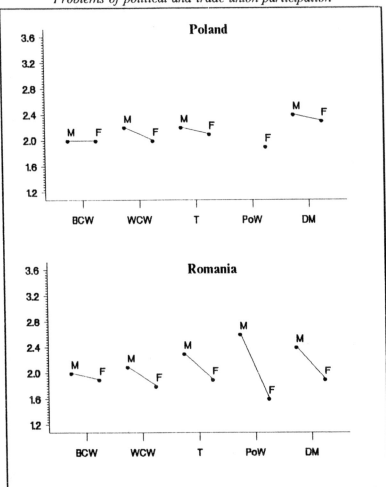

In Poland the differences for T and DM are significant; in Romania only for WCW.
The question asked was the following:
'How much do you think you influence your spouse about the following problems?'
  1 = Not at all;
  2 = Little;
  3 = Quite a bit;
  4 = Much.

Fig. 3 Perception of Influence on the Spouse
Use of free time

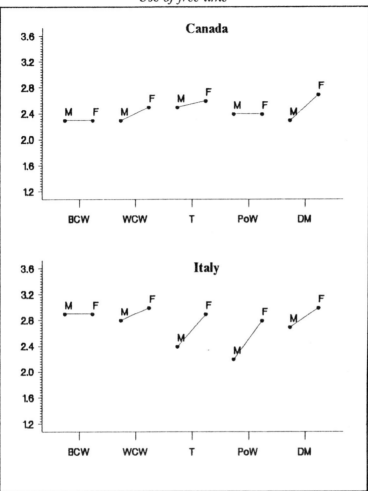

In Canada the only significant difference concerns DM; in Italy they are all significant (T, PoW) or suggestive (WCW, DM), except for BCW.
The question asked was the following:
'How much do you think you influence your spouse about the following problems?'
    1 = Not at all;
    2 = Little;
    3 = Quite a bit;
    4 = Much.

Fig. 3 Perception of Influence on the Spouse
Use of free time

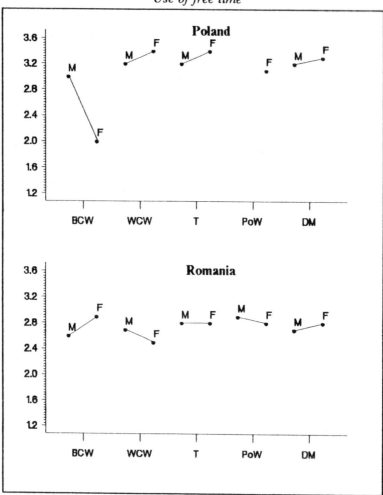

No differences are statistically relevant.
The question asked was the following:
'How much do you think you influence your spouse about the following problems?'
    1 = Not at all;
    2 = Little;
    3 = Quite a bit;
    4 = Much.

tion that in modern times its root is in the capitalist mode of production proves groundless.

Even for the area in which the perception of influence on the spouse is strongest, the pattern is rather uniform in the four countries. It is generally stronger in matters concerning free time, weaker regarding political and trade-union participation: this is true for both men and women.

7 Some General Hypotheses about Income Equality

We turn our attention now to some hypotheses concerning income equality.

The more women achieve income equality with their husbands, the more they are relieved of child care, the less they take care of everyday routine, and the more is the influence they perceive they have on their husbands. In particular, the ideal distribution of chores between husband and wife tends to be more egalitarian.

The hypothesis is proved for all domestic chores in each country: the less males are the main source of income, the less their wives perform the chores. This is true also as far as child care is concerned.

But the hypothesis concerning the influence on the husband is disproved, with the exception of female white-collar workers and decision-makers in Poland. Women who earn about as much as or more than their husbands feel that they exert less influence on them. Two interpretations are possible: one is that in such a case wives have less need, both materially and psychologically, to feel that they influence husbands; the other is that, being in such a condition, they feel they should have more influence on their husbands than they actually have.

Our findings do not uphold the hypothesis that the more wives earn in relation to their husbands, the more egalitarian is the ideal distribution of family tasks. There is a slight tendency in this direction in Canada and to a lesser extent in Romania, but in other cases the opposite holds true: in Poland, for instance, the more female blue- and white-collar workers earn in relation to their husbands, the more they state that wives should take care of domestic chores.

As far as ideal child care is concerned, the hypothesis that women's income parity is matched by a more egalitarian orientation is verified only for Italian blue-collar workers and decision-makers and, at the global level, only in Canada and Italy.

* * *

In conclusion, it seems that in all countries the tendency towards parity of income affects women's behaviour and values regarding traditional roles in the family only in so far as the actual performance of domestic chores and child care is concerned. Its influence on the other phenomena is less homogeneous.

Nevertheless, these findings (and others not presented) in general are not inconsistent with the "normative theory of marital power" (10). In fact, we found that the more women achieve income parity with men, the less they contribute to child care; the more is the likelihood of finding gender equality in the domestic division of labour; the more husbands contribute to child care; and the more women participate in organizations.

8 Religion and Domestic Chores

The four countries in our sample have a variety of religions and two of them have an official atheistic creed which is part , or even the basis, of an egalitarian ideology. Because the performance of domestic chores and child care by women has traditionally been one of the main tenets of all religions, we wonder whether differences exist among people of different religions and in comparison with people who have no religion at all, especially in the two countries where atheism should imply an egalitarian bent. We also wonder how strongly each religion is affected by national culture. In other words, we want to find out not only whether differences exist between Catholics and Protestants or between Catholics and atheists but also whether there are differences between, for instance, Italian and Polish Catholics.

Of paramount importance for us, of course, is to discover whether the impact of religion varies between the sexes (Porter and Venning, 1976). It is a long-established view that women are more religious. We will test this point as well as the hypothesis that, because religions are generally conservative in family matters, practising women are more conservative than practising men.

All in all, when we take into consideration the performance of domestic chores, apart from child care, by people of different religions, Catholics of both sexes tend to be rather traditional. This is true especially for women, except for decision-makers. The same holds true for Protestants, although the inter-sex difference appears to be smaller.

We also validated empirically that women who hold positions of public responsibility generally show a much more open outlook not only than other women but also than men of the same religion. This finding, however, is less true of Greek Orthodox and Jewish female decision-makers.

People with no religion present an orientation that is sometimes traditional and sometimes more progressive, with large gender differences. In actual practice, however, their behaviour tends to be conservative.

The gap between the real and the ideal performance of domestic chores is stronger for women than for men within each religion.

If we take child care into consideration, males within each religion tend to be more conservative than females. As expected, females within each religion take care of children more often than their husbands do.

If we add to this the previous finding concerning the gap between the ideal and the real distribution of chores, we see that in this respect women constitute a group with potential for change within each religion. This comment applies also to people with no religion.

Are there differences between respondents of different nationalities who belong to the same religion? If so, is this difference more marked for men or for women? In answering this question, we limit ourselves to Catholics and to respondents with no religion, because these are the only two forms of belief that exist in all four countries.

Among Catholics, Italians are by far the most traditional in these matters, while Polish Catholics appear more open than Catholics in the other countries. Curiously, Romanian atheists, contrary to atheists in the other countries, are the most traditional.

No marked differences appear between men and women belonging to the same religious group in the cross-country comparisons.

8.1 *Religious Practice*

Thus far we have compared data with reference to religious affiliation per se and, in the case of Catholics and respondents with no religion, across countries. Equally important, however, is the relationship between religious practice and actual and ideal distribution of chores within the household.

As far as the actual performance of domestic chores is concerned, among males the more devout they are, the more traditional the division tends to be, except for Catholics, for whom the opposite holds true. This tendency may be interpreted as the result of the fact that a large portion of the Catholics in our sample come from Poland. There, as we saw, a cooperative attitude prevails, probably mainly for contingent reasons. Among females, however, especially Catholic and Greek Orthodox, the more devout they are, the more they perform domestic chores.

When we turn to the ideal performance of domestic chores, in sharp contrast to what we have seen above, among Catholics and Greek Orthodox there is no difference between males and females: the more they practise, the more conservative is their outlook. Among Protestants, practising males tend to be progressive, practising females conservative. Among Jews, for males, the more they practise, the more conservative they are, while for females there is no significant correlation.

With the exception of Jewish women, the more women practise, the more they take care of children. For men, the opposite holds true among Protestants and Jews. Among Catholic and Greek Orthodox males there is no correlation.

For Catholics, both male and female, the more they practise, the more they maintain that wives should take care of the children. The same holds true only for Greek Orthodox females. In the other cases, there is no correlation between religious practice and ideal child care.

*   *   *

In general, religious practice has different effects on the behaviour and outlook of people in the above-mentioned areas of family life but, tendentially, it exercises a conservative influence. In addition, men and women with the same religious affiliation react differently. As for women, the correlations are much stronger among Catholics and Greek Orthodox than among Protestants and

Jewesses; as for men, they are stronger among Protestants than among Greek Orthodox, with Catholics and Jews in the middle.

9 Determinants of Equality between the Couple

The findings that emerge from this chapter are neither startling nor unexpected. In fact, they confirm our general assumptions. To some people it may come as a surprise to discover that the situation of women in countries where the official ideology stresses egalitarianism differs only slightly from the situation in countries where, if the Marxist approach is correct, the remnants of patriarchy are inextricably interwoven with capitalism.

In all four countries, not only men but also women state unequivocally that mothers more than fathers do and should take care of children. Yet we also note a tendency toward a more egalitarian distribution of this task: when asked about the respondents' actual participation, men, especially in Poland and Romania, answer that they often take care of children.

Domestic chores, both ideally and in reality, are perceived as typically female tasks, with the partial exception of shopping. There are no radical differences among the four countries, but in Poland and Romania the gap between the actual and the ideal distribution of chores is generally smaller than in Canada and Italy. In addition, the ideal distribution in all countries tends to be slightly more egalitarian.

The influence that spouses perceive that they exert on each other is moderate for both sexes regarding work, and especially in political and trade union matters; regarding the use of free time, it is stronger for women than men.

The relevant factor, as we stressed at the beginning of this chapter, is not the lack of substantial gender parity regarding activities that are traditionally portrayed as feminine but the spirit that characterizes the performance of these activities on the part of women: in general, this seems to be no longer a spirit of passive acceptance.

As a consequence, women are beginning to turn to the outer world, although they do not reduce the performance of activities that have been their lot for time immemorial. It is clear that these women take often upon themselves a triple role: mother-wife, employee, active citizen. We limit ourselves here to test the hypothesis that the performance of domestic chores does not present a negative correlation with holding governmental or non-governmental public office or with participation in associations such as political parties, trade unions, and voluntary organizations (Table 3).

Table 3 Correlations between Women's Public Activity (holding an office and participation in associations) and Performance of Domestic Chores

		(a) Holding Public Offices†				
	Cooking	Dish-washing	Shopping	Laundry	House-Cleaning	Child Care
			Canada			
FBCW	-.10	-.02	.05	-.06	-.15	-.39**
FWCW	-.01	-.21***	.14	-.07	-.10	.33
FT	.10	.09	.08	.18***	.17***	-.25***
HW	-.05	-.22*	-.17**	.02	.10	.04
FDM	.03	-.02	.01	.17***	-.07	-.15
			Italy			
FBCW	-.03	.03	0.00	-.04	-.11	-.06
FWCW	.16***	.07	-.02	-.16***	-.21**	-.12
FT	.19**	.05	.15***	.13	.14	.01
HW	-.02	.06	.13	.07	.09	.41*
FDM	.04	-.20***	.22**	.11	-.17	.39*
			Poland			
FBCW	.07	-.16	.17	.06	-.27**	-.14
FWCW	-.21**	-.02	0.00	.16	-.09	.04
FT	.12	.17***	.04	-.06	-.08	.02
HW	-.05	-.04	.02	.03	.15***	-.13
FDM	.04	.13***	-.05	.10	.19	.18
			Romania			
FBCW	.11	.10	.14	.15	.12	.14
FWCW	0.00	-.04	-.05	.09	.19***	.10
FT	.20**	.19**	.30*	.13	.19**	.18
HW	.02	-.10	-.07	-.26*	-.02	-.08
FDM	-.03	-.01	.39*	-.05	-.01	.12

†See App. 17.

*p $\leq$ .01;   ** .05 > p > .01;   *** .10 > p > .05

In fact, in regard both to holding public office and to participation in associations, there is a general lack of significant correlations between the two phenomena, although in general the indication is that women who take care of domestic chores do not undertake the two activities.

In Italy, it seems that women who are active in both kinds of public life are less absorbed by the performance of domestic

Table 3 Correlations between Women's Public Activity (holding an office and participation in associations) and Performance of Domestic Chores

	Cooking	Dish-washing	Shopping	Laundry	House-Cleaning	Child Care
			(b) Participation in Associations†			
Canada						
FBCW	-.05	-.16	-.01	-.25**	-.38*	-.22
FWCW	-.11	-.04	-.19**	-.38*	-.31*	-.32
FT	.03	.04	-.02	.11	.05	-.02
HW	.15***	-.10	.05	.09	0.00	-.08
FDM	-.07	-.10	.04	.02	.17***	-.28***
Italy						
FBCW	-.29*	-.37*	-.14	-.08	-.16	.03
FWCW	-.16***	-.37*	-.08	-.69*	-.45*	-.14
FT	-.28*	-.40*	-.21**	-.20**	-.17***	.12
HW	-.03	.05	-.39*	.06	.08	-.10
FDM	-.09	-.25**	.22**	.01	-.24**	.36*
Poland						
FBCW	.02	-.06	.18	-.22***	-.07	-.35**
FWCW	-.01	.16***	.05	.09	.16***	-.07
FT	.19	-.03	.06	.16***	-.12	.13
HW	-.03	-.13**	-.15***	.09	-.24*	.60*
FDM	-.07	-.12	.05	.08	-.06	.02
Romania						
FBCW	-.07	-.05	.24**	.07	.08	.35**
FWCW	.08	.17***	.01	.10	.18***	.14
FT	.16***	-.02	.07	.02	.01	.20
HW	-.09	-.24*	-.06	.01	-.24*	-.13
FDM	-.11	-.13	.11	.17	.21***	.16

†See App. 16.

tasks. We know from the previous paragraphs, however, that Italian women are generally more absorbed by these tasks than women in the other countries. Therefore, it seems reasonable to discover in this country a more pronounced negative relationship between the two phenomena.

These results coincide with our findings about the reasons for lack of commitment to public life. Family obligations rank first for only a few categories in Canada, Italy and Romania and for none in Poland. A reduction of the domestic burden is a prerequisite but, in general, female respondents seem to be aware that the reason for lack of participation lies elsewhere. The traditional family, as the still largely surviving stereotype prescribes, is only the seal of women's exclusion from public life.

* * *

This chapter, although based on limited data, yields a clear picture. Although there is a marked difference between child care and domestic chores, all systems share the ideal tendency towards a more egalitarian distribution of tasks within the family. In actual practice, however, everywhere both tasks still fall mainly on women's shoulders.

This should not come as a surprise for a number of reasons. Has housework ever been granted equal attention and status with work outside the home? Nowhere has housework been granted the same dignity as production work. Since production has traditionally been a male activity, it is no wonder that equality, in all systems, has been considered by political parties, mass-media and public opinion in terms of production, i.e. of paid work outside the home. The determining factor everywhere has been a male reality and the values that it entails (Keller, 1983: 234-5; Bondy, quoted, ibid.). Nowhere has strong pressure been exerted on men to perform domestic chores (Rosaldo and Lamphere, 1974). At the most, there has been pressure to take care of children.

Even in the socialist countries, "to be a woman" differs little from the condition of women in other countries.

Where have children been socialized in other terms? Girls have been prepared to take some of the male roles in production, but are still taught to perform household tasks as "their lot". Is it surprising to find that they feel more confident in doing housework and are more willing to do it than their husbands and that husbands wholeheartedly agree? Although the mechanism that is internalized through this kind of socialization is checked somewhat when wives work, it is activated fully when wives become mothers and husbands become fathers. Resocialization not only of women but also of men is the main way to promote equality within the family. Another avenue worth exploring is the stimulation of professionally organized agencies to provide services such as food and cleaning (11). By professionalizing jobs that are connected with housekeeping, their prestige may, in turn, also be enhanced.

The case of child care is different, because its essence is psychological and moral. It should be easier, as this research also proves, not only to resocialize men in this respect and to convince their wives to exert pressure on them but also to resocialize women into not thinking that being a mother exhausts their resources. Psychoanalysis has shown that children need both parents and that a woman is not fulfilled just because she is a mother, even a good mother.

Another fact emerges from our findings. In certain respects, Canada appears more progressive than Poland and Romania. One reason may be the pro-natalist policies which are fluctuating in Poland and very strong in Romania. Obviously a pro-natalist policy reinforces the image of women as mothers and strengthens the stereotype that child care and, consequently, domestic chores are typically female activities. But another phenomenon, which is absent in Poland and Romania, must also be taken into consideration: an active feminist movement. Because of feminism, the situation for women has improved even in Italy, although the consequences within the family are perhaps less tangible there than in Canada (Boals, 1975).

A prerequisite for collective action which is aimed at the re-socialization of men is that women should express their dissatisfaction and channel it in "consciousness raising groups", where these problems are discussed and their causes unveiled. This action implies, at least partially, a criticism of the existing order. Obviously, it can take place only in a context where spontaneous mobilization about gender equality is a reality at the grass-roots level. A women's movement that is encapsulated within a political party cannot easily pursue this line, especially if that party is, by constitutional definition, the ruling party in the country and operates on the basis of "democratic centralism".

A feminine organization that is connected to a party lives in the shadow of its official ideology: if democratic, that progress will entail equality between the sexes; if communist, that the "new society" will be characterized by the disappearance of all forms of inequality. The impact of such organizations, although not negligible, has been much more limited than that of the feminist movement.

The importance of the feminist movement is demonstrated very clearly by our findings concerning Canada, which is the only country in our sample where we have a sizeable number of respondents who qualify themselves as feminists. Canadian feminists, not only ideally (average: 3.1) but also in reality (3.6), have a much more egalitarian arrangement with their husbands than the non-feminists, except for child care (3.0). But even in this area, the difference, although not significant, still favours the feminists.

Husbands of non-feminists give even less of their time to children (3.4).

There are, however, no significant differences between the feminists and members of feminine party organizations in Canada. In that country the party structure is known to be very loose.

The comparison between women who belong to both kinds of organizations and women who are not members of any organization is very interesting (Table 4).

Canadian and Italian women who are active in either the feminist movement or a feminine party organization have a much more egalitarian arrangement with their husbands than non-active women, not only ideally (average for Canada and Italy: 3.1) but also in reality (averages for Canada: 3.6, for Italy: 4.0). In Italy this difference even extends to child care on the part of the husband (2.8), but this is not the case in Poland and in Romania. In these countries, women's organizations are affiliated with the party, which does not consider the resocialization of husbands as its task because it is not interested in changes in this area. These women are not different from the rest of the population and, therefore, cannot be considered agents of change.

* * *

In an attempt to identify a constellation of factors favourable to an egalitarian orientation, we considered first only the Canadian data, then the data of each country separately, and, finally, that of the four countries together. We used multiple classification and regression analysis with the variables listed below.

After a number of trials we found the following variables to be significant: country; education; working mother; religious practice; holding a party office; priority of work over family, also for women; the view that men should not have more opportunities to hold leadership positions; mother's political involvement; the view that women should not be fired first in case of unemployment; the respondent's propensity to work even if economically not necessary; and age.

The following variables were found to be insignificant: degree of political involvement in the family of origin; holding office in governmental and non-governmental organizations; importance of present and past party offices; membership in a party; number of children; civil status; and category in the sample.

As a result of these analyses, we dropped almost all the demographic variables we had begun with, in favour of cultural fac-

Table 4 Actual and Ideal Performance of Domestic Chores and Child Care. Women in feminist movements or feminine party organizations v. non-involved women

	df	t	p	df	t	p
	Canada			**Italy**		
Actual chores						
Cooking	41.284	-2.52	.012	27.344	-2.92	.004
Dish-washing	40.277	-2.58	.010	25.320	-4.53	.000
Shopping	41.284	-2.50	.013	28.330	-1.62	.105
Laundry	37.280	-3.25	.001	21.318	-1.64	.103
House-cleaning	37.276	-3.18	.002	22.322	-2.46	.022
Ideal chores						
Cooking	70.410	-4.74	.000	59.461	-5.47	.000
Dish-washing	70.407	-4.38	.000	59.460	-5.35	.000
Shopping	69.403	-7.02	.000	59.456	-3.65	.000
Laundry	70.406	-8.60	.000	56.456	-8.61	.000
House-cleaning	70.405	-7.21	.000	58.460	-7.35	.000
Actual child care from husband	19.129	-1.13	.272	20.206	-2.61	.010
Ideal child care from husband	67.403	-5.71	.000	59.462	-4.65	.000
	Poland			**Romania**		
Actual chores						
Cooking	16.366	- .56	.575	17.330	- .53	.559
Dish-washing	16.365	-1.72	.085	17.332	- .88	.377
Shopping	16.365	-2.78	.005	17.331	-2.67	.008
Laundry	16.363	- .22	.825	17.331	-1.84	.067
House-cleaning	16.325	.42	.675	17.332	- .72	.471
Ideal chores						
Cooking	22.507	- .50	.614	24.426	- .29	.775
Dish-washing	21.497	-1.10	.272	24.425	- .58	.565
Shopping	22.504	- .39	.700	24.425	-1.91	.056
Laundry	22.504	.62	.534	24.426	-1.20	.232
House-cleaning	22.505	.66	.512	24.425	- .65	.510
Actual child care from husband	7.189	-1.29	.199	6.188	- .89	.375
Ideal child care from husband	22.495	1.01	.913	24.426	-1.88	.060

tors. Thus our findings differ from those of other authors (e.g. Rossi, 1982: ch. 6).

The picture that emerged shows clearly that women and men who cultivate an egalitarian orientation at home are also those who maintain an egalitarian orientation in the outside world.

As Table 5 shows, country is an important predictor in all cases, but more so for women than for men. To change men's at-

Table 5 Beta Rank Order of Determinants of Attitudes towards Ideal Performance of Domestic Chores in All Countries (MCA)

Males

	Cooking $R^2 = .10$	Dish-washing $R^2 = .12$	Shopping $R^2 = .14$	Laundry $R^2 = .15$	House-cleaning $R^2 = .12$
Country	2*	2*	1*	4*	3*
More opportunities for men to hold leadership positions	-1*	-1*	4.5*	-2*	-1*
Priority of work over family also for women	3*	6*	6*	5*	6*
Women fired first in case of unemployment	-4*	-3*	4.5*	-3*	-2*
Propensity to work even if economically not necessary	5.5*	5*	3*	7*	5*
Mother working	-7*	-10	7*	-8	-7
Religious practice	-8	-7	8*	-6*	-8
Holding party office	9	8	9	9	9
Mother politically active	-10	-9	-10	-10	-10
Education	5.5*	4*	2*	1*	4*
Age	-11	-11	-1	-11	-11

Table 5 Beta Rank Order of Determinants of Attitudes towards Ideal Performance of Domestic Chores in All Countries (MCA)

	Cooking	Dish-washing	Shopping	Laundry	House-cleaning
	$R^2 = .14$	$R^2 = .12$	$R^2 = .13$	$R^2 = .15$	$R^2 = .9$
			Females		
Country	1*	1*	1*	4*	6*
More opportunities for men to hold leadership positions	-4*	-8.5	-7*	-5.5*	-4*
Priority of work over family also for women	3*	4*	8	1.5*	2*
Women fired first in case of unemployment	-2*	-2*	-4.5*	-1.5*	-1*
Propensity to work even if economically not necessary	5*	3*	4.5	3*	3*
Mother working	-11	-8.5*	-10	-10	-10
Religious practice	-6*	-5.5*	-6*	-7*	-5*
Holding party office	8*	7*	3*	8*	8*
Mother politically active	-10	-10	-9	-9*	-9
Education	9	5.5*	2*	5.5*	7*
Age	-7*	-11	-11	-11	-11

* Significant

The sign - indicates a negative correlation with the egalitarian orientation. The R^2 indicates that the proportion of variation explained by the additive effects of the relevant variables is rather small.

titudes towards gender equality at home, it is more important to reshape their basic attitudes towards gender equality in leadership positions. Being a citizen of one social system or another is for them the second most relevant variable.

It is worth underlining that the country which contributes most to an egalitarian orientation towards the performance of domestic chores is Poland, while the country that contributes least is Romania. This is true for both men and women.

Education is an important determinant for both sexes. For women it is higher education and, to some extent, middle-level education that play a positive role; for men, it is either higher or primary education. For them, obviously, middle-level education tends to transmit a traditional orientation.

A more egalitarian orientation about firing in the case of unemployment is also about equally important for both sexes, but slightly more for men than for women.

Some variables, on the other hand, discriminate strongly between the sexes. Religious practice, for instance, affects women's attitudes negatively in all cases at a significant level, but for men this is so in only one instance. Holding a party office has no impact for males but does have for females in all cases.

Other variables that one might have expected to be relevant play a minor role. Among these are age and a working or politically active mother, although the respective coefficients are significant ($.05 > p > .01$).

However, what results from the multivariate analysis about the mother is extremely interesting. A working or active mother produces both in men and especially in women a reaction away from the egalitarian orientation towards the performance of domestic chores! One might have expected that the example of a mother who is more open to the outside world and maybe less dedicated to traditional tasks should have induced in the children, especially females, an egalitarian orientation towards their performance. What happens is just the opposite.

As far as age is concerned, youth contributes to an egalitarian orientation only for women. For men, it is the middle-aged group that contributes most to it.

It is interesting to note that the propensity to work, even if economically not necessary, is also a significant predictor for men.

Of course, the rank order of the variables changes within each country. We cannot describe this phenomenon here in detail but, with the exception of shopping, values appear to play a very important role in promoting what is, after all, another value: egalitarianism about housework. For men it plays the main role.

As we have already argued, parity between the couple depends mainly, although not only, on a resocialization process. With different nuances, orthodox Marxism maintains that such a transformation is impossible within the capitalist mode of production (Jaggar, 1983; Eisenstein, 1979a; Hartmann, 1981a). Our data disprove this claim.

* * *

In conclusion, equality within the household is part of a constellation of positive attitudes towards equality in general. It is not merely the result of a socio-economic system, of a global political ideology or of demographic factors such as age, number of children, civil status.

For women, involvement in the feminist movement appears as a coagulation point of objective conditions and values that join together to form a more egalitarian orientation in these matters. Obviously, the achievement of such a goal requires a transformation of society at large, but in which sense is a matter still open to speculation --- as the debate on post-industrial, post-materialist, post-modern society shows.

Notes

1 Such as Young and Willmott, 1973, critiqued in Lupri and Symons, 1982; Parsons and Bales, 1955a, critiqued in Aronoff and Crano, 1975; Tiger and Shepher, 1975, critiqued in Palzi et al., 1983. For a comprehensive review, see Glenn, 1987.

2 Orthodox Marxism, starting with Lenin, ignored and still ignores the insights contained in some of Marx's early writings and the feminist outbursts that also emerged in the Soviet Union in the wake of the October Revolution. The following well known sentence by Engels is scorned as a flash of wit by the writers belonging to that current (Delmar, 1976; Sacks, 1974): "The first class antagonism appearing in history coincides with the development of the antagonisms of man and woman in monogamy, and the first class oppression with that of the female by the male sex." (1884: 36) Incidentally, the original text has "Mann und Weib", which might mean, besides 'man and woman', 'husband and wife'.

3 In Italy, for instance, blue- and white-collar workers are the categories in which the earning capacity of the male respondents is significantly greater than that of their wives. In Poland there are practically no differences. Only in Canada and Romania do decision-makers rank above all other male categories. It is interesting to note that men out of work fall below all other male categories in Italy and Romania, but not in Canada. Canadian men out of work, thanks either to part-time jobs or to unemployment payments, still manage to earn more than their wives because the vast majority of their wives are housewives (62%) and some are unemployed (7%).

4 Blue-collar workers of both sexes in Canada and Italy take care of children less than all other categories of the same sex. In Poland and Romania working-class children receive more care from their parents. Housewives in all four countries are more absorbed by child care than all other female categories. Female decision-makers take care of the children less than all other female categories, but the differences are significant only in Romania and, in the other countries, only with teachers and, of course, housewives. Teachers of both sexes everywhere, but especially in Italy, tend to take care of children more than the other categories of the same sex. Obviously, the teachers' working week is shorter than that of other categories in all countries. In addition, their cultural background and training and the kind of work that they do predispose them to child care.

   The cross-country comparisons show a moderate number of significant differences: both for males and females, the respondents themselves take care of children most in Romania and least in Canada.

5 Women in general state that they take care of the children more than anyone else. Yet, there are exceptions: blue-collar workers in Canada rank themselves after a relative, and in Italy at the same level as a relative. This finding in Canada and Italy is interesting because it shows the survival in two different contexts of a tie that many people thought had vanished completely. Decision-makers in Canada rank themselves in third place after domestic help and the school (the husband ranks fourth). This is the only case where tradi-

tional institutions still exist: as we said earlier, domestic help has almost disappeared from all the countries in our study.

On the other hand, especially in women's responses, Canada appears as the country where there is more flexibility in child care: there more than elsewhere women use one of the other children, a neighbour or another person, although still to a limited extent. The recourse to a neighbour (in second place for female white-collar workers and third for female teachers) appears particularly interesting because it shows that in Canada the neighbourhood (Gershuny, 1978) is less evanescent than elsewhere. One should be aware, though, that the custom of rewarding such a service economically is widespread.

6 We confine to a note some hypotheses that may cast light on this delicate issue. We wish to test whether the tendency of women to take care of children is less accentuated for young, educated and higher class women. The hypothesis about age is supported only partially at the category level and even less so at the global level (that is, by country and by sex). Also, if we inspect the first order partial correlations, controlling separately the number of children, the age of the last child, and an index that combines the number of children and their age (App. 10), and if we examine the second order correlations, controlling together the number of children and the age of the last born, we find that no change appears in the results. It therefore seems that the mother's age is not correlated with the frequency of care given to children.

Regarding the impact of education, only if we consider the correlations at the global level do we find a highly significant correlation in Canada, Poland and Romania, while in Italy the coefficient is not significant. We can conclude, therefore, that this is the general tendency (except for Italy) but that strong inter-category differences exist.

As to social class, again only if we consider the correlations at the global level is the hypothesis proved in Canada, Poland and Romania; in Italy the higher the status of women, the more they take care of their children. Obviously, child care has a very positive connotation in Italian culture.

7 As a matter of fact, we find a significant ($p = .05$) correlation between these two variables in 88 cases out of 95 for the 19 male categories in our sample (five domestic chores are considered), and a suggestive correlation in four of the remaining cases. How can we explain such an impressive uniformity, which in 77 cases shows a level of confidence far below .01? It seems that males say one thing but behave in a different way. The more egalitarian they are in words, the more their wives perform all of the domestic chores in reality. It is not surprising, of course, to find a strong correlation (97 cases out of 100) in regard to female categories.

8 The results in the text refer to intracategory correlations. At the global level, a significant correlation exists in all countries, with few exceptions (cooking in Poland for both sexes and for males in Romania, and cleaning the house for males in Poland and for females in Romania).

9 There is one exception. The correlations concerning Canadian and Italian female decision-makers are negative (respectively -.15, $p = .03$; -.20, $p = .007$). A reasonable explanation of this is that female decision-makers in these countries tend to interpret these

statements in universal terms, while the other female respondents tend to interpret them as directed to themselves. Thus, female decision-makers in Canada and Italy who state that work must have priority over family state at the same time that women are sacrificed within the family. The reason why we do not find the same pattern in Poland and Romania lies in the fact that very probably female decision-makers in these countries reflect the official ideology that denies the existence of a contradiction between giving priority to work and being sacrificed within the traditional family.

10 As Andrée Michel brought to our attention in a personal communication, the results reported here support such theory.

For a recent critical review of what has become known internationally as the "normative theory of marital power in cultural context" (Rodman, 1967; 1972), see Lupri (1990), Brinkerhoff and Lupri (1978; 1983), and Eichler (1981).

The resource theory of marital power is a model based on assumptions that are derived from Blau's social exchange theory. The theory was developed initially from data reported in *Husbands and Wives* (Blood and Wolfe, 1960). This classic study showed that a husband's power within marriage tended to increase in proportion to the resources that he could muster: education, income, prestige, social status, and so on. These authors also found that the husband's power was associated with the stage in the life cycle and with the presence of children in the home. More importantly, wives who worked for pay had more power than wives who were not gainfully employed.

When the resource theory was applied to the study of marital power in different societies, the findings were inconsistent. Research results about decision-making from the United States (Blood and Wolfe, 1960; Wolfe, 1959; Kandell and Lesser, 1972; Centers et al., 1971), France (Michel, 1967), West Germany (Lamousé, 1969; Lupri, 1965; 1969) and other countries showed a positive association between the husband's power and his socioeconomic resources, such as education, social status, income, and occupation. However, findings from Greece (Safilios-Rothchild, 1967; 1969; 1970), Yugoslavia (Buric and Zecevic, 1967), and later from Canada (Brinkerhoff and Lupri, 1978; 1983) revealed a negative association between the husband's power and his socioeconomic status. Furthermore, on closer inspection of those studies that reported an overall positive association, there were indicated curvilinear tendencies in the data and weak relationships that lacked statistical significance.

Many cross-cultural studies have examined the association between the wife's employment status and her power in relation to her husband's. Most of these studies indicate that working wives have more power than wives who do not work for pay. Again, however, the findings are not consistent; some divergent relationships were reported, depending on the type of decision that was used to tap the husband's power. Thus several comparative studies found that working wives have less power than non-working wives.

These divergent findings, produced by the application of resource theory to various societies, led Rodman (1967; 1972) to formulate a "theory of marital power in cultural context". He postulated that egalitarian norms are not distributed equally throughout the societies that were examined, but that in certain modernizing societies the middle and upper-status groups are the first to accept the ideology of gender equity. Thus the institution-alization of egalitarian gender norms varies from society to society, influencing the effect of resources on the distribution of marital power. In other words, the effect of resources on the husband's power must be seen in the normative context from which emerge the cultural or subcultural expectations about the distribution of marital power. In a later, more complex theory, Burr (1973) developed a general model of marital power which spells out a set of propositions, taking into account the complex interconnections between the amount of power, the cultural or normative context, and the specific tangible and in-tangible resources that affect the distribution of marital power.

11 Muscott (1983) points out correctly that technology has a liberating effect not in the single household but in collective institutions. Otherwise, the use of technologically advanced appliances merely means the increase of plus-value produced (see also Robinson, 1980).

4 AT WORK

1 Women's Vocational Mobilization

Women's vocational mobilization is the subject of what is by now an extensive body of writing by social scientists and public officials, each of them adopting a wide variety of approaches. Many scholars view the question of women's work merely in economic terms, considering women as an additional source of labour, to be manipulated according to the needs of the market (Amsden, 1980; Beechey, 1978; Boserup, 1970; Bruegel, 1979; Huntington, 1975; Knychala, 1977; Connelly, 1978; Gunderson, 1976; Przedpelski, 1975; Tilly and Scott, 1978). This approach was particularly dominant during periods of fast industrialization and during wars. It was very common in Europe and the United States during and after World War II.

Towards the late sixties, with feminist movements springing up and spreading in many countries, new approaches --- of differing scientific value --- were developed in the study of the changing social role of women. The subject matter of such analysis was "she", her experiences of breaking out of traditional roles (including the obstacles), and the psychological and social price which she has to pay for doing so.

Some researchers, however, maintained that women are not a universe apart, and that only a comparison between men's and women's behaviour patterns and attitudes can provide an answer as to which of them are specifically "female" and which "male" and to what degree. Indeed, many studies showed that gender does not differentiate attitudes (to work, for example: Hatch, 1986), while other individual variables (e.g. age) or social variables (e.g. education, occupation, class, place of residence) do have that result.

Some writers pointed out that women have in fact always performed roles which are thought to have become typically "female" after the industrial revolution in Europe and America. For example, Virginia Novarra (1980) goes as far as to say that women who are gainfully employed "outside the home" perform mainly the same kinds of jobs that their predecessors did for centuries. Women's activities have always concentrated, she says, around the same areas: bearing children; feeding the family; making clothes; caring for children, the sick and the disabled; being responsible for the education and upbringing of children; running the household. Naturally, these activities have at different times taken different institutional forms. For centuries, most of them were performed by women on their own, at home, in the midst of small social groups. Later, as a consequence of the growing division of labour, the activities were taken over by specialized institutions with mostly female staff. Thus, Virginia Novarra argues, the difference between the past and the present lies not so much in the jobs themselves but in the fact that they are now performed in a different institutional context --- outside the home and for pay. Such an approach is controversial. In fact, women have broken away in many respects from their traditional place in society, and it is unquestionable that extra-domestic work is a kind of participation in public life.

We start with the assumptions that the structure of the labour market and the attitudes towards women's and men's work have been differently shaped in each country by its historical development and that, especially in recent times, women's occupational mobilization is, in the socialist countries, a process different from that in the capitalist countries.

2 Models of Women's Mobilization and Attitudes towards Women's Occupational Activity

To borrow an expression from David Riesman, albeit for a different purpose, in the socialist countries we have to deal with a model of women's mobilization which could be called "the other-directed model". Opposite to this is the "inner-directed model", where changes in women's own ideas concerning their role in social life prompt them to seek opportunities to become active outside the family. In the other model, this search takes place mainly under external pressures which depend on political authority (Siemienska, 1985b).

The two models developed, of course, in different ways. In the inner-directed model, it is the evolving consciousness of women, induced in turn by changing living conditions, which produces changes in their behaviour. The other-directed model emerges chiefly as a consequence of sudden changes in life's circumstances, which force women to go beyond accepted traditional patterns and to adjust to new macrostructural situations.

The final result of the operation of both models can be quite similar, producing roughly the same proportion of men and women who are active in various spheres of public life. However, the ways in which the two models come into existence play an important role in producing some basic differences in attitudes towards women's active participation in extra-domestic work.

In the other-directed model, it is less common for women to claim equal rights and equal participation with men, even in family life. Further, men are even less likely than women to support sex equality. Equality is accepted mainly under pressure of external circumstances. The opposite holds true in the inner-directed model, where it is the result of a slow evolution affecting spheres of life.

While we cannot, of course, consider these models as a description of the real situation, they do highlight traits that are important for differentiating two types of women's vocational mobilization. The real processes have similar traits, even though they belong to different syndromes. For example, in socialist countries a highly centralized economic and political system permits rapid social mobility and industrialization to be combined with a strong ideological emphasis on equality, including gender parity (Lapidus, 1978; Heitlinger, 1979; Jasinska and Siemienska, 1983). In the highly developed free market countries, characterized by pluralism at all levels, the combination is different. A certain number of women began to work because of their husbands' low earnings or because they were single mothers. Also, many middle-class women wanted to work in order to become independent from their husbands and/or have a chance to express their creativity and use their talents. Many of them realized, especially in the late sixties, that the position of women resembled the situation of ethnic minorities or other discriminated groups. Their desire to work was caused by a change in the way that they perceived their own situation, and not just by economic necessity. The mass-media continued to disseminate traditional images of the woman as mother and wife, and as a sex object (Burstyn, 1985; Cantor, 1987), but reality was somehow moving in a different direction.

The two models of women's mobilization are open to change. This is especially true of the other-directed model, which is clearly of a temporary nature. It is followed, in fact, by profound changes which produce a more congruent pattern of relationship among various types of behaviour, and between behaviour and attitude.

Obviously, various factors modify the models constantly so that different versions of them exist in real life. These factors may be macrostructural determinants (e.g. economic crises and wars) in those societies in which the inner-directed model prevails, or microstructural factors (e.g. personal preferences and family situations) in the societies where the other-directed model prevails.

An important factor in both models is women's social class. The inner-directed model largely resembles the situation of middle-class women in highly developed Western societies, while the other-directed model may be considered as displaying the characteristics of the working-class women in East European countries.

It can be surmised that the prevailing model of mobilization affects the social perception of the opportunities open to women in various sectors of life.

3 Work Experience

3.1 *Period of Gainful Employment*

Our findings show that work seniority is differentiated, as expected, by the respondents' age and category, but significant differences are only sporadically found between men and women from the same categories.

3.2 *Patterns of Occupational Careers*

Patterns of occupational careers vary from country to country. They are determined, among other things, by differences in expectation about citizens' participation in the labour force (Piotrowski, 1963; Lapidus, 1978; Heitlinger, 1979: Young et al., 1984; Wolchik and Meyer, 1985; Powell, 1988).

In the socialist countries, the attempt to eliminate unemployment has been largely successful, at least formally, while in the capitalist countries unemployment, within certain limits, is considered normal. Moreover, the attempt by the socialist countries to industrialize quickly and, later, to modernize their economies has been connected with a strong pressure on women to enter the labour force. Efforts to mobilize them have been supported by propaganda (Jasinska and Siemienska, 1983) and by general low-wage structures which force women to supplement their family income (Piotrowski, 1963). The Canadian and Italian ways of economic development, on the other hand, have been different. The traditional role of the woman has been emphasized there almost all of the time but, in spite of it, women's participation in the labour market has become a reality (see ch. 1).

These two different types of economic development are reflected in the results of our study. More than half (53.4%) of the Canadian and 40.4% of the Italian respondents have known the experience of being without a paying job, while this is true in Poland for only 30.3% and in Romania for only 23.5% of respondents. Such a high percentage in Canada is caused also by the presence among our respondents of newly arrived immigrants who encountered difficulties in finding a job.

In all countries and categories, women more often than men have found themselves in this situation, with the exception of Italian female white-collar workers. But the gender differences vary strongly. For example, they are almost zero among blue-collar workers in Canada and Italy and teachers in Italy. In other cases, they range from 10% to 25%. The highest differences are found among Romanian blue-collar workers and Canadian decision-makers. Many more women in these categories went through the trial of being without a paying job.

In Poland and Romania, the percentage of respondents who had had such an experience was a little above 60% (only once) and 22.3% in Poland and 14.3% in Romania (twice). Few respondents underwent the experience more than twice. In Canada and Italy, however, respondents were more often without a paying job. This can be partially explained on the basis of the presence in the sample of men out of work. In fact, 36.8% of Canadian and 22.1% of Italian men out of work were six or more times without a paying job. In the Polish sample, as the reader will recall, such a category does not exist; in the Romanian sample, it is made up of disabled men.

The housewives' experience in this respect varies from country to country. Almost all of the Canadian housewives, with the exception of 5.8%, have worked at one point, while in the other countries the number without such an experience is much higher (over 20%). Many of them lost work once or twice before staying at home.

Reported reasons for being without a job reflect systemic differences. Difficulties in finding a job are mentioned by 37.9% of the Canadian and 54.2% of the Italian respondents, but by only 15.3% of the Romanian and 6.7% of the Polish respondents. However, the hypothesis that a woman would be in a more difficult situation than a man in this respect is not supported by our findings. In all categories, it is more common for men than for women not to find

a job. In general, blue-collar and white-collar workers and respondents out of work have more difficulties than others.

The reasons that are mentioned more frequently by women
than men in all four countries are children, especially, but also
marriage. However, only housewives (one-third in Canada and
Romania, almost half in Italy, 13% in Poland) often mention
marriage as a cause of being without a paying job. This means that
marriage, as such, no longer has a strong influence on women's
careers. This result coincides with what emerges elsewhere in this
book (ch.s 3, 5, App. B). Children interfere with vocational careers
more often than marriage, but not as frequently as might be expected.

However, the ways in which countries differ in this respect
is astonishing. One group consists of Italy and Romania, where in
only a few cases do children interfere in all categories. The other
group comprises Canada and Poland, where a quarter of women
in all categories state that having children is the reason why they
had to give up work. In both groups this reason, like marriage, is
mentioned by a high proportion of housewives.

"Needed at home" is another reason which differentiates the
respondents' occupational careers and is mentioned with particular
frequency by housewives (one-third in Poland, more than half in
Romania and Canada, but less than 10% in Italy), and relatively
often by female blue-collar workers. Other women, together with
men, rarely indicate this as a reason to stop working. Other mo-
tives, such as illness, the necessity to move to another town, reluctance of the spouse to have a working wife, or the respondent's
unwillingness to have a paying job, are mentioned by not more
than 12% of the respondents in each country, and that too mainly
by housewives. The correlation matrix reveals in all countries the
presence of a syndrome which has to do with the family (children,
marriage, unnecessary income, spouse's opposition). The influence
of these factors is stronger in Poland than in the other countries,
while it is weak in Canada. This can be explained by the different
orientation of an immigrant society where individual achievement
is emphasized and family members often live far away from each
other.

3.3 Rejected Offers of Promotion

It is generally believed that more women than men turn down
offers of promotion because of their double role, since they obtain

jobs chiefly in order to add to the family budget and are not interested in a career. Our study (Ch. 2, pars 4.2, 4.4) disproves this
view. It shows, rather, that the attitude to an offer of promotion is
largely correlated with a woman's occupational status.

In fact, when respondents were asked: "Have you ever been
offered a chance of promotion at your workplace or elsewhere that
you turned down?", the answers show that male and female members of the same category do not significantly diverge.

The promotion offer was rejected for a variety of reasons
(Fig.1).

Among them, there are some which recur particularly often
in all countries. The first is personal unwillingness. In second place
is the feeling that the promotion offered would be time consuming.
Third, many respondents in all countries, with the exception of
Poland, rejected promotion because they did not want to move to
other towns. Poles, more often than respondents in other countries,
considered it unacceptable to leave their friends in the workplace.

Almost all of the reasons listed in the closed question used
have been mentioned more frequently by men than by women,
with only a few exceptions. In all countries, women slightly more
often than men explain their decisions to turn down an offer of
promotion because of a fear of too much responsibility. Also, in
Poland and Romania more women than men are afraid that a new
position would demand more time or more work.

Sometimes, the differences observed are at variance with the
existing stereotype of female nature. For example, in all countries
male blue-collar workers fear, more often than their female counterparts, that they would not be able to handle new tasks which a
promotion might require. The same difference exists within other
categories but is not so pronounced.

Briefly, the reasons for turning down an offer of promotion
are not consistent with the prevailing stereotype. The expected differences, or even opposite reasons, do not exist in reality. We did
not find two clusters which could respectively be considered "male"
and "female". Reasons vary from country to country and, more so,
from one category to another.

3.4 *Experience of Protesting in the Workplace*

Protesting against unacceptable working conditions or decisions affecting work or both is considered here as a measure of the
respondent's self-confidence and active attitude towards the sur-

Fig. 1 Reasons for Refusing Promotion (percentage saying 'yes')

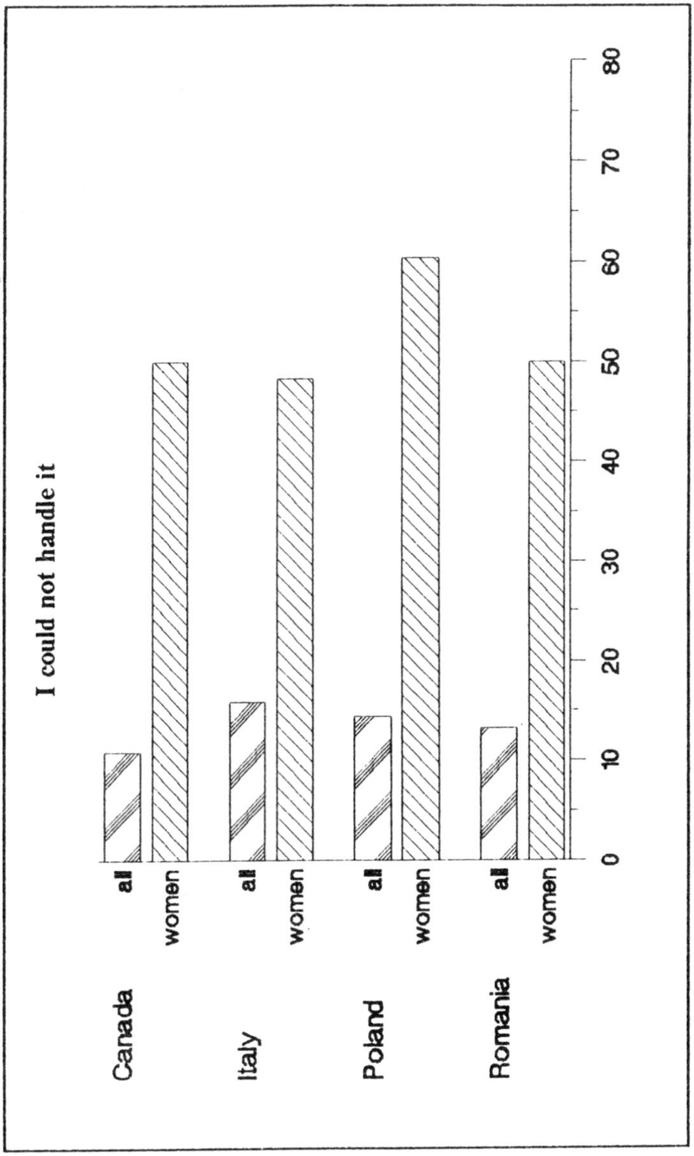

I could not handle it

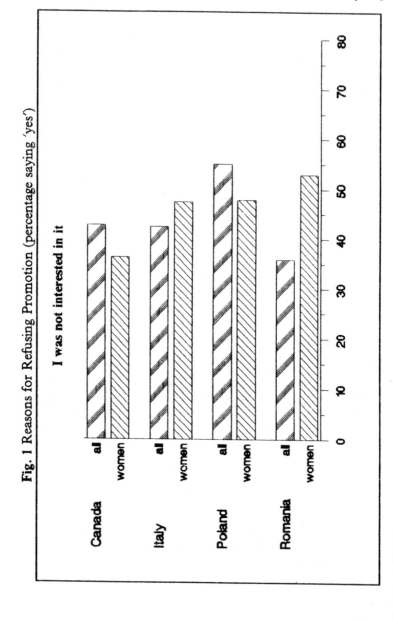

Fig. 1 Reasons for Refusing Promotion (percentage saying 'yes')

I was not interested in it

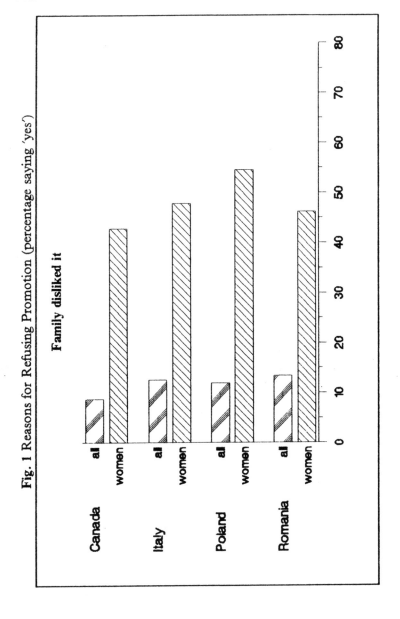

Fig. 1 Reasons for Refusing Promotion (percentage saying 'yes')

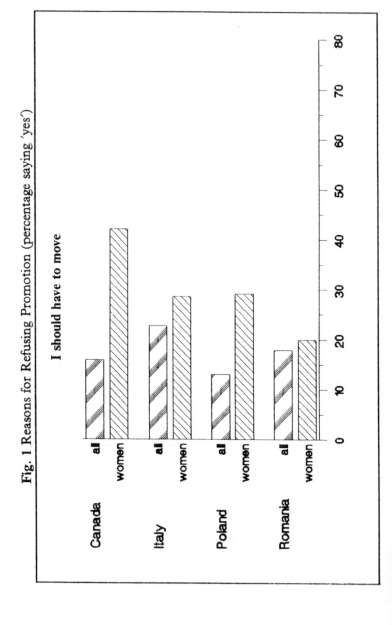

Fig. 1 Reasons for Refusing Promotion (percentage saying 'yes')

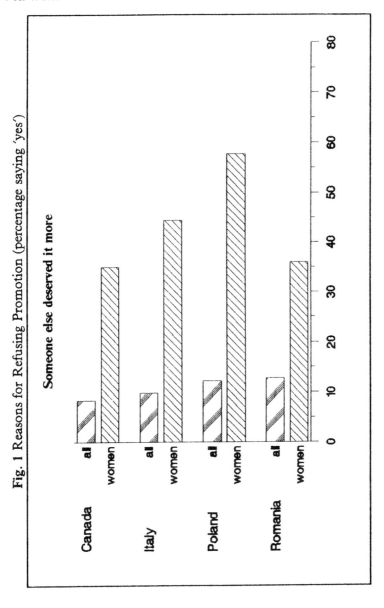

Fig. 1 Reasons for Refusing Promotion (percentage saying 'yes')

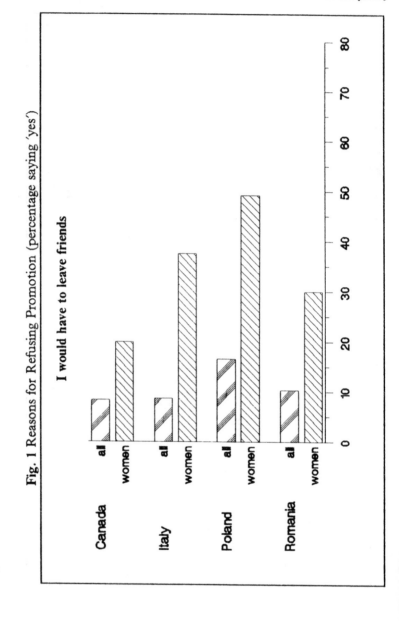

Fig. 1 Reasons for Refusing Promotion (percentage saying 'yes')

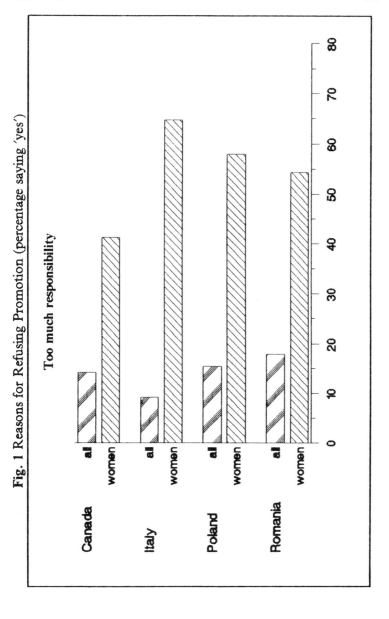

Fig. 1 Reasons for Refusing Promotion (percentage saying 'yes')

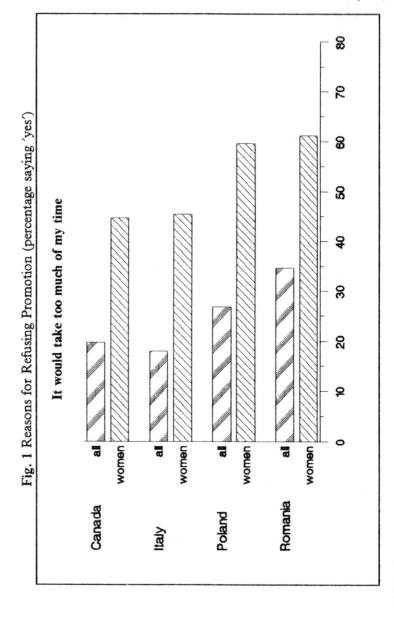

Fig. 1 Reasons for Refusing Promotion (percentage saying 'yes')

rounding world. For a long time women were passive, usually accepting the jobs offered to them, unable to protest. Often their working conditions were worse than men's, the amount of work expected by employers was higher that that expected of men, and wages much lower than those offered to men. But protests by women, in the form of strikes, demonstrations, etc., were less frequent than those organized by men. This has often been explained by citing not only the kind of socialization that is received by women but also women's fear of retaliation by the employers owing to the different opinion that women are less reliant, are more mediocre workers, and have a higher rate of absenteeism.

Our study confirms this pattern only partially. The distribution of answers to a question as to whether respondents ever protested against decisions with which they totally disagreed shows that male respondents protested more often than their female counterparts. However, in certain categories protesting men usually outnumber protesting women by no more than 10%. Some exceptions have been found, though. In Poland, the number of male blue-collar workers who have protested is twice as large as that of female blue-collar workers. Also, in Romania the proportion of protesting male teachers is 20% higher than protesting women in the same profession.

It is symptomatic that such diversity does not emerge between male and female decision-makers, with the exception of Poland. In Canada and Italy, as a matter of fact, female decision-makers protested more often than their male counterparts, although the difference is not significant. In Romania there are no differences at all.

In analysing these results, we have to consider some "systemic determinants". In a country with a long tradition of political liveliness, such as Italy, the protest rate is so high in all the categories that no differences were found between them. The frequency of protest is at its lowest in Romania where no channels for protest are allowed. The same lack became one of the main problems in Poland in the late 1970s, at the time of the collection of the data for this study; one of the demands raised in August 1980 was, indeed, the establishment of an independent trade union.

The character of the social processes that followed World War II and the type of social background of the respondents might also be of some help in explaining the differences between the countries. The peasant background of many people who live in Polish and Romanian cities and their newly acquired social status might prevent some of them from taking action against unacceptable decisions.

3.5 *The Respondent's Boss: Male or Female?*

Various analyses of the structures of employment of men and women have found that even in workplaces with a predominantly female workforce the bosses are usually male (Tannenbaum et al. 1974). The traditional view that women are not suited to holding managerial positions is so strongly entrenched that a major change in this field is hardly accepted by many people. Nevertheless, the situation is changing and more and more women can be found among bosses, even though they are usually at the lowest levels in the hierarchy. Such changes may be conducive to a dismissal of the prevailing stereotypes and to an easier acceptance of women as bosses.

Did our respondents have the experience of a female boss? In all four countries, this experience is not very common among both men and women. However, more women than men in all the categories have had a female boss, though the differences are not always significant. The differences are relatively more pronounced in Canada in all the categories, with the exception of teachers. In Italy, on the other hand, there are no significant differences, simply because most respondents of either sex have had only male bosses. In Poland men and women from the same categories have had a similar experience from this point of view, though a somewhat larger proportion have had a female boss either at the time of the study or earlier. In Romania the experience of male and female blue- and white-collar workers differs sharply, as many more women than men have had a female boss in both groups. In all of the countries under study more male and female teachers and decision-makers than blue- and white-collar workers have had significantly more ($p < .01$) female bosses.

4 Appraisal of Actual Conditions of Work

4.1 *Feeling of Being in Control of One's Conditions of Work*

The fact that the members of most categories have almost the same work seniority lends special interest to the question of their perception of working conditions and of their involvement in the job.

The data in Fig. 2 show that social position determines most strongly the individual consciousness. In fact, no significant differences were found in three of the four countries (Canada is the exception) between men and women from the same category. As had been expected, housewives, followed by female decision-makers, have the strongest feeling that they are in control of their working conditions.

Stronger differences turned up among members of different categories in Italy and Canada than in Poland and Romania. The latter two countries offer a nice contrast, though: the feeling of control is at its highest in Romania and at its lowest in Poland.

4.2 Satisfaction with One's Work

Respondents were asked the question: "Are you satisfied with your work?" Blauner (1960) criticizes the use of a direct question on job satisfaction, but acknowledges that such a question differentiates meaningfully between various occupations (see also Inkeles, 1960).

In general, as it appears also from this study (ch. 3, par. 2), women's earnings are lower than men's. However, when we consider non-monetary rewards as well, our findings confirm the results of other researchers that the overall rewards men and women derive from their jobs are about equal (Sauser and York, 1978; Darcy et al., 1984). An analogy of the differences in men's and women's determinants in job satisfaction is beyond the scope of the present research. Some authors (e.g. Herzog, 1982) maintain that holding jobs that entail autonomy, authority and prestige, and also promotion possibilities affects the degree of satisfaction for men more than for women, while relational, expressive and nurturant features of the job play a more important role for women than for men in breeding a feeling of job satisfaction in employment (Kilkpatrick et al., 1964; Kulpinska, 1975). Whether a compensation takes place between the two sets of variables in such a way that the outcome is the same, we cannot test. We know, however, that women's attachment to work, interest in promotions, and leadership aspirations are not much lower than men's. It is hard to explain, therefore, why women are as content as men with a situation which is objectively more unfavourable to them than to men. An explanation (Crosby, 1982) is that women's expectations from employment are lower than men's, in the sense that women think that they deserve fewer rewards than men who

Fig. 2 Perception of Control over Conditions of Work †

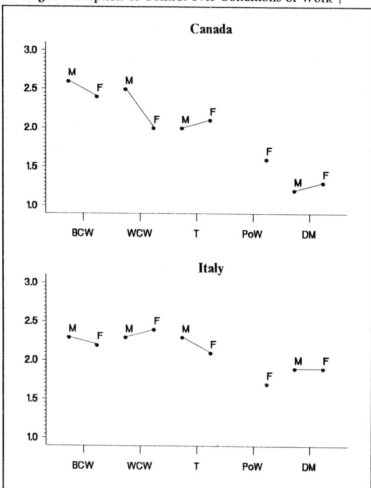

† A low score indicates a high degree of control. The question was not addressed to men out of work.

Fig. 2 Perception of Control over Conditions of Work †

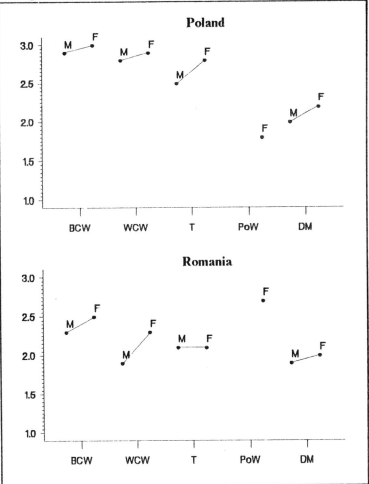

† A low score indicates a high degree of control. The question was not addressed to men out of work.

performed similarly, because they underestimate their own abilities or performance. Thus women, although they gain less overall rewards from their jobs, tend to adjust their feelings of satisfaction to the same level that they perceive in men.

We expected to find in countries with an active feminist movement, resulting in the creation of a feminist consciousness or a strong egalitarian pressure, that women would display a relatively low level of contentment with their employment, often lower than that of men belonging to the same category.

In reality (see Fig. 3), while it is true that significant differences between female and male respondents from the same category are found only in Canada and Romania (i.e. in one country with an active feminist movement and in another where the pressure of the dominant egalitarian ideology is strong), such differences are not in the expected sense: in Canada women in several categories appear to be more satisfied than their male counterparts and in Romania female teachers are significantly more satisfied than their male counterparts and equality characterizes the other cases.

5 Appraisal of Gender Inequality in Job-Related Situations

5.1 *Appraisal of Gender Inequality in Vocational Training and Obtaining Jobs*

Vocational training is a basic necessity for employment. In all societies it is widely held that women, on account of their different life tasks, do not need as much school education as men. It is only recently, in some countries, that women have begun to outnumber men in higher education but even in these countries women still tend to choose to study subjects that accord with the traditional image of female activity.

Apart from this, there is the question of the expenses connected with education. Thus, we are not surprised to find that, in those countries such as Poland and Romania where education is totally free, the opinion prevails, more often than in Italy and Canada, that women and men have equal chances in this respect.

In general, respondents state that women have more equal access to vocational training than to jobs. The correlations between appraisals of opportunities for vocational training and job opportunities range between .36 and .45 (in Italy the correlations are higher: .47 for men and .54 for women).

Fig. 3 Work Satisfaction †

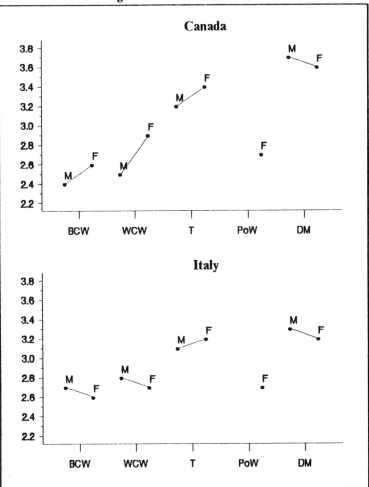

† A low score indicates a high degree of control. The question was not addressed to men out of work.

Fig. 3 Work Satisfaction †

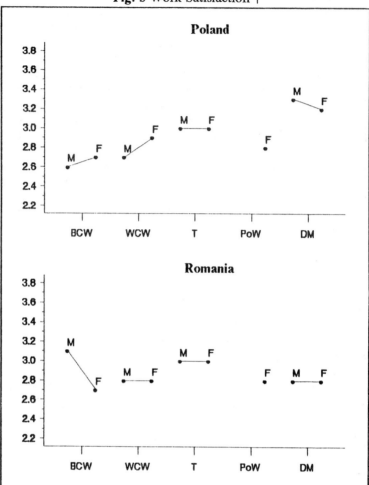

† A low score indicates a high degree of control. The question was not addressed to men out of work.

A perception of gender equality with regard to the opportunity to a job may depend on many factors. While the objective situation must be taken into consideration, social consciousness can also reflect an egalitarian propaganda, if it is persuasive enough. We can assume, therefore, that an egalitarian perception will be more common in socialist countries, while feelings of gender inequality will prevail in Canada and Italy, also thanks to the feminists' attack against discriminatory situations.

This hypothesis is supported by our findings. In Romania the majority of the respondents (68.6%) feel that men and women have equal chances to get a job, and only a quarter hold the view that men have better chances. About 6% state that women are even privileged in this respect. The Polish sample comes next: almost half of the respondents hold that there is no gender discrimination, but the other half (double the figure in Romania) feel that men are privileged.

In Italy and Canada, the egalitarian perception is less common, expressed by about one-third of the respondents in each country. In Canada, fewer respondents than in Italy think that women are better off than men (5% in comparison to 11%), while the number of respondents who assert that men are privileged is the same in both countries (about 60%).

We surmised that the perception of the lack of opportunities for women to get a job will be more often shared by women than by men, because the latter do not experience the discrimination to which women are exposed. By and large, this hypothesis is supported by the findings of our study in all of the countries.

5.2 *Who gets Fired First: a Man or a Woman?*

Overall, the majority of the respondents in all the countries state that women are fired first. Italy comes first, followed by Canada and then Poland. Romania is the exception, with 53% of respondents believing that women and men are treated in the same way. In general, the persuasion that women are treated equally is shared by more people in socialist countries than in the others. This validates our hypothesis regarding the role of the economic and political system and, even more, its propaganda as a differentiating factor.

In some categories men express this opinion (that women are fired first) more often than women, even by as much as three or four times. This is the case for male decision-makers in Canada and

Italy. In Poland, the dissimilarity between male and female decision-makers is smaller, and in Romania it almost does not exist. In general, less educated respondents, e.g. blue-collar workers, tend to consider the situation as more egalitarian than do the better educated.

The feeling that women are discriminated against is strongest among the Italian respondents, particularly female decision-makers. This is true also for female decision-makers in Canada and Poland. In Romania, female decision-makers report this form of discrimination less often than other respondents (with the exception of male decision-makers and men out of work). The results show that women who have succeeded in having a career are also those who are more aware.

5.3 *Are Women and Men Offered Equal Pay?*

The perception of gender equality in regard to wages divided our respondents in a different way than did their perception of job opportunities. As in the previous case, Italian respondents come first: 82.8% consider the situation to be unequal. This time the Poles come next (59.8%) and the Canadians third (46.9%), while an overwhelming majority (83.9%) of Romanians state that in their country women and men receive the same wages. In all countries, save Romania, women in almost all categories claim --- nearly always twice as often as men --- that men are paid better (see also ch. 3, par. 2).

Thus, perceptions concerning equality of chances to get a job and to have equal wages can differ from one another. This is the case for the Canadian and Polish respondents. The latter, more often than the former, regard access to jobs as being equal, but simultaneously feel that the structure of wages is discriminatory for women.

The extremely high percentage of Romanian respondents who hold the situation to be egalitarian, in spite of the fact that objectively there are gender differences in the wage structure, is an example of how propagandized systemic principles can affect people's perceptions.

5.4 *Job-Related Expectations*

The level of optimism or pessimism as to career prospects during a five-year period is different in the various countries.

In Canada and Italy, women, slightly more than men belonging to the same categories, think that they will hold better jobs in the future. This applies to all women, with the exception of teachers and housewives. This is easy to explain: teachers' opportunities for professional promotion are inherently limited by the nature of the profession; and housewives, if they do not plan to start working, cannot expect any change.

In Poland and Romania, the pattern of expectation is different. Almost all male respondents of all categories in Romania and the majority of them in Poland expect, more often than their female counterparts, to have a better job in the next five years. The belief that one will be working in the same type of job in the future is more common among women than men, within the same category, in Poland and Romania than it is in Canada and Italy, with the exception of female decision-makers, who also in the latter countries are less sure that their positions will not change.

The distributions of answers to this question and to that concerning the perception of equality in getting a job are inconsistent with each other. Polish and Romanian women, despite their strong conviction that equal job opportunities exist, are less optimistic than men about their own future. The opposite holds good in Italy and Canada.

The diversity is perhaps owing to the fact that in Poland and Romania the appraisal of the situation is influenced by the state propaganda, while an evaluation of one's own occupational chances of promotion is mainly determined by individual experience and the opportunities that are perceived realistically in the workplace or in comparison with other jobs to which one may aspire.

The opposite pattern found in Canada and Italy can probably be explained by the influence of the feminist movement. Women are aware of their underprivileged situation but at the same time are also aware that some improvements have taken place and, therefore, believe that further improvements are in prospect.

5.5 *Appraisal of the Efforts by Government and Trade Unions to Create Equal Conditions for Women and Men in Job-Related Situations*

One of the goals of this research is to find out the degree to which male and female citizens of countries with different social, political and economic systems evaluate their governments and trade unions in terms of the measures they take to decrease discrimination against women in the workplace. Job-related situations may be regarded as the most basic way through which the majority of women participate in public life. Therefore, a feeling that the government and the trade unions actively support an anti-discrimination campaign is important for women in that it encourages and facilitates their entry into the labour force.

Two questions, in which the respondents were asked to evaluate the performance of the government and the trade unions, formed the basis for an index of "system performance related to sex equality". We conjectured that the perception of attempts by government and trade unions to create equal conditions would be related to a perception of actual equality.

Our hypothesis was supported by the results of our study. In Romania, where the highest number of respondents maintain that women and men are treated equally, the percentage of respondents who state that the government and the trade unions are committed to equality in the workplace is also the highest (87.3%). Romanian women, even more than men, hold that the government and trade unions are concerned with this problem.

Poland is the next country in this respect, with 51.5% of respondents (Siemienska 1985a), but unlike Romania there is a relatively higher percentage of respondents (28% v. 16%) who consider that neither the government nor the trade unions have adequately dealt with this issue. Also, unlike Romania, men slightly more often than women report that the government and the trade unions have taken steps to achieve the goal of non-discrimination.

Canada comes third (26%) but the difference between Poland and Canada is less striking than that between Romania and Poland. In Canada, there is a higher percentage of respondents who believe that the government and the trade unions do not care about unequal opportunities for women (39.1%), while 19.5% think that they are making some efforts to improve the situation. Female decision-makers, more often than males, state that the two types of institution are not concerned about sex equality.

Italy is the country with the largest group of respondents who express a negative view about the government and the trade unions in this area (45.1%). This opinion is shared to the same degree by members of different categories but, in all of them, more often by women than men (the difference is usually 15% to 20%).

These results are congruent with what we know about the countries in our study. Italy is a nation where dissatisfaction with political institutions is traditionally high (Inglehart, 1977). The difference between Poland and Romania can be easily understood if we remember that the data were collected on the eve of a crisis in Poland. This was characterized by the effort to create a new trade union, which included among its first demands the recognition of the right of young women to stay at home (first agreement signed by the government and the delegates of the striking committee in Gdansk in 1980; Siemienska, 1986).

5.6 *Factors Determining the Perception of Gender Inequality in Job-Related Situations*

The above-mentioned questions about inequality in job-related situations were used for the construction of an index called "Appraisal of Gender Inequality in Work-Related Situations" (App. 22).

As shown in Fig. 4, the perception of work inequality is the highest in Canada. Italy comes second, followed by Poland and then Romania.

Women, particularly those in leadership positions, affirm more often than men the existence of sex differences in job-related situations.

The perception of inequality on the job may depend on many different factors. We can divide them into the following groups:

(a) demographic variables (sex, age, length of residence in the neighbourhood, education, occupation);
(b) social background (mother's and father's occupation, religious practice);
(c) perception of work conditions (work satisfaction, control over work conditions);
(d) perception of the performance of the political system with regard to gender equality (efforts of government and trade unions) and political alienation;
(e) country.

We formulated the hypothesis that the impact of these factors in explaining the perception of gender inequality on the job varies from country to country. Our hypothesis appears validated.

Fig. 4 Appraisal of Gender Inequality in Work-Related Situations †

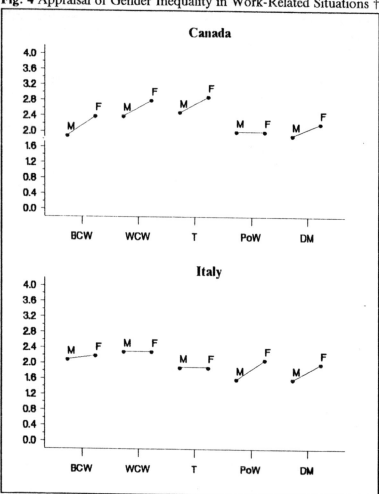

† Index, see App. 22.

Fig. 4 Appraisal of Gender Inequality in Work-Related Situations †

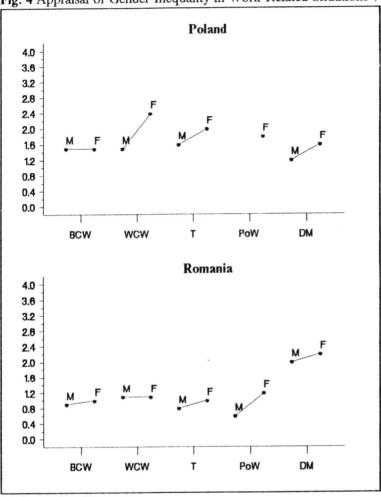

† Index, see App. 22.

From the analysis made separately for each country (Table 1), it appears that, while there are no two countries with exactly the same ranking of predictors, Italy and Canada are more similar to each other than Poland and Romania. In Canada and Italy the respondents' occupation, sex, length of residence in the neighbourhood, and frequency of religious practice are the most important predictors. With the exception of religious practice, the same applies to Poland. In Romania the most important predictors are not only the respondents' occupation and length of residence in the neighbourhood but also education and mother's occupation.

In general, in Poland and Romania religious practice plays a significantly minor role as a differentiating factor. The reason is that in Poland the majority of the respondents practise often, while in Romania the opposite is true.

The higher role played by the respondents' education in Poland and Romania than in Canada and Italy may be explained by the influence that schooling exerts on the formation of social consciousness. In the absence of feminist movements in the socialist countries, it seems reasonable to suppose that the formation of a social consciousness in the matter of gender equality would strongly be influenced by schooling.

Another finding worthy of consideration is the relatively more significant role of the mother's occupation rather than the father's in almost all countries. Mothers, especially if they have held or still hold high positions at work (and we may assume that, as a consequence, they have learned more about the unequal treatment of women) inevitably affect their children's perception of reality in this field.

The analysis presented in Table 2 shows that the country is the most important factor followed by the perception of the performance of the system in the efforts to equalize women's and men's conditions. The third most important factor is the respondent's occupation. Sex comes fourth. The ranking order shows that political alienation and education, contrary to what we expected, play an insignificant role. Social background, i.e. the type of socialization received, is more important.

6 Conclusion

According to our model concerning the mobilization of women in the labour force in socialist and capitalist countries, the position of women in Poland and Romania should be more egali-

Table 1 Predictors of Appraisal of Sex Inequality in Job-Related Situations
(MCA)

Predictors	Ranks of betas	Respondents seeing inequality more often
	Canada	
Occupation	1	Decision-makers, teachers, housewives
Sex	2	Women
Years in neighbourhood	3	1-2 years, 8-18
Religious practising	4	Less practising
Control over work conditions	5	Having more control
Mother's occupation	6	Professionals, middle-level managers, white-collar workers
Work satisfaction	7	More satisfied
Education	8	More educated and middle-level managers
Father's occupation	9	High professionals and middle-level managers, professionals
Alienation	10	Less alienated

$R^2 = .11$

Predictors	Ranks of betas	Respondents seeing inequality more often
	Italy	
Occupation	2	Decision-makers, teachers, white-collar workers
Sex	4	Women
Years in neighbourhood	3	1-8 years
Religious practising	1	Not at all practising
Control over work conditions	8	Having some and little control
Mother's occupation	7	High-level managers, skilled workers, professionals
Work satisfaction	9	Less satisfied
Education	10	More educated (especially university education)
Father's occupation	6	High and middle-level managers, professionals
Alienation	5	Less alienated

$R^2 = .14$

Table 1 Predictors of Appraisal of Sex Inequality in Job-Related Situations (MCA)

Predictors	Ranks of betas	Respondents seeing inequality more often
Poland		
Occupation	4	Housewives, decision-makers, teachers
Sex	1	Women
Years in neighbourhood	3	16-21 years
Religious practising	9	Not at all practising
Control over work conditions	7	Having moderate control over work conditions
Mother's occupation	2	Professionals, middle-level managers
Work satisfaction	8	Somewhat and rather satisfied
Education	5	More educated (especially university education)
Father's occupation	6	High-level managers
Alienation	10	Less alienated

$R^2 = .07$

Predictors	Ranks of betas	Respondents seeing inequality more often
Romania		
Occupation	1	Decision-makers, men out of work
Sex	9	Women
Years in neighbourhood	2	3-6, 10-15, 20-23 years
Religious practising	8	Not at all and little practising
Control over work conditions	10	Having no control over work conditions
Mother's occupation	4	High-level managers, unskilled workers, white-collar workers
Work satisfaction	6	Somewhat satisfied
Education	3	Having university or primary school education
Father's occupation	5	Men out of work, unskilled workers, high-level managers
Alienation	7	Moderately alienated

$R^2 = .02$

Table 2 Predictors of Appraisal of Sex Inequality in Job-Related Situations (ranks of betas in MCA analysis)

Independent variables	Rank	Beta	Respondents who perceived sex inequality more often
Country	1	.3685	Italians most often, Canadians next, followed by Poles and Romanians
System performance	2	.2023	More critical respondents
Category in the sample	3	.1524	Decision-makers, teachers
Sex	4	.1307	Women
Religious practice	5	.0718	Less religious
Length of residence in neighbourhood	6	.0658	Less than 7 years
Mother's occupation	7	.0642	Working mothers
Father's occupation	8	.0449	Managers, professionals, white-collar workers
Control over work conditions	9	.0357	Having more control
Work satisfaction	10	.0249	Very satisfied
Education	11	.0194	More educated
Alienation	12	.0075	Less alienated

Multiple R^2 = .31

tarian than in Italy and Canada. We surmised also that this should be reflected in the social consciousness, despite the presence of the feminist movement in the latter countries.

Another assumption in our model was that Polish and Romanian women, owing to the other-directed nature of their labour mobilization, should be less interested in their careers than their Western counterparts. We also expected a profound difference between men and women as far as behaviour and perception of job-related situations are concerned.

Our analysis shows that socio-political systems do not always divide the countries of our sample into a dichotomy. This is understandable, considering the different past of each country and the complexity of their recent political developments. It is enough to think of Poland and the structure of the political scene there, with the unique role played by the Church and other organized movements, and of the frequency of Polish political crisis to realize the difference from Romania. The system differentiates the countries as far as the respondents' history of employment and the opportunity to get vocational training or jobs are concerned, but not with respect to the reasons for stopping or interrupting work and the reasons for rejecting offers of promotion.

Also, when the respondents evaluate equality in wages we find a different dichotomy from that expected: Italians and Poles perceive inequality much more than Canadians and Romanians.

Usually, the Romanians consider their job-related conditions to be more egalitarian than the others; our Polish respondents are sometimes fairly close to them, but sometimes also far away. In this context it is interesting that, when the respondents are asked about their evaluation of attempts made by the government and the trade unions to equalize job opportunities for men and women, Poles and Romanians stand out with favourable assessments. Such a result can be viewed as a proof of the effectiveness with which the system succeeds in convincing its members that the ideological principles that justify it are actually implemented.

All in all, it seems correct to stress that, despite the divergences in political systems, women, according to their own and also their male counterparts' opinions, do not enjoy equal access to and equal treatment at work . In general, the feeling is slightly stronger among women than men. Yet, there are cases in which the perception of gender inequality is more common among men than among women. This is so in all four countries, at least in some categories, when, for instance, opportunities for getting a job are considered.

The literature dealing with the differences in women's and men's approaches to work tends to present men as highly motivated and women as interested only in gaining an additional income. Consequently, men aspire to be promoted, while women avoid promotions as much as possible. Our analysis, to some extent, gives opposite results. Indeed, the analysis of the reasons why people refuse to be promoted shows that a difference between men and women almost does not exist in the Italian and the Polish samples and is just visible in the Canadian and Romanian samples. There are even cases where men, more often than women of the same category, mention reasons which are commonly considered as "typically female" (e.g. fear that they would not be able to cope with the new tasks that a promotion would entail). In general, the reasons for turning down a promotion do not accord with the traditionally accepted "female" and "male" patterns.

The same happens with protest. Men protest more often than women. However, in the majority of categories, protesting men usually outnumber women by no more than 10%.

As far as the impact of a feminist movement is concerned, our findings are inconclusive. There are issues, such as opportunities to a job, in which such a movement presumably played a role in making people aware of the existing discriminations; however, there are other issues, such as job satisfaction, in which it seems irrelevant.

While there are differences between men and women in attitudes to work, the differences are not as relevant as is commonly believed. Social variables, such as the respondents' occupation, play a stronger role than sex. A conception of female and male worlds as two separate entities is exaggerated, if not completely false (Hatch, 1986). We agree with Feldberg and Glenn's (1979) conclusions that a more careful analysis of not only women's and men's appraisals of their work conditions and attitudes towards work but also their behaviour in job-related situations reveals a tendency towards a resemblance between men and women performing similar types of work. Both the traditional "job model" applied mainly to men and the "gender model" applied mainly to women appear to be based on a number of false assumptions which start with the deeply ingrained one that women's and men's involvements in work are different by definition.

If this is so, it remains to be explained why women are not found in the higher echelons of hierarchy in the workplace.

5 PUBLIC PARTICIPATION

1 Modes of Public Participation

This chapter deals with participation in public life and especially with the exercise of power, from the specific angle of gender differences.

The vast majority of political systems claim to be egalitarian. But, in actual practice, there are many differences in the degree to which people participate in public life and in the power that they exercise. We deal with one item that traditionally has been taken for granted as "naturally" associated or not associated with participation in public life and with power: gender, in the sense that where participation in public life and also power is found a specific gender is also normally found. Through the ages these activities have been considered as typically masculine (1) (Ackelsberg and Diamond, 1987; Azmon, 1981; Acker, 1981; Blanquart, 1974; Bourque and Grossholtz, 1974; Cook, 1985; Haavio-Mannila, 1970; Merkl, 1976; Milbrath, 1965; Stacey and Price, 1981; Welch, 1977; 1978).

The exclusion of at least half of humankind from the shaping of public life, if not "the making of history" (as some people say), is found in all latitudes. And in all latitudes we find corresponding ideologies which, in a variety of ways, tie women to the family and to the menial tasks of everyday life.

Yet, following the nineteenth-century bourgeois revolution in the West and the advent of socialist regimes in other parts of the world in this century, something has started to change. Women's equality with men in the public realm has slowly become an issue which has recently moved into the foreground. The first outstanding cry for women's emancipation came from one of the most prestigious intellectuals of the liberal-democratic brand, John Stuart Mill. It was followed by the work of Engels and socialist authors such as Bebel, Luxemburg, Lenin, Zetkin, Kollontay --- to mention just a few names belonging to the period before or during the October Revolution. Yet, in spite of these doctrinal speculations that equated women's emancipation with socialism, one is entitled to wonder why there is today more women's participation in a liberal-democratic regime than under socialism.

The problem is complex because the definitions of participation in public life and access to power vary radically between the two systems. For some people, obviously, it is right to claim that under socialism the level of women's participation is low, because it is open only to people who accept the so-called "dictatorship of the proletariat". Others will maintain that this is so for the "bourgeois" regimes where power is said to be the monopoly of the ruling class and of its representatives. We will not pursue this line of argument. Instead, we will ask ourselves whether discrimination between men and women disappears or at least is attenuated after switching from one system to another in different areas, such as work, political parties, voluntary associations, and public and semi-public associations, and we will look for the correlates of the differences in the spheres of values and role distribution within the family.

Our concern is with participation in public life in general but, as we said already, we focus our attention on the phenomenon of power. By access to power we refer to the holding of offices in the public or semi-public sphere (such as government, public administration, agencies such as hospitals, opera houses, schools) and in organizations such as political parties, trade unions, professional associations and the like. In other words, we restrict our analysis to "official" establishments, leaving out economic organizations as well as the certainly very interesting but research-wise almost impracticable sphere of informal and/or illegal actions that are aimed at influencing public policies.

Our study concentrates on the factors that decrease the gender gap in office-holding. The reason for this is that, in complex modern societies, where power is formalized, institutionalized offices are the seat of authority for recognized processes of decision-making in the public fields. We will concentrate on participation and incumbency in political parties, because in all four countries parties are the crucial seat of power, despite the deep differences between them. In fact, recruitment of national leaders and governmental personnel as well as the definition of public policy take place through them.

However, women and men also differ as far as other aspects of public participation are concerned (2). We will try to explore what follows from these differences. To state that women have less power or participate less than men in all societies is not to deny that there are differences between countries. We are interested precisely in how these differences vary and in relation to what.

In a study of this issue, which was conducted in the framework of a much broader international research, Verba et al. (1978) (3) showed that "the male/female gap increases as one moves from the relatively easy political act of voting to the more stringent acts contained in the scale of overall political participation" such as campaign activity, communal activity, contacting officials on personal matters. They go on to ask: "Why should there be such a pervasive difference between male and female participation rates? How can we account for the variation in the extent of that difference across the nations?" (1978: 236).

While acknowledging that they cannot offer "a comprehensive explanation" of that difference, the authors try to offer a "more limited explanation":

> If we find sex difference in resources and in the ability to convert resources into political activity, we shall have some explanation of the lower levels of political activity among women. Differences in ability to convert resources into activity will be especially interesting. If such differences exist, they would suggest some special inhibition for women when it comes to political matters. It would mean that even when women attain parity in individual and institutional resources, they do not convert their comparable resources into political activity as well as do men. (Verba et al., 1978: 236)

Our study, started in 1973, when the work by Verba et al. had not been written, can be considered as an expansion of their effort. However, while the line of reasoning is the same, our set of variables is larger than that used by them.

For us, as for Verba et al., class (in the Weberian sense) plays a pre-eminent role and, for this reason, it was important to have socialist systems in our sample. These authors (Verba et al., 1971; 1978; Verba and Nie, 1972) and others (Milbrath, 1965) have pointed out the association between high status and political participation. The fundamental reason appears to be the availability of resources. If a person belongs to a low stratum, resources will not be available, and she or he will also have a poor feeling of personal efficacy and a low level of belief in groups. It appears reasonable to surmise that this is even more true for women than men. Consequently, women in general, and those from the lower strata in particular, can gain access to power only through a change in or evolution of society in the direction of a more egalitarian set-up. We will discover that this is exactly what has happened.

We expected to find under socialism, relative to the liberal-democratic countries, not only a greater readiness on the part of women to transform into public activities the socio-economic opportunities they find available but also fewer obstacles in their path and a greater equality in the socio-economic opportunities themselves. The result of this should have been a lessening of traditional gender differences in terms of participation and power.

Individuals enter political activity through membership of or involvement in political organizations. We have parties in all four countries of our sample. We also have movements, more or less loosely organized, where women give vent to their specific interests. These, like the parties, vary widely from one country to another. Some of them, in Canada and Italy, differ from protest movements only because of a loose structure which secures for them a certain continuity of commitment on specific issues on the part of their members, and because of their political articulation which gives them some weight in national events such as elections and referenda. There is no doubt that their adherents have, or develop, a keen consciousness of their being women, identify themselves with the "movement", and breed an ideology of their own. Other movements or organizations are more emanations of parties (this is true particularly in Italy, Poland and Romania). But, whatever their differences, all these movements work towards a common goal (4).

The importance of having feminist organizations in our sample lies also in the fact that within them women are not faced with the male dominance that permeates the party structures.

The reader may be surprised to find in this study no coverage of electoral turn-out, often considered a key indicator of political participation. In this instance, however, the use of this indicator would have been misleading, since in two countries of our sample voting is for many merely an enforced ritual.

In paragraphs 2 and 3 below, we describe the modes of participation that were used in this study but some preliminary remarks are necessary here. We know that in two countries of our sample organized opposition is not permitted. It is reasonable to surmise that in these countries, while many people will not join the only existing party or coalition of parties, it follows not that their political interest is low, but merely that there is no party corresponding to their ideas. However, this is again a complex issue, because the same can also happen in countries where a plurality of parties exists. We will not enter into the motivations of why people join or do not join a party: they may be the noblest or the basest, an index of ideal or utopian commitment, of solid political realism, of apathy, or of opportunism.

Also, the fact of holding a party office in a party organized along the principle of democratic centralism is quite different from that in a party organized along liberal-democratic lines. Again, however, it is very difficult to say that the incumbent's freedom is more limited in the first case than in the second, because we know that there are factions within the second type of party, allegiance to which is stimulated by the risk of not being re-elected and of seeing one's political career jeopardized. Furthermore, one must take into account pressures exerted by the "vested interests".

The reader must always keep in mind that our focus is limited and that we pursue only one line of analysis: the difference between women and men in terms of participation and exercise of power in public life (5).

2 Public Offices

Let us start with a description of gender differences in public office-holding. We consider first non-governmental organizations such as schools, hospitals, opera houses, etc., and then governmental organizations. Access to each type depends on either appointment or election. Both forms are considered here.

Our respondents in all countries hold non-governmental offices of low importance (Table 1, see also App. 8) but what matters from the point of view of our research is that, within each category, the gender differences are very small and almost none is significant.

We found exactly the same results for the governmental offices, as shown in Table 2 (see also App. 17).

* * *

Among our respondents, the number of people who were unsuccessful candidates for office is low in all countries. Aside from Italy (both for governmental and non-governmental offices) and Romania (limited to governmental offices where the average is higher for women), there are no differences between men and women. Once more, this is a finding that runs against our expectations.

Table 1 Non-Governmental Offices†

	Canada Elected N Office-holders	Canada Elected N Offices	Canada Appointed N Office-holders	Canada Appointed N Offices	Italy Elected N Office-holders	Italy Elected N Offices	Italy Appointed N Office-holders	Italy Appointed N Offices
Low								
MBCW			3	3	6	14	1	4
FBCW			3	5			1	1
MWCW			10	16	11	27	2	6
FWCW	1	1	4	5	7	26	2	12
MT			6	13	22	34	5	11
FT			3	9	13	18	2	2
MOW	1	1	2	8	2	4		
HW			9	11	2	2		
MDM	8	12	58	195	15	25	7	17
FDM	5	7	42	133	24	32	12	19
Middle								
MWCW	1	3	1	5				
MT	2	2	2	3				
FT								
MDM	2	2	24	40	7	16	3	3
FDM	2	4	36	93	8	10	5	7
High								
MDM	3	4	17	37	2	2	7	7
FDM	4	9	31	82	6	8		

†Levels and categories with no respondents have been eliminated.

Table 1 Non-Governmental Offices

| | Poland | | | | Romania | | | |
| | Elected | | Appointed | | Elected | | Appointed | |
	N Office-holders	N Offices	N Office-holders	N Offices	N Office-holders	N Offices	N Office-holders	N Offices
Low								
MBCW	5	7	4	10	14	41	3	5
FBCW	3	4	4	25	6	20		
MWCW	5	12	3	5	22	50	2	2
FWCW	5	7	3	9	12	27	1	4
MT	8	18	7	16	10	25	4	9
FT	12	17	3	4	6	18	2	6
MOW					5	10	7	21
HW	9	17	2	8	19	75	1	2
MDM	28	49	30	53	25	33	3	3
FDM	36	94	16	30	8	19	1	1
Middle								
MBCW			1	1				
FBCW			1	2				
MWCW					3	9	1	4
MT	1	2	1	2				
FT	3	5	1	1	1	4	1	1
MOW								
HW					1	5		
MDM	3	4	1	2	12	17		
FDM	3	6	1	2	2	5		
High								
MBCW			1	1				
FBCW	1	1						
FT	1	2						
MDM					3	7		

Table 2 Governmental Offices†

	Canada Elected N Office-holders	Canada Elected N Offices	Canada Appointed N Office-holders	Canada Appointed N Offices	Italy Elected N Office-holders	Italy Elected N Offices	Italy Appointed N Office-holders	Italy Appointed N Offices
Within City (i.e. district)								
MWCW					1	1	1	
FWCW								
MT				1	2	1		
MDM	2	2	1	1	1	2	2	1
FDM	6	21	1	1	2	2	1	
City								
MWCW					1	2	6	10
MT					7	11	1	1
FT					1	1		
MDM	10	44	10	20	41	114	4	5
FDM	17	47	7	10	47	81	5	5
Intermediate (i.e. province, county, state in a federal system)								
MT					1	1		
MDM	13	22	17	29	23	53	5	15
FDM	15	28	25	44	22	29	2	2
National								
MWCW			1	3	1	1		
MOW								
MDM	11	21	20	29	48	92	12	32
FDM	4	15	16	30	62	108	5	8

†Levels and categories with no respondents have been eliminated.

Table 2 Governmental Offices

	Poland Elected N Office-holders	Poland Elected N Offices	Poland Appointed N Office-holders	Poland Appointed N Offices	Romania Elected N Office-holders	Romania Elected N Offices	Romania Appointed N Office-holders	Romania Appointed N Offices
Within City (i.e. district)								
MBCW	1					2		
MWCW		1						
FWCW								
MT	1	4	1	1	1	1		
FT	2	2			2	3	1	1
MOW					1	3		
HW					1	1		
MDM	10	12	1	1	6	7	8	9
FDM	5	7	2	4	6	16	4	17
City								
MT	1	3			2	3		
FT	1	4			1	1		
MDM	5	6			2	6	1	2
FDM	3	4	1	1			2	2
Intermediate (i.e., province, county, state in a federal system)								
MT	5	6	2	2	1	5	1	3
MOW	1	1					1	1
MDM			2	2			1	1
FDM	1	2			1	1		
National								
MT					1	1	1	4
FT					1	1	1	4
MOW					1	4	1	1
FDM		2			1	5		

The question arises whether, among the candidates who failed at least once, there is a higher average of males who at a certain point succeeded in getting elected. The average of the ratios between the two frequencies shows that, while there is no difference in Poland, males are slightly privileged in Romania and more privileged in Canada and especially in Italy where the ratio for males is about twice that for females. There are, however, very few cases where the ratio for women is below 1: in other words, female candidates who initially failed have been subsequently elected about the same number of times as they were candidates.

3 Party Affiliation and Office-Holding

In the following paragraphs we will use a global measure, called "Political Participation" (which in reality refers to party activities, see App. 3). In this paragraph we pause to consider the variables that make up that measure.

3.1 *Party Affiliation in General*

Affiliation is defined in terms of either formal membership (which is the typical form of affiliation in Italy, Poland and Romania) or personal involvement. Fig. 1 gives a picture of the situation.

As the histogram shows, aside from decision-makers, the level of party affiliation is in general moderate or low, being at its lowest in Canada and at its highest in Romania. In all countries, within each category, a higher percentage of men is affiliated. This is true everywhere, except for decision-makers (save in Poland) and for Canadian blue-collar workers. Gender differences, however, are significant for all categories (except teachers) only in Poland, while this is so in Romania only for white-collar workers and teachers and in Canada only for teachers. No significant difference appears in Italy. Once more, we have a result that runs against the stereotype.

The difference for decision-makers is not significant anywhere. Women who hold office are affiliated to a party to the same degree as men.

Housewives in general rank low (Baxter and Lansing, 1983: 29, 183-184). However, the difference between them and the other female categories is seldom statistically significant in Canada, Italy and Poland, while it is always so in Romania.

Fig. 1 Party Affiliation

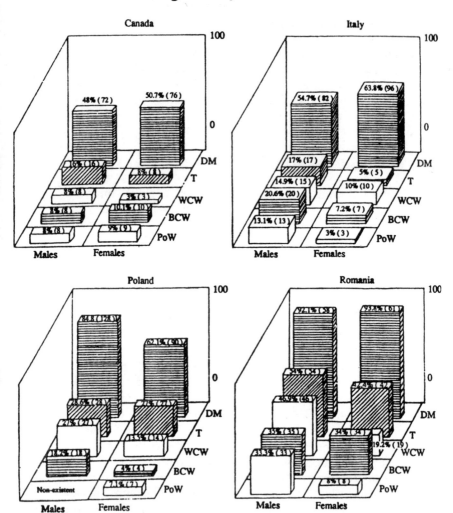

Female teachers in Poland are a somewhat special case. Their affiliation is high, close to that of men. The reason is that in Poland the teaching profession is a good channel of access to a political career (Siemienska, 1983a).

3.2 *Party Seniority*

All in all, there are almost no significant differences in party seniority between men and women belonging to the same categories, with the exception of Italy where men have a significantly higher party seniority than women (6).

3.3 *Degrees of Involvement*

We turn now to more difficult acts of participation. Simply becoming involved in a party, even though more exacting than voting, is a relatively easy act, largely influenced by the environment. Taking the floor at meetings and giving free time to the party, on the other hand, imply a much greater degree of initiative.

These two forms of participation, with the exception of Romania where they are expected from members, present rather low rates, especially in Canada.

Almost no significant gender differences emerge within the categories, save in Poland with respect to taking the floor. This is an activity which women seem to be more reluctant to carry out than men.

Among the categories, workers (including those in the socialist countries) and housewives rank below the other categories, while decision-makers occupy the opposite end of the spectrum.

We used, in addition to these objective indicators of participation, a measure of self-evaluation. The picture coincides: in general, our respondents feel that their involvement is rather low. In Canada, and especially in Italy, women hold this opinion significantly more than men do. Again, workers and housewives rank below the other categories, while decision-makers rank above.

Romania stands out as the country where the self-evaluation is the highest (7). The suspicion that our Romanian respondents reckon their involvement more positively than it is in reality appears to be supported by the correlations with the global measure of participation (App. 3), which are less strong than elsewhere.

In fact, in all countries and for both men and women there are significant correlations between these two variables. What is particularly striking is the symmetric ranking in strength of the correlations for both sexes by country, which is much stronger in Italy, followed by Canada, than in Poland and especially Romania. In other words, in the latter two countries much more than in the other two, there are people who state that they are active but in reality are hardly so.

We must, therefore, conclude that in Poland and especially Romania such self-evaluation is the result of a stereotype: if one is a party member, one cannot but be high in participation. This is also the consequence of propaganda which presents participation in party activities as compulsory. Furthermore, in countries where a party is in power without any danger of losing it, people may derive a feeling of involvement by merely being in it and, all the more so, the more they hold offices or carry on activities which depend on the party.

It is interesting to remark that the correlations are stronger for women than for men: contrary to popular prejudice, it appears that women are more consistent than men. It is possible that men tend to exaggerate their self-evaluation of political activity because the social pressure to participate and to claim to have done so is stronger for them.

3.4 *Party Offices*

3.4.1 *Past Offices*

Power tends to perpetuate itself. This is a matter not only of the network of relationships that people build around the offices that they hold but also of the experience that office-holders accumulate. From the point of view of our research, therefore, an exploration of gender differences in the past is crucial for an understanding of actual differences in party offices (Table 3).

All in all, in Italy and especially Canada very few party members held offices previously, while in Poland and particularly Romania many more did. In general, men appear favoured, although significant gender differences by category are few, the main exception being Italian and Romanian decision-makers. Another exception is found in Poland among teachers, but surprisingly it is in favour of women (t = 1.96, df = 55, p = .055).

We expected to find decision-makers ranking significantly above all other categories but this is only partially true. It is true

Table 3 Number of Times and Level of Actual and Past Party Offices Held by Party Members in the Four Countries†

	Canada				Italy				Poland				Romania			
	Males		Females		Males		Females		Males		Females		Males		Females	
	A	P	A	P	A	P	A	P	A	P	A	P	A	P	A	P
Blue-collar workers																
Once at the district level					2				9	1			8	4	7	4
Once at the city level										1					2	2
Twice or more at the district level							1		3				1		3	2
Twice or more at the city level	1															
White-collar workers																
Once at the district level	1	1			1	2			9	3	2	2	17	7	4	5
Twice or more at the district level					2	1			3	8	1	1	5	12	2	4
Twice or more at the city level													1			
Twice or more at the intermediate level (province, county, state)													1			

†Levels with no respondents have been eliminated.
A = actual
P = past

Table 3 Number of Times and Level of Actual and Past Party Offices Held by Party Members in the Four Countries†

	Canada				Italy				Poland				Romania			
	Males		Females		Males		Females		Males		Females		Males		Females	
	A	P	A	P	A	P	A	P	A	P	A	P	A	P	A	P
Teachers																
Once at the district level					3	4			3	9	10	12	12	6	12	9
Once at the city level			1		2	1	2		2						1	
Once at the intermediate level (province, county, state)	1				1				1							
Once at the national level					1											
Twice or more at the district level	1		1				3		1	5	2	9	1	8		5
Twice or more at the city level							1									
Twice or more at the intermediate level (province, county, state)																1
Twice or more at the national level					1											
People out of work																
Once at the district level	1	2	2	1	1							1			8	1
Once at the city level						1									1	
Twice or more at the district level	1										3					
Twice or more at the national level					1										1	1

Table 3 Number of Times and Level of Actual and Past Party Offices Held by Party Members in the Four Countries†

Decision-makers

	Canada				Italy				Poland				Romania			
	Males		Females		Males		Females		Males		Females		Males		Females	
	A	P	A	P	A	P	A	P	A	P	A	P	A	P	A	P
Once at the district level	2	8	1	3	5	11	7	5	36	40	27	37	19	8	26	13
Once at the city level		3	3	2	11	10	21	10	2	7	3	9		1		2
Once at the intermediate level (province, county, state)	11	4	9	7	16	13	18	13	6	8			1	3		2
Once at the national level	12	3	9	3	20	14	24	13	14	12	3	2	3	27	2	19
Twice or more at the district level	1	7		1		4		6	5	47	2	22				1
Twice or more at the city level		1	2	5	6	7	3	11		4						
Twice or more at the intermediate level (province, county, state)	4	19		20	3	16	3	11	2	7	1	2				
Twice or more at the national level	2	8	2	8	2	14	5	9	3	5		2	2			1

for both sexes only in Canada and in Italy, while in Poland and Romania it is true only for males. In other words, in the latter two countries a more balanced distribution prevails for women in the party: the percentage of female decision-makers who held office in the past is not significantly higher than the percentages in the other female categories. This is because in all Polish and Romanian categories there are more women who held some offices in the past.

But what happens when we take into consideration the importance of the offices? Our quantification of the importance is based on the territorial level of the office (district; city; province, region or state in a federal system; and nation) and the number of times it was held (once or twice or more; see App. 2).

In all countries, offices held by party members in the past concentrate at the lowest level (district), with the exception (less strong in Romania, more pronounced in Italy) of decision-makers who also held offices at the other levels. That decision-makers held offices of more importance does not come as a surprise, since it is built into the sample. What is surprising is the uniformity we find everywhere as to the other categories. In all countries, the picture looks astoundingly similar.

From the point of view of gender, no differences emerge, except among Italian and Polish decision-makers (males held offices of greater importance than females). This is another unexpected finding, which reveals that, from the gender point of view, a deep change has taken place.

3.4.2 *Present Offices*

There is a sharp distinction in our sample between Italy and Canada, on one side, and Poland and Romania, on the other. In the latter countries, there are many more party members other than decision-makers who hold an office in the party, while, by and large, in Italy and Canada only decision-makers hold such offices (the only exception being male teachers in Italy).

The picture looks quite different in the other two countries. First of all, workers in office (in Romania of both sexes, in Poland male) are, if not numerous, a sizeable minority. In Romania, for instance, workers in percentage terms do not differ from decision-makers, although in absolute terms they are far less numerous. In Canada and Italy, workers do not hold offices at all. Also, white-collar workers and teachers of both sexes in Romania and females of the same categories in Poland fare pretty well. The situation of these categories in the other two countries, with the exception of Italian male teachers, looks quite miserable.

Turning our attention to the specific topic of this research, the result presented in the previous paragraphs holds also for present offices: in no country, with only a few exceptions in Poland, do we find statistically relevant gender differences.

As regards the importance of the offices, with the exception of decision-makers, our respondents generally hold offices at the lowest level. Also, in this case, no significant gender differences emerge within the categories, with the exception of Poland where female teachers and male decision-makers rank above their counterparts (8).

* * *

As previously stated, the items examined above go to make up a global measure called "Political Participation". In the following paragraphs, we will refer to this index, described in Appendix 3.

3.4.3 *Interconnections between Past and Present Offices*

Power clings to those who have it, while it wriggles out of the hands of those who do not. Consequently, we expect to find a strong correlation between holding an office now and having held an office in the past and the importance of the respective offices. The stereotype would require a stronger correlation for men than for women, because it maintains that the former will try more than women not to let power slip from their hands.

As far as the first hypothesis is concerned, the cross tables (not shown here) reveal for both sexes a highly significant association between the two variables in all countries. The lowest coefficients concern Polish and Romanian women (respectively, phi = .17, p = .05 and phi = .21, p = .02).

As for the second hypothesis, the picture is shown in Table 4.

This is a startling result. Everywhere, except in Romania, the coefficients for women are stronger than for men. In Canada and Italy the difference for decision-makers is even significant. The more important the offices held by party members in the past, the better they manage to keep them, and in achieving this goal women are superior to men.

Table 4   Correlations between the Importance of the Present and of the Past
              Party Office

| Canada | | Italy | | Poland | | Romania | |
M	F	M	F	M	F	M	F
			For all office-holders				
.28**	.43*	.42*	.56*	.69*	.70*	.69*	.04 ns
			For decision-makers only				
.13 ns	.37**	.31**	.55*	.66*	.70*	.72*	-.10 ns

*p $\leq$ .01; **   .05 > p > .01; ns not significant

Comparing the findings used to verify the two hypotheses,
we see that, as far as the actual holding of an office is concerned,
the association between present and past is stronger for Canadian
and Italian women than for Polish and Romanian women, while,
with respect to the importance of offices, the turnover is highest in
Romania, followed by Canada, Italy and Poland. In other words,
once a woman is in office, it is easier for her to stay there in Canada
and Italy. However, the chances of holding offices of the same importance are highest in Poland, followed by Canada and Italy; they
are lowest in Romania. From this point of view, Romania looks
more democratic than the other countries but this may only be a
consequence of the fact that the offices that are held by women in
Romania are of minor importance. Indeed the picture is quite different for men (9).

3.4.4 *Interconnections between Participation and Office-Holding in the Party*

The hypothesis that the higher the level of participation in
party life, the higher the importance of the offices held proves true
in all countries, especially in Poland and Romania (10). But the
correlations are stronger for men than for women, with the exception of Poland. In other words, if a man participates actively, he
has more chances than a woman to move up the party hierarchy.
It means also that men with important offices are more active in
party life than women.

In all countries, however, and for men and women equally, the correlations are very strong. Thus, if both men and women must make a large investment of energy in order to count in the party, it becomes relevant to consider the difference between them in terms of offices held as an outcome of participation. Our study of this matter produced very interesting results.

The regression analysis (not presented here) initially shows that it is only at a certain point of political participation that the lowest levels of party hierarchy are reached. From that point on the increment is rather sensitive, and, especially in Canada and Italy but also in Romania, the gradients are stronger for women than for men. In terms of party offices, women in these countries tend to benefit more than men from political participation. In Poland and Romania, obviously, women's political careers do not depend as much as in the other two countries on their political participation.

A closer look at the data reveals that in all countries offices are held almost exclusively by people in the higher band of participation. Here, all have an office. In this respect, the inter-sex differences are impressive (Table 5).

Table 5 Top Party Offices Held by People with High Participation†

	Canada	Italy	Poland	Romania
M	10 (37)	7 (14)	19 (22.1)	12 (18.8)
F	13 (50)	16 (30.3)	8 (15.4)	10 (19.2)

†The percentage in brackets refers to the total. For instance, in Canada 37% of all male members with high participation hold top offices.

In Canada and Italy politically active women hold, in both absolute and relative terms, more important offices than men in the same band of participation. The same is not true in Poland but in Romania it is true in relative terms.

As far as governmental offices are concerned office-holders, both male and female, are politically active everywhere. This is again more true for women than for men except in Poland. However, but for Italy, where women with a high level of political participation hold important governmental offices, there is no significant correlation between these two variables.

3.5 *Socio-Demographic Variables and Party Involvement*

3.5.1 *Family*

It is often maintained that women who are married or have children are driven away from political life. This is not true. In the overwhelming majority of cases there is no interconnection between the phenomena (Rogers, 1978: 136-7; Sapiro, 1984; see also ch. 3, par. 9 above) (11). It is even possible to find cases where the opposite situation prevails. In Canada, for instance, there is a suggestive association (phi = .15, p = .07) for female white-collar workers between being married and being in a party; a strong association for female teachers between having children and party membership (phi = .30, p = .01) as well as between having children and office-holding (phi = .45, p = .000); and a strong association for female decision-makers between having children (phi = .22, p = .01) and being married (phi = .19, p = .01), on one hand, and party membership, on the other. But Canada is the only country where this happens to an impressive extent. No such strong associations are found, for instance, in Poland. Such differences between countries can be explained by differences in levels of modernization, one important feature of which is the thriving of feminism in the more advanced societies.

There are, of course, also cases where married women do not participate, but their significance is rare (altogether five correlations).

For men, indifference, as expected, is the rule. However, especially in Poland and Romania, a positive association may be found more frequently for them than for women.

Since children are usually considered one of the main obstacles to women's participation, let us consider their impact on some key aspects of being active in public life, such as the importance of the offices held in the party, the unions, and governmental organizations, and the number of hours devoted to the party.

We correlated four variables concerning children --- child-burden (App. 10), number of children, age of smallest child, presence of children --- with the importance of the offices held in the above-mentioned organizations. The hypothesis that children are an obstacle to a woman's public career is not validated, although in some countries a tendency in that direction is more accentuated than in others. This is the case especially in Italy and, as far as the age of the smallest child is concerned, in Poland and Romania. In other words, children are a slight problem in Italy for a woman who wants to pursue a public career; Polish and Romanian mothers with small children are disadvantaged in comparison to mothers in the other two countries.

It might seem reasonable to conjecture that, especially for women, age affects these results: young women, even if they have children, can be more active than older women. Controlling age, however, does not basically change the picture. From our analysis of the impact of child care on the number of hours devoted to the party, we find further evidence that children are not a major obstacle to women's political participation. First, not even the sign is negative in all countries: in Poland the more women take care of their children, the more they give time to the party; second, the only correlations that are statistically relevant are in Italy, at a suggestive level (-.21). The amazing result for Poland probably stems from the pressure exerted in this country on highly committed party members to comply with their family obligations lest they jeopardize the image of the party.

In this case also, age does not substantially alter the results.

3.5.2 *Education*

Another current belief is that women need more schooling than men in order to move up the party hierarchy. In reality, for both sexes, schooling is a poor predictor. All office-holders are persons who have completed high school at least and often also university. A few more years of schooling do not make much difference and can even be detrimental to a career in the party.

To check in more detail how much education discriminates between men and women, we divided our respondents into three bands of education --- low, middle, and high (App. 18) --- and looked at the gender differences for the two phenomena under consideration: importance of party offices and political participation.

As far as the former is concerned, we found only one significant difference, namely in Poland, where men in the middle band of education hold offices of more importance than women ($t = 2.89$, $df = 247.91$, $p = .004$). As for the latter, in Canada and Italy no significant gender differences were found in any band of education. In Poland, however, men in the middle and high bands transform their educational assets into participation in party activities better than women do, while in Romania the same happens in the low and middle bands (in Poland: middle band t = 3.52, high band t = 1.81; in Romania : low band t = 2, middle band t = 2.04).

Moving up the educational ladder, nowhere do we find an increase in difference between men and women. In other words, men and women transform education into occupancy of offices and political participation at about the same rate. This finding runs against the hypothesis that the rate should be about the same at the lowest level, while a gender gap should appear on moving to the higher levels.

We obtained the same results from a similar analysis of governmental offices.

3.5.3 *Age*

In all systems, middle and high positions are held by rather elderly people. But is age more important for women than for men? Men, it is usually thought, start to hold offices when they are younger than women.

Our data (not shown here) reveal, first, that the gradients are almost flat for both sexes and, in some rare cases, are even negative. Second, the hypothesis that women start political careers at a later age is only modestly true in Italy, Poland and Romania, while the opposite tends to be true in Canada.

3.5.4 *Religious Affiliation*

The traditional image of religions tends to portray them as perpetuating the customary dichotomy: "women = private, man = public". Is this still true today?

Gender differences are not in general very strong, except in Poland, where male Catholics are very much more active than female Catholics, and in Romania, where, again for Catholics, the opposite is true. Religious affiliation in itself does not explain much. (For further discussion of this topic, see par. 9.2.2 below.)

3.6 Milieu and Participation

It might be argued that the importance of offices held depends more for women than men on the level of political commitment of the family of origin during childhood and adolescence. Men, it is believed, are motivated by the male culture surrounding them to develop an interest in politics, to acquire knowledge and skills, and to enter networks that are indispensable to achieve political success; this is irrespective of the political commitment of their family of origin. Women, on the contrary, are allegedly hindered by that very culture. Therefore, a favourable milieu during childhood and adolescence may work for women as a spur towards that achievement which men attain "naturally".

A short description of the situation in the four countries from this point of view is timely here. The measure used is described in Appendix 4.

With the exception of Canada and of decision-makers in all four countries, our respondents, both men and women, come from families where the political involvement was rather modest. This is especially true for Italy. Interestingly enough, Canadian women, with the exception of teachers, come from families in which the political involvement was not only rather marked but also significantly higher than for men. This is almost the only instance of a generalized significant gender difference. However, of great interest is the fact that decision-makers in all the countries come from families with a strong political commitment (Kirkpatrick, 1974). Apart from male decision-makers in Romania, both male and female decision-makers everywhere rank significantly above the other categories of the respective sex.

Does the importance of party office also depend on the political commitment of the family of origin? Is this more true for women than for men? Contrary to what we might have surmised at this point, we found that this is not the case in any country. For both sexes, everywhere the gradients are close to zero. The logic of power in society at large is different from the logic of power in the party. Public dignitaries come from families where political commitment was high, but for party office-holders it does not make much difference whether the family of origin was politically committed or not.

One might think that the mother's political involvement during a respondent's childhood or adolescence should make a difference, at least as far as women are concerned, but this is not borne out by our data. As a matter of fact, where the gradient for women is rather strong, as in Canada, it has a negative sign. In Italy and Poland the sign, while positive, is only modestly so.

The involvement of the father is practically irrelevant, except for Canadian males. The same is true for the commitment of other people around the respondent. The picture is no different if we consider the political involvement of the present environment (spouse and friends).

Although the political involvement of the milieux of party members both during their childhood and adolescence and at present, does little to explain the importance of the offices that are held, we might still reasonably surmise that they are correlated at least with the very holding of a party office and, above all, with party membership. In particular, we would feel inclined to think that the fact of having had a politically active mother should be correlated, especially for women, at least with party membership. But, again, the results do not fit our expectations, at least not completely. With the partial exception of party membership, the hypothesis that women's participation might be influenced by their mothers' or their husbands' participation is not upheld.

4 Political System, Class, Gender and Participation

4.1 *A Model*

Gender parity is one aspect of a broader movement towards equality in all spheres of life. Therefore, where there is more equality in general there should also be more gender equality. But to speak of equality implies speaking of class and its discriminatory effects.

We do not wish to enter here upon a discussion as to whether or not socialism has achieved the goal of creating an egalitarian society. It is a fact, however, that in those societies which proclaim themselves socialist this goal is officially pursued. It seems reasonable to think that the following steps should make a difference: the abolition of private ownership of the means of production; the adoption of measures to prevent the private accumulation of wealth on a macroscopic scale; a policy of full employment; parity of access to education for both sexes; the insistence through all state agencies of socialization around the concept of the "New Man", that is, a person characterized by solidaristic habits of mind (Menschik, 1971; Sacks, 1974; Delmar, 1976). While it is true that what we know about socialist countries is not at all encouraging (Heitlinger, 1979; Jancar, 1974; Karchev and Yasmaya, 1982; Molyneux, 1984; Sas, 1981; Scott, 1979; Siemienska, 1985a; Sokolowska, 1981; Szalai et al., 1972; Wolchik, 1981 : 470), it might well be that in certain respects and for certain categories the difference between men and women has decreased under socialism.

While policies aimed at promoting equality are also pursued in the liberal-democratic societies, they are not necessarily interlinked in deliberate fashion within an overall plan which is directed to that goal. In other words, to use the traditional Marxist terminology, equality in the liberal-democratic societies is purely "formal".

Thus someone in line with the orthodox tradition might expect that socialism, by eliminating classes (at least in the "bourgeois" sense), entails the decrease of class differences and consequently an increase of egalitarianism in all spheres of life, including public participation, between men and women. Class differences are defined, as the above authors do, in Weberian terms as the whole of socio-economic opportunities available to a person (Weber, 1921, ch.IV, par.1) .

For women, however, class is not enough: the way in which they are situated structurally in relation to men is another important variable that must be taken into account. The conventional indication of class, referring to the husband's and/or the woman's occupation, catches only a part of the truth. Very often, for instance, husbands do not share their income equitably with their wives, while, if wives earn, they soon find out that their money is not regarded as their own to the same extent that it is for men. Nor does the level of women's education translate into an equivalent position in the occupational hierarchy. Women are kept in a subordinate position, and the common opinion (disproved by our findings, though) is that women, as oppressed people, are not interested in participating in public life, irrespective of class. Yet, since participation in public life presupposes the availability of certain opportunities, it is reasonable to expect that whatever participation there is will be found among upper- and middle-class women, but we cannot posit for them a correlation of the same strength as we do for men. The stereotype maintains that, for women, participation is always an exception, even when the socio-economic resources are available to them.

Thus, while it is correct in general to assume that the more socio-economic resources are available, the more individuals become active, we cannot suppose that no difference exists between women and men, because women's political motivation and skills are not the same as those of men, and women meet more obstacles than men do.

It sounds logical also to assume, with Verba et al. (1978), that there are acts, e.g. membership in a party, in which socio-economic resources should play a minimal role because it is the system that largely succeeds in bringing people to action, thanks to the pressure exercised through custom and the mass-media and to the advantages accruing from being a party member, etc. Individual resources in this case should not be so important. On the other hand, if we examine acts such as giving free time to the party or taking the floor at meetings, we should find that the involvement demanded at the individual level is greater. Consequently, participating in these acts should depend on socio-economic resources to a larger extent than for party affiliation. When we turn, finally, to the most exacting act, participation in decision-making, this is even more true for office-holders.

If it makes a difference whether people live in a system that is strongly committed to promoting social equality or in a system that is mildly committed to it, then the impact of socio-economic resources on the various acts should be as shown in Table 6.

Table 6 Impact of Socio-Economic Resources on Four Acts†

| | Strong pressure | | Mild pressure | |
	Males	Females	Males	Females
(a)	nil	very low	nil?	very low
(b)	very low	low (very low)	low	medium (low)
(c)	low	medium (low)	medium	high (medium)
(d)	medium	high (medium)	high	very high (high)

†Bracketed grading: hypothetical situation, see text.
(a) Party membership
(b) Taking the floor
(c) Voluntary work for the party
(d) Office-holding

The main grading indicates the strength of the impact of class for men and women in the four acts under consideration, according to the degree of pressure that the system exerts on *social* equality.

The grading in brackets indicates the hypothetical impact of a system that succeeds in exerting a real pressure on *gender* equality: if women were as motivated to participate as men, had the same skills, and met the same obstacles, there would be no differences between the sexes in terms of the socio-economic resources required to perform the various acts. Since presumably even a strong egalitarian system has not yet instilled in men and women an equal motivation to participate, nor made available to them an equal acquisition of the necessary skills, nor achieved a total elimination of the obstacles on the way to women's participation, it seems reasonable to expect that women need more socio-economic resources than men to accomplish the same acts, even in a strong egalitarian system. But there should be a difference between a mild (liberal-democratic) and a strong (socialist) system. For the purposes of simplification, we use a dichotomy, although we have serious doubts about its correspondence to reality. What we know about Poland and Romania, as far as these phenomena are concerned, is based mainly on aggregate data. It is quite possible that at the micro-level, that is, the level of our survey, things appear in a different way from the specific viewpoint of the topic under consideration, i.e. gender equality.

Other dimensions of specific interest to us, always in relation to class, are gender differences in non-governmental and especially governmental office-holding. In this respect we adopted the model used by Verba et al. (1978: ch. 5) (12), which can be summarized as follows. A "dominant system" is a system where party affiliation (at least *de facto*) is both a necessary and a sufficient condition to hold governmental and/or non-governmental offices, where socio-economic resources play no role, and where, consequently, only the affiliated are active and share the same level of participation in terms of the importance of offices held. An "additive system" is one where the affiliated hold more important offices than the unaffiliated, but the effects of class are felt by both groups; in other words, where the institutional and individual forces operate in an additive way. Obviously, the impact of institutions has an equalizing effect in the dominant, but not the additive, system. A "restrictive system" is characterized by the fact that party affiliation is a necessary, but not a sufficient, condition for holding office: i.e. a system where the unaffiliated are locked out no matter what their individual resources, but where the affiliated still convert socio-economic resources into offices. For the affiliated, this system differs from the additive system only as far as the impact of class on incumbency is concerned: in the restrictive system it is stronger than in the other. A "weak" system is, as the name implies, a system where affiliation does not have any impact on the importance of the offices, which depends on the resources available to individuals.

Although not completely, Poland and Romania should be close to the "dominant" system; Canada to the "weak" system for men, to the "additive" system for women; and Italy to the "restrictive" system for both sexes, but with a huge difference between the two. In all countries we expect to find men privileged, but the impact of socio-economic conditions on sex differences should perhaps follow a different pattern in Canada and Italy, on one hand, and in Poland and Romania, on the other.

The interplay between country, membership in a party, importance of governmental offices, socio-economic level and sex can be graphically represented in the "ideal-type" scheme shown in Fig. 2.

The impact of the socio-economic level should be stronger in Canada and Italy than in socialist Poland and Romania. Party membership is relevant mainly in Italy, Poland and Romania because in these countries public life is dominated by parties, while this is much less so in Canada.

In all countries, parties make a difference for women more than for men. In other words, the distance between real and expected office-holding (expected for the population in general) should increase more for female than for male party members, because women who are in a party are more eager and ready than men to climb up the public structure. In Poland and Romania, though, the institutional constraint should favour women and men of low social extraction. In Canada, as a consequence of the longer democratic tradition, the expected rate of female office-holding should react more than elsewhere to the socio-economic level.

Of course this is an abstract representation of reality. Other variables need to be introduced. For instance, as Verba et al. point out (1978: 88-91), the results change, depending upon where the majority of women and men are located along the dimension of socio-economic level. Let us illustrate, with their words, just one case. If, in a country close to the dominant model, the majority of affiliated people happens to be of a higher socio-economic level than the unaffiliated, then the asymmetry between the affiliated and the unaffiliated will increase:

Fig. 2 Hypothetical Model concerning the Impact of Party Affiliation on the Relationship between the Importance of Offices Held and Social Class, by Sex

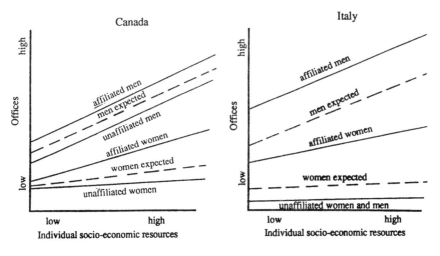

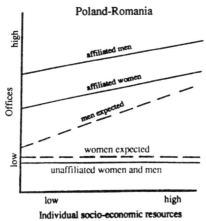

Since socio-economic level plays a role in determining who becomes affiliated, a larger number of affluent and well-educated citizens take advantage of the participatory boost given by institutions and a larger number of less affluent and less well-educated citizens are kept out of political activity by their lack of party affiliation. The result is a participatory system stratified by socio-economic level as should be a participatory system in which only individual forces were working. But in this case the stratification takes place through the process of recruitment to institutions. (1978: 91)

The interplay of these factors is further complicated by the fact that in Canada and Italy parties differ widely both in ideology and social composition. Some parties may be more interested than others in the issue of gender equality. This interest may be manifested in one party in a global way, in another mainly with respect to work conditions, in still another in the form of concern for family law. Some parties may have a large percentage of women in them, others very few; some may over-represent low-status groups, others upper/middle-status groups. But, as we already stated, an analysis of individual parties is beyond the scope of this research.

4.2 *Empirical Validation of the Model*

4.2.1 *Class and Party Activities*

First, our hypothesis about party membership as an "easy" act does not fully hold (see Table 7 and Fig. 3). In all countries, party members have a pretty high socio-economic background and the chances of being in a party increase remarkably with it. Except in Canada, this is slightly more true for women than for men. In this respect, there is a vague correspondence with our hypothesis. We will comment further on this point below.

Second, our hypothesis about the growing impact of socio-economic background in concomitance with the growing difficulty of the acts performed is also disproved (Table 8). Nowhere do we find this kind of progression.

Third, in general the assumption that women need more socio-economic opportunities than men to perform the same acts is not proved. This is true especially for highly participative women (Table 8, part 2: no chi-square is significant or even suggestive). It seems that we are in the presence of a process of democratization

Table 7 Socio-Economic Background and Party Membership
(correlations and regressions for the whole sample, frequency distributions in brackets (%) for party members)

	Canada		Italy		Poland		Romania	
	M	F	M	F	M	F	M	F
r	.20	.14	.16	.24	.19	.24	.21	.28
beta	.221	.137	.106	.163	.170	.242	.207	.269
Social class:								
Low	19 (17)	27 (25.5)	32 (21.8)	19 (15.8)	12 (6)	11 (7.7)	79 (35)	56 (34.1)
Middle	42 (37.5)	33 (31.1)	38 (25.9)	28 (23.3)	120 (59.7)	81 (57)	84 (37.2)	52 (31.7)
High	51 (45.5)	46 (43.4)	77 (52.4)	73 (60.8)	69 (34.3)	50 (35.2)	63 (27.9)	56 (34.1)
χ^2	2.567		2.228		.511		2.055	

All χ^2 are non-significant. All r are highly significant.

Fig. 3 Regression of Party Affiliation[†] on Social Class

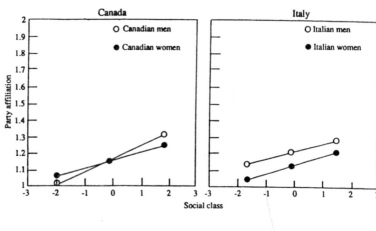

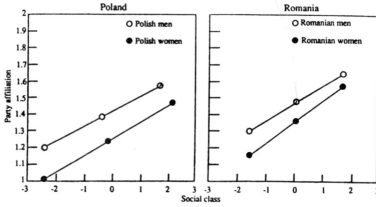

†1 = No ; 2 = Yes

that has made the individual resources that are necessary for women to take part in party activities equal to those that are necessary for men.

The above comment concerns the overall picture. Going into a detailed analysis act by act (see paragraphs below) shows that in some cases differences exist.

Table 8 Socio-Economic Background and Acts of Political Participation (members only)

Part 1: correlations and regressions

Act of Participation	Canada		Italy		Poland		Romania	
	M	F	M	F	M	F	M	F
				r				
Taking the floor	.18**	.13***	.54*	.30*	.03	.09	.12**	.22*
Voluntary work	.10	-.07	.19*	.08	.07	.17***	.13**	.12***
Number of hours	.20*	-.02	.32*	-.03	.08	.02	-.01	.04
Office-holding	.01	.20**	.45*	.17**	-.07	.04	0.00	0.00
Importance of offices	.03	.17**	.33*	.21*	-.02	.03	-.02	0.00
				beta				
Taking the floor	.244	.131	.548	.344	.054	.146	.121	.229
Voluntary work	.102	-.067	.193	.089	.070	.174	.136	.096
Number of hours	.201	-.020	.323	-.015	.076	.023	.055	0.00
Office-holding	.007	.201	.421	.161	-.066	.040	-.013	-.013
Importance of offices	.077	.139	.414	.138	-.007	.035	-.030	.008

*p $\leq$ .01; ** .05 > p > .01; *** .10 > p > .05

Table 8 Socio-Economic Background and Acts of Political Participation (members only)

Part 2: distribution by social class of politically highly committed respondents (number with % in brackets)

Social class	Canada M	Canada F	Italy M	Italy Ḟ	Poland M	Poland F	Romania M	Romania F
Often taking the floor								
Low	11 (19)	11 (19.6)	8 (9)	11 (12.5)	2 (2.6)	3 (8.6)	42 (29.8)	31 (31.3)
Middle	15 (25.9)	18 (32.1)	20 (22.5)	19 (21.6)	50 (65.8)	21 (60)	58 (41.1)	30 (30.3)
High	32 (55.2)	27 (48.2)	61 (68.5)	58 (65.9)	24 (31.6)	11 (31.4)	41 (29.1)	38 (38.4)
χ^2	.662		.569		2.003		3.436	
Voluntary party work								
Low	13 (15.5)	22 (25.9)	17 (17.9)	10 (12.5)	7 (4.5)	5 (5.1)	30 (25.2)	25 (28.7)
Middle	32 (38.1)	28 (32.9)	25 (26.3)	21 (26.3)	96 (61.1)	58 (58.6)	57 (47.9)	30 (34.5)
High	39 (46.4)	35 (41.2)	53 (55.8)	49 (61.3)	54 (34.4)	36 (36.4)	32 (26.9)	32 (36.8)
χ^2	2.791		1.041		.178		3.959	
More than 30 hours per month of voluntary party work								
Low	1 (5.3)	1 (5)	4 (10.8)	2 (12.5)	0	1 (16.7)	3 (17.6)	3 (23)
Middle	7 (36.8)	13 (65)	11 (29.7)	6 (37.5)	14 (58.3)	3 (50)	11 (64.7)	6 (42.2)
High	11 (57.9)	6 (3)	22 (59.5)	8 (50)	10 (41.7)	2 (33.3)	4 (23.5)	4 (30.8)
χ^2	3.247		.415				.682	
Holding party offices								
Low	5 (17.2)	3 (10.7)	2 (3.2)	8 (11.1)	7 (8)	2 (3.6)	21 (28.8)	19 (30.6)
Middle	11 (37.9)	10 (35.7)	15 (24.2)	15 (20.8)	53 (60.2)	37 (70.9)	37 (50.7)	22 (35.5)
High	13 (44.8)	15 (53.6)	45 (72.6)	49 (68.1)	28 (31.8)	14 (25.5)	15 (20.5)	21 (33.9)
χ^2	.673		3.041		2.07		4.044	
Highly important offices								
Low	1 (11)	0	2 (22.2)	0	0	0	0	0
Middle	4 (44)	7 (50)	0	5 (25)	4 (80)	1 (50)	0	0
High	4 (44)	7 (50)	7 (77.8)	15 (75)	1 (20)	1 (50)	0	1

Let us examine separately each of the dependent response variables studied.

Party Membership

The gradient is positive everywhere, being slightly stronger in Poland and especially Romania (Fig. 3).

It is interesting to observe the height of the phenomenon in these countries, where low-status people have more chances to be in the party than even high-status people in Canada and Italy. This is in line with the ideology of the ruling parties and corresponds to what we know from the aggregate data in Poland and Romania. If we divide social class into three bands and examine the frequency distributions of party members, we see (Table 7) that in Canada and Italy there is a rather strong association between party affiliation and high social class. In Poland no such association exists and in Romania there is a negative association for male party members and no association for female party members. This means that in Poland and Romania class discriminates more than in Canada and Italy when we consider the totality of the sample, but these former countries present more egalitarian conditions than Canada and Italy when we consider those who adhere to the party.

As far as gender differences are concerned, the gradients in each country are about the same but the intercepts, except in Canada, are higher for males. This means that lower-class women do not join a party as much as men do and that men and women with the same socio-economic resources do not belong to the same extent to the party throughout the spectrum of socio-economic opportunities.

Taking the Floor

As shown in Fig. 4, everywhere there is a positive slope. It is more marked for both men and women in Canada and Italy, especially the latter; in Poland and Romania the gradient is steeper for women. In all four cases, upper-class women take the floor as much as men, but in Canada and Italy lower- and middle-class women take the floor more than men. The frequency distributions of party members who often take the floor (Table 8, part 2) show that in Canada and Italy the association with high class is much stronger than in the whole sample, and that it is rather strong also

Fig. 4 Regression of Taking the Floor on Social Class

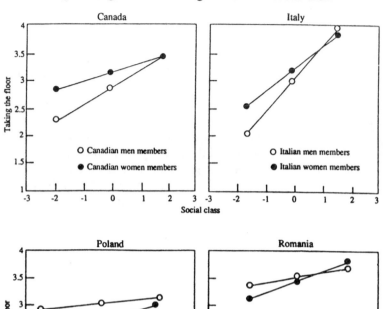

in Poland. Once more, no significant gender differences emerge anywhere.

Amount of Free Time Given to the Party

Fig. 5 shows that there is a strong resemblance between Canada and Italy, on one hand, and Poland and Romania, on the other. The divergence between the two groups of countries is marked. In Canada and Italy the slope for women is negative: upper-class women give less time to the party than lower-class women. In all four cases class works the other way for men: but in Canada and especially in Italy its impact is incomparably stronger.

The frequency distribution by class of party members who give more than 30 hours of their time to the party shows that the impact of class is not relevant in Canada and Italy, especially for men, while it is relevant in Poland and Romania. Again, no significant gender differences appear.

Importance of Offices

The picture is somewhat diverse in the four countries (Fig. 6). The gradient is almost flat in Poland and Romania and the intercepts much lower than in the other countries, but women's intercepts are higher than men's in Romania and vice versa in Poland. Social class discriminates considerably in Canada and Italy, but in the former more for women, in the latter more for men. Since the intercepts are the same for men and women in Canada, while they are higher for women in Italy, the result is that in Canada upper-class women hold more important offices than upper-class men, whereas in Italy both groups hold offices of the same importance. Poland and Romania present a more egalitarian picture from the gender point of view also.

4.2.2 *Class and Governmental Offices*

Effects on the System

Fig. 7 shows that, in general, the results fit our model pretty well (13). The "restrictive" type that we find in the socialist countries is a (realistic) variant of the "dominant" type. Table 9 shows it clearly.

Belonging to a party is an element which "adds" to the strength of socio-economic resources for our Canadian respondents. The affiliated hold more important governmental offices than the unaffiliated at each class level, but the effects of the socio-economic level are felt at the same time by the affiliated and

Fig. 5 Regression of Free Time Given to Party on Social Class

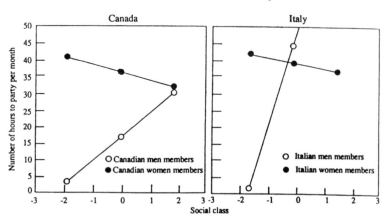

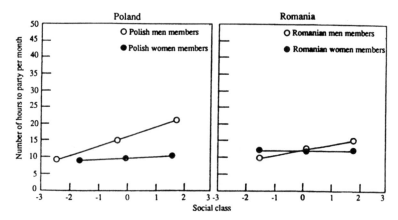

the unaffiliated. The institutional pressure is strong but not enough to eliminate the ability of people to convert their individual resources into a public career.

In the other countries, the restrictive system prevails for all, with the exception of Polish women for whom we had to invent a new type, which we called "withholding". In this model, as for the

Fig. 6   Regression of Importance of Party Office on Social Class

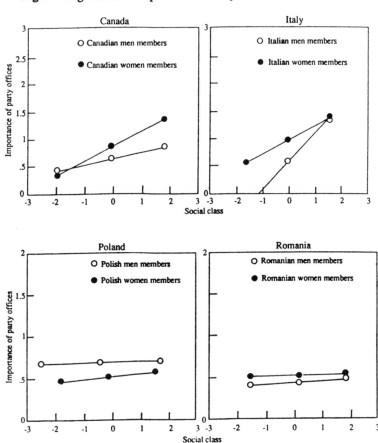

dominant model of which it is a variant, affiliation is necessary and sufficient for holding governmental offices but the lower-class affiliated hold offices of more importance than the upper-class affiliated. To use once more the words of Verba et al., "This illustrates one way in which institutions, when they are strong, can reduce inequality across socio-economic levels" (1978: 86). It is

Table 9 Expected and Found Systems

	M	F	M	F
	Canada		**Italy**	
System expected	Weak	Additive	Restrictive	Restrictive
System found	Additive	Additive	Restrictive	Restrictive
	Poland		**Romania**	
System expected	Dominant	Dominant	Dominant	Dominant
System found	Restrictive	Withholding	Restrictive	Restrictive

interesting to note that this happens for women, not for men. There is a possible explanation: for men, becoming a party member is enough to allow entry into the competition for high position in the public structure, thanks to the support of the party leadership combined with personal resources; for women, on the other hand, promotion responds largely to the logic of tokenism which induces the party leadership to prefer women from the lower class.

In the other cases, affiliation is a necessary, but not sufficient condition for this kind of activity. If a person is not affiliated to a party, socio-economic resources do not lead to this form of participation. But being in the party does not neutralize the impact of socio-economic resources (14).

All in all, party affiliation helps people everywhere to hold governmental offices, but everywhere also class makes a difference in terms of the importance of the offices held. This is slightly less true in the socialist countries (15).

As far as gender differences are concerned, no differences appear, except, as we said, in Poland.

Social Composition of Affiliated and Unaffiliated

What we have done up to now is to compare the relationship between socio-economic resources and importance of governmental offices for party affiliated and unaffiliated

Fig. 7 Regression of Importance of Governmental Offices on Social Class

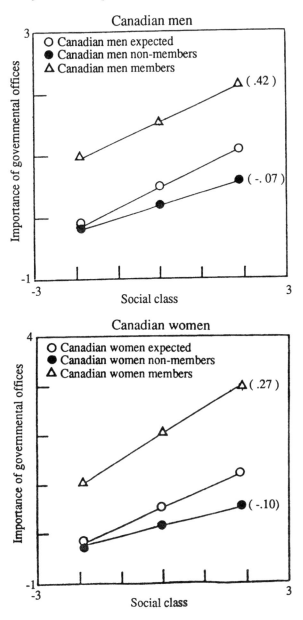

In this figure, the scales of the abscisses differ from graph to graph in order to allow a better presentation

Fig. 7 Regression of Importance of Governmental Offices on Social Class †

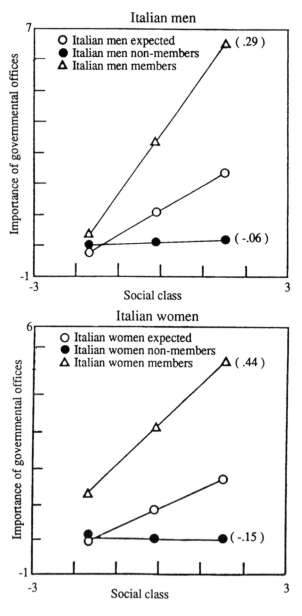

† In this figure, the scales of the abscisses differ from graph to graph in order allow a better presentation

Fig. 7   Regression of Importance of Governmental Offices on Social Class †

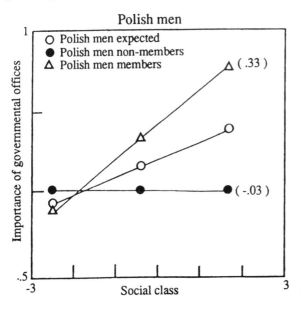

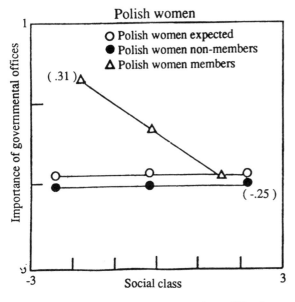

†|In this figure, the scales of the abscisses differ from graph
 to graph in order to allow a better presentation

Fig.7   Regression of Importance of Governmental Offices on Social Class †

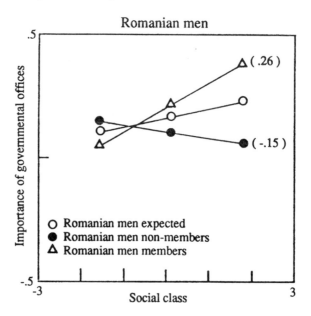

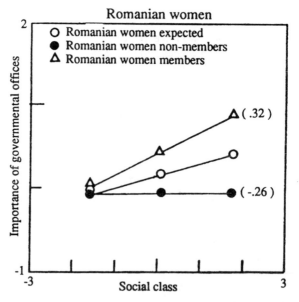

† In this figure, the scales of the abscisses differ from graph
  to graph in order to allow a better presentation

respondents with the same relationship that exists for respondents in general. However, as Verba et al., point out, this

> is not sufficient to tell us what effects institutions would have on the overall shape of the relationship between socio-economic resources and participation [in our case, importance of offices held] --- that is, whether they will make participation rates more equal across the socio-economic levels, less equal, or leave them unchanged. The reason is that much depends upon the social composition of those who are affiliated and those who are unaffiliated with institutions. In a strong institutional system, the activity rate of the affiliated is boosted, that of the unaffiliated reduced. But the impact on intergroup political equality depends on who is affiliated and who is not. (1978: 88)

The numbers in brackets in Fig. 7 indicate the average socio-economic level of the affiliated and the unaffiliated in the four countries (see App. 1). As the reader can easily see, the unaffiliated are of a lower socio-economic origin *everywhere*. This means that everywhere there tends to be a middle/upper-class bias in affiliation.

This, of course, has different implications depending on the system. When we have an additive or a restrictive system (that is, in all our cases, except Polish females), the resulting relationship between socio-economic resources and this form of participation will be stronger. In these cases the system increases inequality by increasing the difference in the importance of offices held between middle/upper and lower-class people. A higher proportion of people from the upper and middle classes are boosted because they are over-represented among the affiliated.

From the point of view of gender differences, in all countries, except Canada, relative to their men peers, middle- and upper-class women are more favoured in relation to lower class women, as can be seen from Table 10.

This means that in all countries parties look for members in the middle/high layers of the social scale or alternatively people of higher social background are themselves keener to enter a party than those in the lower layers. In the latter event, this is more true for women than men, except in Canada.

Table 10 Class Difference between Affiliated and Unaffiliated People

	Canada	Italy	Poland	Romania
Males	.492	.354	.353	.409
Females	.361	.589	.555	.583

5 Other Forms of Participation

We consider here participation in trade unions, women's organizations and voluntary organizations (see Tables 11, 12, 13).

Table 11 Trade Union Membership (number with % in brackets)

	Canada	Italy	Poland	Romania
M. blue-collar workers	68 (68)	75 (76.5)	66 (66.7)	99 (99)
F. blue-collar workers	43 (44.3)	50 (51)	74 (76.3)	96 (96)
M. white-collar workers	32 (32)	63 (62.4)	72 (72) ·	96 (96)
F. white-collar workers	8 (8)	62 (62)	89 (86.4)	97 (98)
M. teachers	49 (49)	41 (42.3)	64 (64.6)	97 (97)
F. teachers	78 (78)	34 (34.3)	89 (89)	93 (93.9)
Men out of work	18 (18)	13 (13.3)	--- ---	61 (61.6)
Housewives	1 (1)	2 (2)	35 (35)	11 (11.1)
M. decision-makers	22 (14.7)	52 (35.6)	138 (91.4)	62 (98.4)
F. decision-makers	19 (12.7)	60 (41.4)	138 (95.2)	64 (100)

An overall evaluation of these, as well as other forms of participation concerning intervention at the local level, shows without any doubt that in the whole sample, except for Poland with respect to trade unions (App. 7), men participate more than women.

A comparison of gender differences in these other forms of participation and gender differences in party activism (App. 3) yields an interesting result. In Canada and Italy, the scores for men for party activism are higher than for women but the difference is not significant, while trade union participation in the same countries discriminates significantly in favour of men. In Poland, on the other hand, trade union participation discriminates in favour of women, while political participation does so in favour of men. In

Table 12 Membership in Different Kinds of Women's Organizations

	Canada	Italy	Poland	Romania
Feminist	69	2	0	0
Political	11	59	8	22
Cultural and Charitable	34	1	0	5
Professional	2	1	0	0
Other	12	0	0	2
Total	128	63	8	29

Romania all forms of participation discriminate significantly in favour of men with about the same intensity. This means that in Canada and Italy, when it comes to struggling for particularistic claims, as trade unions usually do, men become much more active than women (Cook, 1980; Hunt, 1984; Beynon and Blackburn, 1984).

Table 13 Membership in Different Kinds of Voluntary Organizations

	Canada		Italy		Poland		Romania	
	M	F	M	F	M	F	M	F
Cultural	19	23	6	6	40	44	8	4
Charitable	22	20	3	4	5	7	6	9
Sport	31	7	0	1	34	8	10	3
Veteran	2	0	0	1	14	7	3	3
Religious	23	18	4	12	0	1	2	0
Professional	71	97	12	12	73	40	5	3
Ecological	7	4	0	1	5	2	1	0
Other	67	71	0	0	65	52	12	9
Total	242	240	25	37	236	161	47	31

6 Interrelations among Various Forms of Participation

We now face another problem. Is there a gender difference as far as the "diffusiveness" of participation is concerned? We are especially interested in the issue of the relationship between trade union and party participation (Olsen, 1972).

6.1 *Membership*

The pattern that emerges is very interesting and reflects what we know in general about the four countries. Everywhere, except in Canada, if a person belongs to one organization, that person also belongs to the others. In Poland this is true for all kinds of organizations we have examined; the only exceptions are in Italy and Romania, where there is a lack of correlation between being in a trade union and being in a voluntary association. No significant gender differences emerge in this picture. In Canada, on the contrary, the correlations among membership in the various organizations reflect a less monolithic society. For both men and women there is no significant correlation between party and trade union membership. But people of both sexes in voluntary associations are also in parties and trade unions, and women who are in women's organizations also belong to all of the others (however, the correlation with trade union membership is weak: $p = .04$). It appears clearly that in Canada the link is not the party or the trade union but the voluntary associations and, in the case of women, women's organizations.

6.2 *Participation*

The general tendency is that people who participate in one organization also participate in the others. This is highlighted in Appendix B. The exceptions concern women in all countries except Italy, and men in Canada. In these cases there is no correlation between participation in trade unions and in voluntary associations.

6.3 *Office-holding*

Although with regard to membership and participation the tendency is towards diffuseness, in the case of office-holding some people in one organization hold offices in another, while others do not.

6.4 *Importance of Offices*

The contrast with the findings commented upon in the previous paragraph is very interesting. First, for both men and women, those who hold important offices in the party tend also to hold important offices in the other organizations, trade unions excluded. However, there are other forms of interlocking. For men, in all countries, those who hold important offices in non-governmental organizations also hold important offices in the others, trade unions always excluded.

What is surprising is that the interlocking is stronger for women than for men. In fact, in Canada and Italy, besides party, governmental and non-governmental organizations, women who hold important offices in voluntary associations and women's organizations also hold important offices in the other organizations, trade unions excluded. In Poland the interlocking is among party, governmental organizations, voluntary associations and women's organizations; in Romania between party and women's organizations.

For different reasons, in all countries the holding of important offices in trade unions does not imply either for men or for women the tendency to hold important offices in other organizations.

6.5 Protest on the Job and Participation in Party and Trade Union Activities

The hypothesis of a stronger link between protest on the job and trade union participation, at least in Canada and Italy, than between protest on the job and party participation is rejected with the only exception of men in Italy, where we find a weaker correlation for party activities (.07, p = .05) than for trade union activities (.16, p = .000). Everywhere, for men and even more for women, protest on the job is correlated more with the commitment to party than commitment to trade union activities.

Yet there is a difference between men and women: in Poland and Romania the coefficients between protest on the job and trade union activities are not significant for men, while they are for women. For party and trade union activities, therefore, women appear to be more consistent and assertive than men.

It is interesting to note that, in all countries and for both sexes, protest on the job seems to elicit not so much a particularistic interest as represented by trade unions, but an interest in problems concerning the whole of society of the kind parties deal with. But maybe a more realistic interpretation is that people turn to the organization they think is most effective.

7 Feeling of Influence in Organizations

7.1 *In General*

In the previous paragraphs we examined gender differences in terms of participation in various kinds of organizations. We wonder now whether there is a difference between men and women in terms of the influence that they feel that they exert within them (16).

In general, with the exception of Romania where people tend to have the feeling that they have influence, the tendency is towards a moderate (in the case of Italy, a very moderate) feeling of influence. In all countries, except Romania, female blue-collar workers report the lowest level of influence.

Within each category there are only a few significant gender differences. They are all in favour of men, with the exception of female decision-makers in Italy.

7.2 *In Relation to Membership, Incumbency and Degree of Participation in Different Kinds of Organizations*

In general, all forms of involvement are correlated with the feelings of influence. The exception is membership in trade unions: men and women affiliated to them do not feel they have much influence on the other members (women only in Poland and men only in Romania feel they have some). As to the other two forms of involvement, what is at first sight intriguing is the fact that, with the exception of feminist organizations, this feeling goes together more with participation than with office-holding. A possible explanation is that holding an important office, while it allows people to give orders, does not necessarily entail a greater feeling of being influential than being assiduously immersed in a network of face-to-face relationships from which people may derive the impression of holding tight in their hands the daily life of the organization. After all, it is participation that creates the general will of an organization, while giving orders is to a large extent the expression of that will, an activity more detached from the boisterous clashes of interests that one has to face in participation.

The crucial result, from the point of view that concerns us here, is that in both cases this is more true for women than for men.

8 Reasons for not Participating

A study of the motivations for people to join an organization is beyond the scope of the present research. We limit ourselves here to the reasons that are alleged by our respondents for not participating.

The following question was asked:

"If you do not participate in those organizations or your participation is not as you would like, why does this happen?
1 I have too many commitments with my family.
2 I have not found the organization that fits me.
3 I am not well physically.
4 My spouse does not want me to participate.
5 I am not interested in participating.
6 My work tires me too much.
7 I do not have time.
8 It is all talking of people who do not like to work.
9 My participation would not change anything.
10 I participate as much as I want".

The answer "yes" or "no" to each item was requested.

We begin with the last item. Everywhere, but especially in Canada and Italy, our respondents do not participate as much as they would like. There are basically no gender differences on this issue. It is interesting to note that in Poland and Romania blue-collar workers are content with their level of participation, while in all countries, except Italy, male decision-makers give a negative answer more than all other male categories.

The examination of the ranking of the items in each country (not shown here) reveals that everywhere, for both men and women, the most frequently mentioned reason for not participating is lack of time, not family commitment.

We saw above (par. 3.5.1) that, objectively, the family is no longer the hindrance to women's participation that it used to be. It is amazing to discover that this is true also at the subjective level. A really momentous transformation has taken place.

To analyse better this aspect, we built an index of the family as an obstacle (App. 9). Everywhere women more than men are hindered by family reasons (with the only exception of male decision-makers in Italy) but the significant differences are few. Respondents of both sexes in Romania, followed by Canada, appear to be the least affected by such factors.

*   *   *

We tried to investigate more thoroughly the reasons that would favour women's political participation with the following questions:

"Do you think that a greater number of women would be interested in politics if:
(a) They had the feeling that the political problems concern their daily life?
(b) A greater number of women were involved in politics?
(c) The political structures were different?
(d) They were encouraged by political parties?
(e) They had more trust in themselves?"

The scores ranged from 1 = "totally disagree" to 4 = "totally agree".

In general, both men and women agree with all five items, but women agree more than men and very often the difference is significant.

Which conditions are seen as the most important? The picture is very interesting. The last item receives the largest agreement in Romania (all categories) and Canada (females) but also stands out in the other countries for both sexes. This means that the opinion that if women are not interested in politics then it is their own fault is widespread not only among men but also (in the case of Canada much more so) among women. The first item has priority for several categories, slightly more for males than females. To change political structures in order to have more women interested in politics has priority only in Poland for female teachers and in Italy for female white-collar workers and teachers and for men out of work.

It is interesting to note that in Canada the fourth item, implying for women a passive and somewhat minority-like status, comes first for four categories (two male and two female).

It looks as if a kind of inferiority complex prevails among women as to the reasons for their supposedly lower political involvement. The "passivity" image, spread by the literature and more importantly by daily practice, seems to be internalized by them. This may be easily understood, because to enter politics means to enter a world alien to women.

9 Women's Low Level of Participation in Public Matters: a Stereotype with a Hard Core of Truth

As Verba et al. (1978) point out, there are two possible explanations for what they suppose to be the lower level of political activity and office-holding found more among women than men:

> One explanation is based on apathy: women do not care about political matters and, therefore, *abstain* from politics...
>
> Another explanation is that women are *inhibited* from taking part in political life....The inhibition can be external or internal. Women may be externally restrained from taking part in political life by formal or informal rules barring them from channels of political access or from political organizations. Or they may be externally restrained by social norms against female political activity. Women, however, may accept the social norms against female participation. In such a case the inhibition to political activity derives from self restraint. (1978: 254)

We will deal first with the crude fact of political concern. The other hypotheses will be examined in detail in the last paragraphs of this section.

9.1 *Political Interest*

If women are apathetic about public matters, their level of interest in being informed about such matters should inevitably be low.

To measure this phenomenon we used a scale (Appendix 6). The results are shown in Table 14. Generally, in our sample the interest is moderate, with the exception of Italy, where it is more pronounced. Decision-makers are more interested than all other categories, while men out of work and housewives are at the other end. It is surprising to find that in Romania there is no significant difference between blue-collar workers and men out of work and that in Poland blue- and white-collar workers are the least interested categories.

The level of political concern is everywhere significantly higher among men than women. The difference is especially strong in Poland; it is slightly less, although still highly significant (p = .001), in Canada.

Table 14 Level of Political Interest

The questions asked were the following: "Do you regularly follow, through radio and television, political and economic events?" and "Do you read books or articles concerning political and economic matters?"

The scores were:

1 = "very often"; 2 = "at times"; 3 = "seldom"; 4 = "never".

	Canada d†		Italy d†		Poland d†		Romania d†	
M. blue-collar workers	2.5		2.1		2.2		2.3	
		-.2***		-.4*		-.6*		-.2*
F. blue-collar workers	2.7		2.5		2.8		2.5	
M. white-collar workers	2.4		1.9		2.0		1.9	
		-.2**		-.4*		-.2**		-.2**
F. white-collar workers	2.6		2.3		2.2		2.1	
M. teachers	2.1		1.5		1.9		1.9	
		-.3*		-.4*		-.3**		-.2*
F. teachers	2.4		1.9		2.2		2.1	
Men out of work	2.6		2.5		---		2.4	
		-.2***		-.3*				-.5*
Housewives	2.8		2.8		2.6		2.9	
M. decision-makers	1.4		1.3		1.4		1.7	
		0		-.1		-.3*		-.2***
F. decision-makers	1.4		1.4		1.7		1.9	

† d means difference. The levels of confidence are:

*p ≤ .01; ** .05 > p > .01; *** .10 > p > .05.

A question comes spontaneously to mind: is there a generational difference so that the gender gap decreases in comparison between, for instance, the pre-war and the post-war generations? The answer seems positive. Everywhere, but especially in Canada (pre-war: t = 3.11, df = 886, p = .002; post-war: t = 1.84, df = 162, p = .068) and above all Italy (pre-war: t = 5.83, df = 924, p = .000; post-war: t = 1.64, df = 132, p = .103), the gender difference has decreased from the generation born in the first half of the century to that born in the second half. But it must be underlined that it is on the basis of a lower level of political concern that the gender difference has decreased.

Among the socio-economic variables that affect such concern, education is one of the most thoroughly investigated factors. A harvest of research shows that people with more education tend to become more engaged in political participation than those with less education. Milbrath (1965) lists 23 sources as evidence of empirical uniformity about such a correlation. The same link between the two phenomena was found by Verba et al. (1971; 1978) as well as by other scholars committed to women's studies (Klein, 1984: 110-111; Sapiro, 1984 : 88-93; Baxter and Lansing, 1983 : 43). The reason why education everywhere has a strong impact on political involvement is obviously because the more people are educated, the more competent they are to understand public matters, the more they look for mass-media of greater sophistication, and the more they occupy positions with higher status and responsibility. Is this true to the same extent for women?

The correlations between education and political concern are positive in all countries in the vast majority of categories (Jasinska and Siemienska, 1983: 63). The few exceptions are found among decision-makers and teachers, obviously as a consequence of their high level of education and/or political information. The number of significant correlations is high, especially in Italy. Contrary to common prejudice, no substantial difference appears between men and women.

Unlike the situation for political participation and office-holding (par. 3.5.2 above), education is a good predictor of political concern, as is clearly shown by Fig. 8. In all countries, women and men with higher education do not differ very much, but at the lower levels of education women show less interest in politics than men. An increase in education thus affects women more than men. This is especially true in Poland where the gap at the lower levels of education is larger than elsewhere, but where

Fig. 8 Regression of Political Interest† on Education

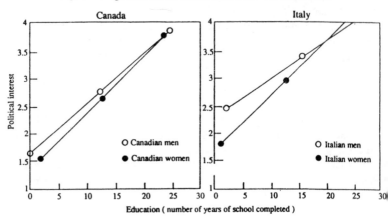

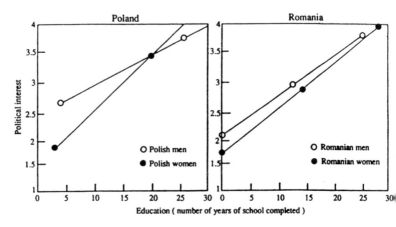

† For convenience of presentation, the direction of the scale has been inverted:
a high score means a high interest

women with higher education need less years of schooling than men to reach the same level of political interest.

The resemblance between Canada and Romania, on one side, and Italy and Poland, on the other, is indeed noteworthy. In the former countries, education discriminates to about the same degree and the interest in politics is rather low; in the latter, it discriminates more for women than for men and both sexes appear to have a higher degree of interest in politics.

However, in all countries women are concentrated much more heavily than men in the lower levels of education. As a result, in spite of the effects of education, women show a much lower interest than men. Thus, as found by Verba et al. (1978:257-260) and Baxter and Lansing (1983:43) found, women convert education into political interest at a greater pace than men. However, to equal men, women need to reach the upper echelons of higher education. Apathy is not the cause of women's alleged lack of interest in politics.

We chose to present here only the results of the regression of the political concern on education. If we use the index of social class, the results are not dissimilar, although education explains better the variable under examination. For both sexes, the more socio-economic opportunities are available, the stronger is the concern for politics. This is more true for women than for men in all countries, but especially so in Italy and Poland.

9.1.1 *Political Concern, Political Participation, Party Offices*

Let us now turn to the impact of political interest on political participation and the importance of party offices held. (Note that, for the sake of brevity, in this and in many of the following paragraphs the data on which the exposition is grounded are not presented.)

As far as participation in party activities is concerned, the impact of political interest is very small for both men and women. Yet, while in terms of gradients there are no gender differences, the intercepts differ: women who are highly concerned about politics tend to be more active than men with the same level of interest. This is another finding which runs counter to the apathy hypothesis.

It is logical to wonder about the influence of education on this gradient. To examine this aspect, we divided education into three bands, low, middle, and high, and replicated the regression within each. In general, the impact of political interest on political participation remains small but an increase in educational level strengthens it: moving up the educational ladder, gradients become slightly stronger. They are about the same for both sexes.

Gender differences emerge when we consider the intercepts. Except in Poland, women in the three bands of education start at a higher level of political participation than men with a similar amount of political interest: in other words, the increase in women's political participation depending on political interest equals that of men but women are able to transform political interest into political participation better than men with a corresponding level of education.

Is this result also true for party offices? It is, but only to some extent. The impact of the level of political interest on party office-holding is minimum. Only in Italy do the gradients increase for both men and women with an increase in education, but the rise is very small. Within each band of education, there is no gender difference as far as the gradient is concerned. Here, too, the differences concern the intercepts which, save in Poland, are higher for women than for men. Furthermore, on moving up the educational ladder, the intercepts increase and do so more for women than for men. Women with a high degree of political interest know better than men how to transform it into important party offices.

The next question is whether a strong interest in politics goes together with a wish to participate more in a political party, a trade union, or a feminist organization. As far as a political party is concerned, the answer is positive, for both males and females of all categories. In all countries, with the exception of Italy, within each category the correlation, significant or suggestive in all cases, is generally stronger for women than for men.

As regards trade unions, the correlation exists but it is weaker than in the previous case and in many instances it is not even suggestive. Here, the correlation is slightly stronger for males than for females.

Obviously, participation in women's organizations concerns women only. On this matter there is an interesting difference between Canada and Poland, on one side, and Italy and Romania, on the other. In the former there are too few statistically relevant correlations but in the latter practically all categories are affected by such connections. A possible explanation is the strong political bent of women's organizations in Italy and Romania, whether connected with a party or not, as compared to women's organizations in the other two countries.

9.2 *Ideal Participation*

Is the actual level of participation satisfactory for our respondents? Is there a difference, and in which direction, between men and women? (17)

In all categories more men than women aspire to a higher level of participation. In Canada and Romania the differences in this area are all significant. But when we take into consideration the impact of a party affiliation, we see that the desire increases remarkably for both sexes, indeed to such a conspicuous extent for women as to make them overtake men. The same result obtains when we examine the impact of education and of political concern. It is clear that the desire to have a higher participation depends on favourable circumstances and that some of them may advantage women more than men.

9.2.1 *Experience of Offices and Ideal Participation*

Does experience of governmental office increase significantly more in men than women the desire to hold offices? The answer is no. Only among respondents with no experience of governmental office do we find that women want offices less than men do. Once women have accumulated some experience, they want to hold offices more than men do, although the differences are not significant.

Having held party offices also tends to generate a wish to participate more in party life, except in Poland and Romania. Even if the differences are not significant, in Canada and especially in Italy women with the same kind of party office-holding in the past are more stimulated than men. However, the only significant difference in favour of women is found among Polish women with high-level party office experience in the past.

It is noticeable that in the band of high-level party offices women everywhere want to participate in party life more than men (but the level is significant only in Poland).

The experience of past party offices does not stimulate men more than women to hold governmental or party offices. Within the four bands into which we divided party offices (no offices, low-, middle-, high-level) there are no significant gender differences, except in the low-level band in Italy in favour of women, and in the 'no offices' band in Romania in favour of men (merely suggestive). Among the remaining non-significant differences, the majority are in favour of women.

The same holds good for incumbency in governmental offices. The more women hold important governmental offices, the more they would like important party offices.

* * *

It is not true, consequently, that experience in handling power drives men more than women to want more participation or more power. The fact remains, however, that women are neither allowed nor placed in a position to have such experience to the same extent as men.

9.2.2 *Religion and Desire to Participate*

It is traditionally believed that women are more sensitive to religion than men, and that religions, particularly Catholicism (Porter and Venning, 1976), Greek Orthodoxy and Judaism, exert a conservative influence on women. There is, in two of the countries of our sample, an institutionalized atheistic belief which is directly connected with their official ideology of egalitarianism. Are atheistic women in Poland and Romania more participative than religious women?

Fig. 9 shows that the answer is negative. As far as gender differences are concerned, men are in general more eager to participate than women from the same denomination. The only exception is found among atheists in Italy.

The conservative impact of religion, especially on women, is even more evident when we compare religion with the desire to hold governmental or party offices.

If we go further and examine the impact of religious practice *within* each denomination upon political participation, upon the desire to hold offices, upon the desire to participate in party life, and upon the belief that politics is a matter for men (Table 15), we see that religious practice exerts a conservative influence, irrespective of affiliation, with the exception of Protestantism in Canada for men. This influence appears to be stronger for women (Baxter and Lansing, 1983: 204-206).

Fig. 9 Religious Affiliation and Desire to Participate More in
Party Life†

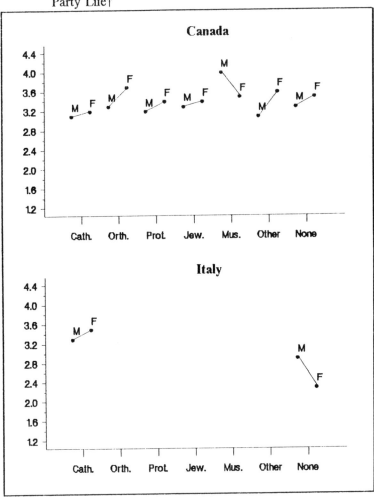

† A high score indicates a low desire to participate.

Fig. 9 Religious Affiliation and Desire to Participate More in
Party Life†

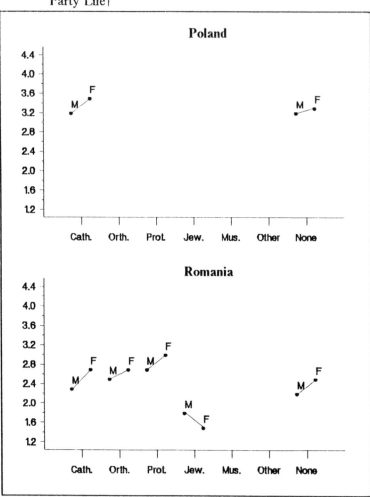

† A high score indicates a low desire to participate.

Table 15 Correlations between Religious Practice and Certain Variables†

	Political participation		Desire for offices		Desire for party participation		Politics: business for men?	
	M	F	M	F	M	F	M	F
Canada								
Catholic	.18**	-.09	-.01	.06	.02	-.02	.17	.25*
Greek Orthodox	.45	nc	.58	-.43	-.58	-.25	.46	.41***
Protestant	.08***	.02	-.16*	-.03	-.06	-.05	-.15*	.10**
Jewish	.00	.13	-.47**	.05	.13	-.20	.09	.41**
Muslim	nc	nc	-.65	-.32	nc	-.89**	-.63	-.77
Italy								
Catholic	-.05	-.21*	-.01	.16*	-.02	.14*	.17*	.17*
Poland								
Catholic	-.45*	-.48*	.33*	.37*	.33*	.26*	.07***	.16*
Romania								
Catholic	-.37***	-.34***	-.06	.45**	-.50**	.44**	.08	.46**
Greek Orthodox	-.24*	-.20*	.18*	.04	.30*	.11*	.06	.15*
Protestant	-.87		.00	.17	-.65	.47	.98***	.33
Jewish	-.17		.50		.89*		.43	

† The negative sign depends on the direction of the scores: 1 = much; 4 = not at all.

*p $\leq$ .01; ** .05 > p > .01; *** .10 > p > .05.

nc means that the coefficient was not computable (N too low).

9.3 *Inhibiting Values*

The presumption that women do not participate because they are apathetic does not hold. Another explanation is that women are blocked by the values that they have internalized.

There is little doubt that, with regard to the role of women in society, the values that traditionally have been predominant in the four countries of our study portray what is typically masculine as being at the other extreme of what is typically feminine (Tresemer, 1976). One activity considered typically unfeminine is political participation. But in all the countries, as we have seen, there has been an evolution towards a more or less explicit parity between men and women (in particular, see ch. 2, par. 4.1). To what extent have these changes affected what is traditionally considered inappropriate for women?

We asked whether people agreed with the following statement:

"Politics is a matter more for men than for women."

Fig. 10 shows that, while disagreement generally prevails in Italy and Canada, there is a surprising tendency to the opposite point of view in the two socialist countries. As expected, in all countries decision-makers of both sexes disagree with this statement more than all other categories. This being said, it is important to note that within all the categories, men, more than women, tend to agree with the statement, with the difference between men and women on this matter being significantly greater in Canada and Italy than in Poland and Romania. Indeed, in two Romanian categories women agree more than men! On the whole, there is good evidence of a psychological barrier put up by men that makes it difficult for women to enter politics. Male ostracism is a more powerful factor than the inhibitions of women themselves.

One might wonder whether there is a difference between decision-makers and working people (i.e. blue- and white-collar workers and teachers in our sample). A difference does exist: decision-makers of both sexes are more open than both male and female working people but, with the exception of Romania, men are significantly much more traditional than women in both groups

Fig. 10 Scores on the Statement:
'Politics is a matter for men more than women'

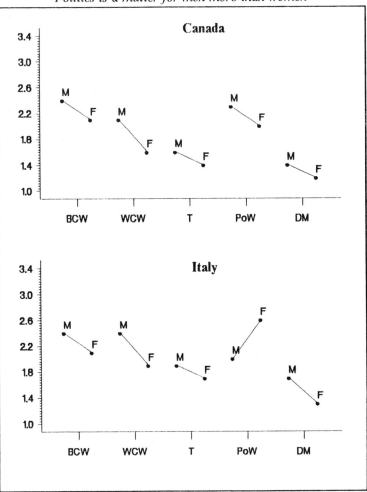

In this figure all differences are significant, except the one concerning Italian
teachers which is merely suggestive.
The scores are as follows:

    1 = **Totally disagree**;
    2 = **Rather disagree**;
    3 = **Rather agree**;
    4 = **Totally agree**.

Fig. 10 Scores on the Statement:
'Politics is a matter for men more than women'

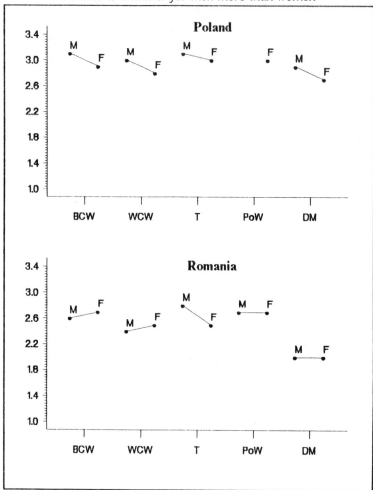

In this figure only two differences are significant (Poland DM, Romania T).
The scores are as follows:
    1 = Totally disagree;
    2 = Rather disagree;
    3 = Rather agree;
    4 = Totally agree.

(in Poland, however, the difference is smaller than in Canada and Italy).

It is reasonable to imagine that party membership makes a difference. In all countries, in fact, working people who are party members hold a more progressive attitude on this issue than non-party members. For decision-makers, however, that is true only in Italy. Party members with power in society adhere to a traditional viewpoint in this decisive area. The shift towards a more open mind among working people is stronger for women than for men, with the consequence that the gender difference is greater among party members than among non-party members! (The only exceptions are working people in Poland and decision-makers in Italy). In other words, women in the party are less inhibited than non-party women, but run into resistance from men; men in the party, although more open than non-party members, uphold an attitude which, relatively speaking, represents an obstacle for women more than is true outside the party. After all, parties are a male construct.

Since this belief is of fundamental importance for our study, we pause to consider its implications. First, what is its impact on political participation?

Table 16 shows that, as expected, irrespective of gender, the more people share such a view, the less they participate. This is true for both women and men but the gradients, except in Poland, are steeper for women than for men. In other words, this belief has more negative consequences, as we might have expected, for women than for men. But we concentrate on men and women who disagree with the statement, we discover that they show pretty much the same level of participation (except in Poland where men outrank women). This means that, since women are more numerous than men among those who totally disagree, women show a slightly higher level of participation relative to the total population of participating men.

Is this also true with regard to its impact on the importance of party offices held? In this case, it might be argued that the answer is different. Values should have less to do with holding positions of responsibility in the party than with political participation. On the contrary, as shown in Tables 17 and 18, although the impact is much smaller, it is again true that the more people hold a conservative view, the less important are their offices in the party. This holds true for both men and women but the gradients, except in Poland, are once more steeper for women than for men, especially in Italy and Romania.

Table 16 Regression of Political Participation (overall measure) on Holding a Conservative View about the Relation between Women and Politics

	Males		Females	
	a	b	a	b
Canada	.76	-.21	.75	-.25
Italy	1.01	-.24	1.05	-.31
Poland	1.50	-.17	.78	-.08
Romania	1.33	-.17	1.39	-.29

Table 17 Regression of Importance of Party Offices on Holding a Conservative View about the Relation between Women and Politics

	Males		Females	
	a	b	a	b
Canada	.33	-.10	.35	-.12
Italy	.55	-.16	.69	-.21
Poland	.50	-.06	.18	-.01
Romania	.37	-.06	.45	-.11

Table 18 Comparison of the Impact of Holding a Traditional View about the Relation between Women and Politics on Political Participation and Party Offices (beta weights)

		M	F
Canada	Political participation	-.23	-.25
	Party offices	-.16	-.14
Italy	Political participation	-.26	-.32
	Party offices	-.23	-.24
Poland	Political participation	-.13	-.08
	Party offices	-.09	-.03
Romania	Political participation	-.17	-.29
	Party offices	-.13	-.22

Again, if we concentrate on the men and women who disagree totally, we discover that, among those holding office, women have offices of about the same importance as men, with the consequence just highlighted about participation.

In general, we have seen that women share this prejudice less than men in all countries, and in Canada and Italy tend to get rid of it. Since it is reasonable to ask how much this is because of experience of the management of power, we divided the respondents into four bands with respect to having held party offices in the past (no offices, low-, middle- and high-level) and checked the gender differences within each band.

With only one exception (Polish women with no office), everywhere women disagree more than men. The management of power, it would seem, is beneficial for women. But moving up the party hierarchy also induces men to disagree with this statement to a point that, in the high-level band, no gender difference is significant in any country. The same is true for experience of governmental offices. As a matter of fact, it turns out that this experience benefits women even more than the experience of party offices.

It is reasonable to conclude that it is not inhibition which blocks women from political participation but rather lack of opportunities in political and public life.

10 The Exclusion of Women from Power

If the idea that women are much more behind men in terms of public participation proves to be a stereotype, and we have enough evidence to state that it is, then the answer to the question why women do not hold leadership positions to the same extent as men do must be that they are excluded from power. This follows logically but is also reflected in our respondents' perceptions.

We asked the following question:

"In your opinion do women in this country have the same chances men have to hold a position of leadership?"

Fig. 11 shows that in all countries women are disadvantaged in the judgement of both men and women, but much more so in Italy and Canada than in Poland and Romania. This is one of the few cases in our research where social systems make a clear-cut difference.

Within each category women everywhere are more aware of their disadvantage than men are, although the differences are not always significant. This awareness, as we expected, is especially acute among female decision-makers who rank in all countries significantly above their male counterparts. This is true also for

Fig. 11 Men's and Women's Chances of Holding a Leadership
Position

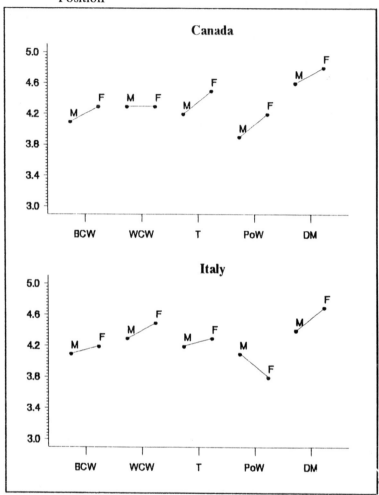

In Canada all differences are significant except for WCW (BCW merely suggestive)
in Italy only the differences concerning PoW and DM are significant.
The scores are as follows:

    1 = Women are definitely favoured;
    2 = Women are somewhat favoured;
    3 = Women and men are treated equally;
    4 = Men are somewhat favoured;
    5 = Men are definitely favoured.

Fig. 11 Men's and Women's Chances of Holding a Leadership
       Position

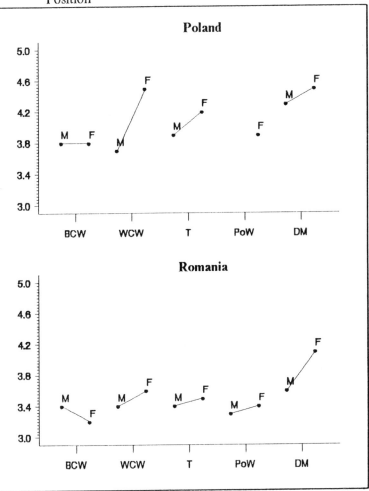

In Poland all differences are significant, except for BCW; in Romania the difference
concerning BCW is suggestive, the one concerning DM is significant.
The scores are as follows:
    1 = Women are definitely favoured;
    2 = Women are somewhat favoured;
    3 = Women and men are treated equally;
    4 = Men are somewhat favoured;
    5 = Men are definitely favoured.

teachers in Canada and Poland and for a few other cases, none of which is found in Italy.

Everywhere housewives and blue-collar workers of both sexes are the least aware that women are disadvantaged. The same applies to men out of work in Italy and Canada.

Thus, we can conclude on the basis of the answers to this question that the barrier exists. Both men and women acknowledge it. We can also conclude that, if women perceive more than men that the opportunities for holding leadership positions are more open to men than to themselves, then the barrier is reinforced because women will probably be that much more discouraged from pursuing a public career.

The fact that in Italy we do not find any gender difference is not surprising: the chances of women in this country look grim and both men and women realistically agree on it. However, a gender difference does emerge in Italy if we split the sample into two parts: working people and decision-makers. Interestingly enough, it is stronger for the latter (working people: $t = 1.98$, $p = .049$; decision-makers: $t = 2.28$, $p = .023$). In the other countries also, women in both groups feel that they are more disadvantaged than men (the only exception is Romania, where there is no difference among working people). However, the gender difference is stronger among decision-makers than among working people. In general, men, and especially decision-makers, are less inclined than women to admit that women are disadvantaged.

What is the impact of party membership on this phenomenon? One might reasonably expect that it is tangible. In fact, as Table 19 shows, the gender difference tends to disappear in Canada and Romania for both working people and decision-makers and, in Italy, for working people. Party membership induces a more realistic attitude in men also. The increase of awareness seems slightly stronger among working people than decision-makers.

*   *   *

The question comes spontaneously to mind as to whether the ideal attitude of our respondents on this issue reveals a diverse picture. To answer this, we asked the same question but substituted "should" for "do".

As we saw in ch. 2, in all countries the overwhelming majority tends to favour an equal distribution of leadership positions between men and women. Yet, except in Romania, there is still a

Table 19 Perception of Objective Possibility for Women to Hold Leadership Positions (scores and absolute figure); comparisons between Men and Women by Country and Party Membership[†]

	Working people				Decision-makers			
	Party members		All		Party members		All	
	M	F	M	F	M	F	M	F
Canada	4.2 (32) t = -1.47	4.5 (20) p = .149	4.2 (294) t = -3.08	4.4 (294) p = .002	4.7 (71) t = -1.50	4.8 (75) p = .137	4.6 (147) t = -3.43	4.8 (147) p = .001
Italy	4.3 (52) t = -1.31	4.5 (22) p = .195	4.2 (299) t = -1.98	4.3 (295) p = .049	4.5 (81) t = -2.77	4.7 (93) p = .006	4.4 (148) t = -2.28	4.6 (148) p = .023
Poland	3.8 (72) t = -2.14	4.2 (45) p = .034	3.8 (296) t = -3.76	4.1 (300) p = .000	4.3 (128) t = -2.16	4.5 (90) p = .032	4.3 (151) t = -2.60	4.5 (145) p = .010
Romania	3.4 (135) t = -.48	3.4 (95) p = .630	3.4 (300) t = -.29	3.4 (299) p = .771	3.6 (58) t = -.47	4.1 (60) p = .635	3.6 (63) t = -3.29	4.1 (63) p = .001

† The negative sign indicates that the score is higher for women: that is, that women state, more than men, that men are favoured.

sizeable minority who think that men should be favoured. However, in all countries men resist changing the traditional set-up more strongly than women do (Goode, 1982)(18).

This finding seems to contradict the results --- favourable for women --- obtained from the question about a more tangible presence of women in positions where decisions are taken. When confronted with the possibility of an egalitarian distribution of leadership positions, the preference still lies with men. The contradiction can be explained by the disposition of people to have more women, but not as many women as men, in the power structure.

The data in Table 20 show that there are people, especially men, who are in favour of letting more women into leadership positions but who still maintain that men should be favoured overall.

Table 20 Percentages of Respondents who are in Favour of More Women in Leadership Positions, but Oppose an Egalitarian Distribution of Them

Canada		Italy		Poland		Romania	
M	F	M	F	M	F	M	F
More women in leadership positions							
72.4	91.8	60.7	83.2	31.2	54.9	44.7	65.1
Men should be favoured							
6.4	4.0	9.4	6.5	15.8	7.8	4.4	6.4

The gap between the ideal and the real situation is conspicuous for all categories in Canada, Italy and Poland, but only for teachers and decision-makers in Romania.

* * *

The gap also exists everywhere between the present situation and the situation in five years' time. Everywhere people think that the situation of women will improve in the future. The difference is small in Poland and Romania, a little larger in Italy, and much larger in Canada, but we have to recall that in the latter two countries women have less chances of holding a position of leadership than in Poland and Romania.

There are very few significant gender differences.

* * *

In all countries, in spite of the belief that things will improve, the expectation in five years' time falls behind the ideal (but the gap is smaller in Romania than everywhere else). Women, especially decision-makers, are in general more pessimistic than their counterparts. This means that they are well aware of the resistance that they meet while trying to reach a position of parity in the area of power (19).

* * *

An important query is whether the experience of holding party offices in the past induces a different perspective in women. It does not seem so. We divided the respondents into four bands (no offices, low-, middle-, high-level offices) and within each band checked the differences between men and women and the differences between people of the same sex in different bands. All say that women are disadvantaged, but in all cases women feel that they are disadvantaged more than men.

Yet, the difference is much sharper among people with no offices: in all countries, except Italy, the differences are significant (although in Romania only suggestive). On moving up the hierarchical ladder, men become more realistic, that is, more pessimistic about the chances that women actually have of holding leadership positions on a footing of equality with men.

As far as values are concerned, practice teaches women to modify the traditional conception of the woman's role in society; as far as reality is concerned, practice teaches men to become aware of the inferior status of women.

The same result obtains in examining the impact of the experience of governmental offices. The only difference from the case just examined is that, on moving up the hierarchical ladder, men and women become even more aware of the gender discrimination.

The next obvious question is to what extent people who see men as favoured in the actual distribution of power would like to redress the situation in a more egalitarian direction.

Table 21 shows that only in Canada and Italy do the respondents of both sexes who state that men are favoured also say that there should be more women in positions of leadership. In Poland only women do. In Romania there is no significant correlation between the two variables for both men and women.

Table 21 Correlations between Ideal and Real Chances for Women of Having Access to Leadership Positions

Canada		Italy		Poland		Romania	
M	F	M	F	M	F	M	F
-.24*	-.09**	-.19*	-.24*	-.04	-.12*	-.02	.03

*$p \leq .01$; ** $.05 > p > .01$

While in Romania the majority of both men (57.9%) and women (55.8%) answer that the sexes are treated equally, that is not the case in Poland. There the majority of both men and women state that men are favoured, but men do not like the idea of having more women in positions of leadership.

The case of Romanian women deserves comment. While the majority of them (65.2%) state that there should be more women in leadership positions, the lack of correlation shows that there are women who state that the sexes are treated equally and at the same time state that men should be favoured!

Men's resistance to a redistribution of power is present everywhere, and it is stronger in Poland and Romania than in Canada and Italy. This may be owing to the fact that, as we saw at the beginning of this paragraph, women have made more inroads in the power structure in the former countries than in the latter. The more they threaten the most jealously guarded monopoly that men have, the harder the barrier becomes.

11 Conclusion

This chapter has shown reasonably convincingly that women are not apathetic and that the traditional values they have absorbed about the marginal role of women in public life tend to vanish if women are exposed to the experience of holding power. It is not so much the system, whether capitalist or socialist, that really matters but rather political participation and political concern. From this point of view, in opposition to a widespread belief that we too shared at the beginning of our study, men and women do not make up two worlds which are basically separate from each other.

Yet, women meet a barrier: everywhere power, and especially the ultimate seat of power, is indisputably a male monopoly.

Consequently it is understandable why, in the feminist movement, a strong tendency has emerged which contends that it is necessary for women to organize themselves as women, and to devise a strategy on the specific issue of how to win leading positions. In fact, without a struggle for the adoption of radical measures in this sense, the situation is likely to perpetuate itself (Brenner and Holmstrom, 1983; Boneparth, 1982b, ch. 16; Elshtain, 1979; Kahn, 1984; Peattie and Rein, 1983, chapter 6; Rossi, 1982; Sapiro, 1984). The political implications deriving from this are obvious.

As social scientists, we can only urge those who are interested in women's studies to investigate, more thoroughly than we have been able to, the issue of women's access to leadership positions in governmental, party, trade union, business, professional, and entrepreneurial organizations.

Notes

1   Hierarchy appears to discriminate between the sexes even in a uniquely egalitarian and indeed 'communitarian' arrangement such as that of the kibbutzim (Tannenbaum et al., 1974: 115), an arrangement which seems to spring out of Karl Marx's early writings (unknown at the epoch of the foundation of the kibbutzim).

2   In 1965 Milbrath was able to cite 21 pieces of research with data drawn from nine countries to prove that statement. We could easily add another dozen in the following years. The reader may see Haavio-Mannila, 1970; Sartin, 1967; European Federation of Soroptimist Clubs, 1972.

3   See on this topic the whole of ch. 12: 'Men and women: sex-related differences in political activity' (in cooperation with G. Shabad).

4   In contrast to the women's organizations existing in all of the countries (Austria, India, Japan, the Netherlands, Nigeria, the United States, Yugoslavia) that were studied by Verba et al., (1978), who perhaps too hastily state that these organizations are non-political (1978:246), the women's movements in the countries of our study are certainly 'political', although in ways which differ from country to country. In Canada, women's organizations are mainly protest organizations, in Poland and Romania they are support organizations, in Italy they are both protest organizations and support organizations (mainly connected with the Christian Democratic Party and especially with the Communist Party). If it is questionable to maintain that, even in countries such as Canada and Italy, sex-related differences are the basis of much explicit political cleavage (also for the simple reason that in contemporary industrial societies global cleavages are very rare), there is certainly no doubt that they have been the object of much inflamed political struggle, around which parties have attempted to mobilize female political activity, looking for the support of their organizations. See Verba et al. (1978:245-251) for a discussion of the whole point of the impact of institutional forces; also Caldwell (1978).

5   Of course, radical feminists who claim that the question is not to give power (a male construction) to women but to destroy power will find our approach inappropriate. We should like to stress that, in doing research, we can deal only with what can be observed. This does not mean that such a stand is not important nor that we are insensitive to it. As a matter of fact, the results of this research may in some senses be interpreted as being in support of such a stand.

   We are aware that for different reasons it has unfortunately not been possible to include in this study some important aspects of the phenomena of participation in public life and the exercise of power, aspects such as: matters over which the offices of the respondents have jurisdiction; mechanisms of co-optation by the male élite; political alignment of the respondents; campaigning; communal activities.

6   The structure of the parties in Poland and Romania, and as far as the male component is concerned in Italy, appears to be gerontocratic.

7 The correlations between age and party seniority project, as we have seen, an image of rigidity in Poland and Romania. Such an image is confirmed by the correlations between the self-evaluation of participation and seniority. In these two countries, more than the others, people who have been in the party for a long time state also that their level of involvement is high, which is not congruent with the objective amount of participative behaviour.

8 The inspection of the differences among categories of the same sex within each country reveals that the importance of the offices held by decision-makers of both sexes ranks above the importance of the offices held by party members in the other categories, with the remarkable exception of our male respondents in Romania. In this country male decision-makers too are concentrated at the lowest level. This is, of course, a result of the design of the sample: we randomly selected male decision-makers from the organization and the level within it where female decision-makers were found, following the specifications indicated in the Introduction. If female decision-makers' offices, as in the case of Romania, are of a low level, then those of the corresponding men are of the same level. This means that in Romania not only are there no women in high positions of power in the country, at least none agreeing to be interviewed, but also men of corresponding importance do not generally hold high-level offices in the party.

9 These data lend themselves to another remark. The correlations concerning men in Poland and Romania (and also women in Poland) are much stronger than the corresponding correlations in Canada and Italy. All differences are significant. In other words, there is once more a hint at the centralized character of the party in Poland and Romania with respect to the party in Italy and especially in Canada.

The comparison between Canada and Italy is also interesting. In both countries power viscidity is higher for women than for men, though in Italy it is much higher (also for men) than in Canada.

10 The monolithic nature of the party in Poland and Romania is again demonstrated by the fact that the correlations are much stronger in these countries than the others.

11 As far as Italian women in management are concerned, these findings are confirmed by a recent investigation (CRORA, 1987). About 60% of women managers are married and only 28% are single; about 53% have at least one child. The inspection of civil status by age shows that the percentage of managers who are married is higher among the younger than the older women. This is further evidence that the traditional antagonism between family and career is beginning to wane. The same result is conveyed by the reaction to the statement 'Becoming a manager negatively influences the woman's role in the family'. This is held to be a false statement. Besides, the distribution of civil status by hierarchical level shows a substantial homogeneity between single and married women.

These findings tally with those that emerged from similar research in the UK and USA (Powell, 1988). It is reasonable to assume that the picture is not different in Canada.

12 The questionnaire used in this research, prepared in 1976, was frozen after the pre-test in 1978, before the publication of this book. However, we found in it a clear formulation of what we ourselves had in mind and so adopted it.

13 Intercepts of affiliated respondents that are much higher in Canada and especially in Italy than in the other two countries do not mean that to be a party member in Canada and Italy increases the chances of holding more important governmental offices in comparison with being a party member in Poland and Romania. There is a lack of comparable samples in terms of the importance of the offices held.

14 Another exception concerns Italy, where we do not find the gap between affiliated men and women in the framework of the restrictive system that we had predicted. Being in the party has practically the same impact for both sexes.

15 The picture is quite different when we consider the impact of the party and the social class of origin on non-governmental offices. We summarize the findings in Table 22 but will not pause to comment upon them. This is not only for brevity's sake but also because these offices are so heterogeneous that it is doubtful whether this kind of analysis is relevant.

Table 22   System Found

	M	F
Canada	Additive	Additive
Italy	Dominant	Dominant
Poland	Dominant	Withholding
Romania	Dominant	Withholding

Let us just note the recurring exclusion of the unaffiliated, except in Canada, and the fact that the system has an anti-elitist impact on women in Poland and Romania. In the latter country, the intercepts for affiliated women are about the same as for unaffiliated women and furthermore the gradient is negative.

16 To gauge this issue, we asked the question: 'If you are a member or actively participate in political or voluntary associations do you feel you succeed in convincing the others of your point of view?' The scores ranged from 1 = 'always or almost always' to 4 = 'never'.

17 To explore this issue further, we asked the following questions:

'If you could, would you like to participate more than you actually do in:
(a) A political party?
(a) A trade union?
(a) A feminist or women's association?
(a) Other voluntary associations?'
and

'If you actually do not hold any public or party office, would you like to be elected or appointed to one?'

The results imply that the general tendency is to be content with the actual level, but that men are significantly more eager than women to participate and hold offices. Yet, if we restrict an analysis to party members, women show a higher inclination to become involved in both kinds of activities.

Education exerts an influence, especially among women, while social class does not.

18 Blue-collar workers of both sexes in Canada and Italy, and male decision-makers and teachers in Poland and Romania are more conservative than all other categories.

Decision-makers of both sexes appear more egalitarian than the other categories in Canada and Italy.

19 Decision-makers of both sexes are more pessimistic than all other categories. Blue-collar workers tend to be the most optimistic, except female blue-collar workers in Canada.

CONCLUSION

The principal aim of this research has been to discover factors that facilitate women's access to power, as well as factors that hamper such advance. Office-holding in governmental organizations and more importantly in political parties is the prime measure used.

We knew in advance that in all four countries of our sample women are disadvantaged in this respect.

The design of our research, based on a comparison between male and female behaviour, attitudes, and perceptions, has allowed us to escape from the basic limitation of many other studies of this type. These are concerned only with women, leaving the world of men unexplored and thereby helping to keep alive many stereotypes about gender differences. The underlying assumption in such studies is that men are different from, even opposite to, women.

This belief, which is widely held by sociologists and political scientists, and even by some feminists, creates the notion that the human world is made up of two separate sub-worlds and this notion is commonly taken to be a self-evident truth. Our study proves that it is, in reality, a prejudice.

First of all, whether in terms of behaviour or attitude, sex does not in an extreme way differentiate between men and women, irrespective of such delicate topics as female nature, gender parity in the ideal division of household chores, work, or politics. A difference exists in the expected direction but to look upon this difference as a dichotomy is an ideological exaggeration which only perpetuates the notion of "natural" spheres.

In reality, the categories in the sample, which correspond to socio-occupational layers in society, play a much more fundamental role than sex. Men and women within each category resemble one another much more closely than men resemble men and women resemble women in different categories. This is particularly true for decision-makers.

We had formulated the hypothesis that the more educated people are, the more easily they accept non-traditional approaches to women's roles in society. Contrary to our expectations, however, the respondents' behaviours, perceptions and attitudes are not strongly correlated with education: this is further evidence that the socialization process is dominated by the male culture (1).

Another stereotype is that socialist and capitalist countries present two profoundly different, even divergent, constellations of behaviour, perception and attitude concerning gender parity. The situation is much more complicated, however, and the demarcation is at best extremely blurred. As a rule, we observe a continuum of patterns that places Canada at one extreme and Romania at the other, while Italy and Poland alternate between the second and third places.

Some differences, however, can be linked to the specific political features of the four countries. For instance, the positive perception of the attempt by the government and/or trade unions to equalize women's and men's socio-economic conditions is much more pronounced in Poland and Romania than in the other two countries. We interpret this finding as an effect of both a policy of full employment, which puts pressure on women to work outside the home, and of the egalitarian ethos prevailing in both socialist countries.

Another finding that is linked to the political system concerns membership in trade unions, which in Poland (at the time of our research) and Romania is automatically linked to employment. But this very fact curtails real participation in terms of free time devoted to the union, frequency of taking the floor in union meetings, and office-holding in the union. A very different picture prevails in Canada and Italy.

Attitudes to work are another example. Romanians in particular, but also Poles, show a higher pro-work orientation than Canadians and Italians. This, too, may be seen as a product of the ruling ideology.

We also wondered to what extent the acceptance of the traditional stereotype about female nature and traditional ideas about the division of household labour are correlated with the political system. While the official ideology in Poland and Romania does not advocate these traditional views, some of these views are more widespread in the two socialist countries than in Canada and Italy. In Poland and Romania there is no real mobilization over these issues, which remain frozen among the many other egalitarian and progressive issues that make up the official ideology. On the other hand, in Canada and Italy governments, parties and trade unions deal only to a moderate extent with such problems and the situation is strongly affected by feminist movements, for which the traditional patterns are exclusive targets.

Other factors, however, cannot be overlooked. One of the most important is the level of socio-economic development. Before World War II, both Romania and Poland were mainly agricultural countries. A strong peasant culture predominated there, while industrialization and urbanization were already widespread in the other two countries. After the war, both Romania and Poland underwent rapid modernization, which radically altered their structures, but, as we well know, personal values lag behind social and economic transformations. It does not come as a surprise, therefore, to find a frequently awkward mixture of old and modern cultural patterns in the two countries.

Although we found that the discriminating power of religion over gender differences is not as overwhelming as might have been expected, it still plays a significant role. We should, however, underline that religious attachment has different meanings in different countries. For this purpose, it may be helpful to distinguish three dimensions of the problem: believers v. non-believers, practising v. non-practising individuals, and people who simply practise v. people who extend their religious commitment to organized political action. While we did not deal with the last dimension, which would have required a study in itself, we know from our experience that, especially in Italy and Poland, this combination is a diffused reality and that it tends to prevent progress towards gender parity.

Our findings also shattered another stereotype: the "woman = private", "man = public" dichotomy, according to which women are secluded at home, taking care of their families, while men are active in business, politics, culture, etc. We raise the following questions. Where are such women who stay totally out of public life? Where are such men who ignore the family? In which society do they constitute a large part of the population, if not a majority? They are certainly not in the countries of our sample and we do not believe that those countries are exceptional in any way.

Moreover, family activities, the domain of women which is more or less scornfully called "private experience", deal with basic processes which are relevant to public life, such as socialization in general, political socialization in particular, and redistribution of economic resources.

Nowadays generations of women have experienced work and public life outside the family. It would be strange indeed if these experiences had not influenced their expectations, at least as much as if we assumed that their values had totally changed. Present-day women tend to live in a net of contradictory forces. It would be naïve to think that their public experiences leave their home experiences unaffected or that the opposite does not occur.

An inspection of the reasons why people turn down promotions and/or discontinue work shows that men too are "private", if by that we mean that family considerations exert an influence in determining the course of one's career. Also, the results we obtained about readiness to protest and the desire to continue working outside the home suggest the conclusion that women cannot be considered to be merely "private".

Our main finding is that the degree of access to power is not determined by differences of behaviour, perception and attitude. The barrier confronting women in this area seems to lie in the *modus operandi* of the interconnected male-controlled structures that dominate society through a network of power relations. Women, by and large, know little about the functioning of these organizations. Even if they are promoted to leadership positions, they have not accumulated enough knowledge about the rules of the game, and so do not play it.

* * *

Multivariate analysis (presented in Appendix B) allows us to specify better the "barrier" theory about gender differences in public participation. We recall that our analysis is based on two separate types of latent dimensions or factors. First, we measure the degree of participation and power of each individual by means of factorial scores which are computed on the basis of several items related to public participation. Second, each individual is classified according to his/her score by a factor which can be denominated potential disposition to power, mediated by closeness or openness towards society and public life, the determination of which is linked to a set of variables concerning attitudes and opinions about some relevant social and political issues. In this framework, by taking into account other variables (such as sex, country, category, work), we have been able to cast more light on the "barrier" model, as this is presented in chapter 5.

An initial barrier has been identified at the lowest level of power and participation. "Work" is the variable that mainly discriminates between males and females at this level.

A second barrier is at the highest level of power. Here, the discriminating variables are the "potential disposition to power", on one side, and the personal curriculum, on the other. We have also verified that this distinction interacts with the social system (capitalist v. socialist).

Within the group of persons who are located at low power levels, the gap between males and females which shows up among people out of work is bridged among working people. Since the gap is larger in the socialist countries, we argue that a greater importance is attached to "work", in terms of power, in these as compared with capitalist countries. This statement holds true with particular reference to the generation which was the object of our investigation. On the other hand, if we look at the highest levels of power, the gap between males and females is bridged, provided that a woman not only scores high on the factor that we call "potential disposition to power" but also is able to present a distinguished "personal curriculum". Thus, within the group of people located at a medium/high level of power, the above mentioned variables act as equalizing factors. Since the discrimination, in that group, is stronger in the capitalist countries, we argue that "disposition to power" and "personal curriculum" play a more important role in the capitalist system as compared with the socialist system.

Along with the above-mentioned "barriers", a major role with respect to access to power is played by some key organizations. In the first place, party membership and activity seem to act as a filter for achieving a higher degree of participation and power, especially in governmental and public offices. Indeed, if we examine a group of people characterized by the same social background and opportunities, we see that, on average, party members are located at a higher level of power vis-à-vis the remaining persons in the group. This holds true in both social systems. In this connection, at a given level of power, no gender differences exist as to the role of the organization in the individual's career. A similar filtering role is played, at the highest levels of power, by women's organizations and cultural associations.

The social system as such seems also to have an influence on the degree of public participation, particularly in the range "medium to high". The access to this band of public participation turns out to be easier for working people (white- and blue-collar workers, and teachers) in the socialist countries than in the capitalist countries. This holds true for both females and males. However, at the highest level of power where the barrier effect takes place, the capitalist system seems to benefit the women who, in that system, score even higher than men, once they have overcome the barrier.

This finding partly contradicts the traditional pattern which assigns to males a consistently higher degree of participation and power as compared to women.

* * *

As we have just said, there is a basic tenet concerning women: they belong to the sphere of the private, that is, to the sphere which is "deprived" of public interest (etymologically, in Greek private means "isolated": the stem is the same as "idiot"). The findings of this research prove abundantly that the tenet is an ideological shibboleth, certainly functional to a conservative outlook, vastly diffused, certainly among women, but without any root in reality (Rogers, 1978: 152-153).

In reality, as already stressed, most women are active in public life. Even if we define public life in the traditionally narrow way that excludes the family from it, we find women active not only in the economic sphere outside the home but also in that part of public life which has traditionally been considered as the realm of men: namely, political life (Baxter and Lansing, 1983: 46; Sapiro, 1984: 189).

Among the myths that have been dispelled by this research is the central one that portrays women as passive and men as active. We have proved that women are not less interested than men in vital issues concerning public life.

The findings of this research go beyond mere critical analysis; they are loaded rather with positive suggestions. A principal suggestion is that women will never achieve parity with men as long as they do not consider their gender identity as a public subject in its own right.

This research has also dispelled the view that socialism (at least of the kind that we know) is a prerequisite for women's emancipation. Leaving aside the question of the desirability and feasibility of socialism, it is clear that women make more progress in countries where a feminist movement is active than in countries where the problem of gender parity is subsumed under the general problem of equality. Obviously, living in a country where the ruling ideology stresses equality makes a difference for women but our findings show abundantly that socialism by itself does not help women to overcome the barrier (2).

From the point of view of women as public subjects, the speculation concerning the family appears to be particularly important (Elshtain, 1981). We still have a very scanty knowledge of human nature, and especially of what is specific to men's and women's natures. Unless we have more knowledge on these matters, neither a fully-fledged theory about women's political participation nor a mature political theory can be adequately developed.

Yet, it seems proper to concentrate on what is a crucial reality in life for both men and women: the family, about which women have accumulated more experience than men. Two excesses must be avoided: first, ignoring the family as a subject for public life and considering it outside politics; second, reducing women's experience to the family as if it were their only world.

The family is here to stay. Rather than becoming trapped in the absurd dream of its elimination, women must require their partners to be prepared to share everything on a footing of equality (Sapiro, 1984: 183-193). But this is not enough: they must become aware of the social, economic and political problems connected with their daily experiences in the family --- problems they have to face personally.

The family is and must remain the core of private life. The personal cannot become political, except at the risk of tragic distortions (3). Should this demarcation be violated, the totalitarian system, whatever its label, that would ensue, would certainly not favour the cause of women. However, this does not mean that the family is not connected with social, economic and political problems, and that it is consequently not relevant to the polity. A faint consciousness of this appears in the claim of some streams of feminist thinking that housewives' work should be paid and rewarded like work outside the home.

Although it has often been said that the family is the cell of society, no political theory has been elaborated on this assumption. This may not be accidental, since the whole history of political thought has been written by men.

Rejecting utopian proposals, which border at times on mental illness and at times on fascist attitudes, women have before them the opportunity of intervening in the relationship between the family and the public domain. Health, pensions, and welfare programmes are some of the areas which come immediately to the mind as directly of concern to women. If a basic principle of democracy is that people must exert control on what affects their life directly, then women must devise new modes of participation in public life in order to control these areas, in the same way that workers have found in the unions a channel to express their specific claims as workers.

Our research has shown that family commitments and children do not represent such great obstacles for women as are commonly imagined, to the point of eliminating any possibility of participation in public life. Resocializing men to perform domestic chores is not, therefore, mainly a question of time-saving but of re-defining women's identities and moral dignity.

These are just some possible areas of intervention for women. Women will soon discover that it is not possible to deal adequately with health, pensions and welfare programmes without exerting some influence in other areas, ranging from the apparently very remote area of international affairs to the clearly more immediate one of economic policy. In handling these problems, which are typical of all advanced societies, a new style and a new perspective could be developed by women (Baxter and Lansing, 1983: 53-56), if they do not submit to male-dominated organizations, incapable of changing the traditionally power-centred approaches to politics.

We do not like dichotomies, but there is some truth in the statements that public power has historically been male-dominated and that its main characteristic is to serve the interests of those who hold it rather than the interests of the common people. We believe there is some truth in maintaining that the exercise of power would change, were women allowed to manage it on a mass scale. Of course, we have sensational examples to the contrary but these examples are merely individual cases and do not represent a mass phenomenon.

This research has shown that male power-holders do not allow women such forms of supreme and decisive participation. The usefulness of our sampling lay exactly in the opportunity that it gave us to test whether women themselves are responsible for their absence from the top positions.

Of course, we knew in advance that women do not hold key political positions. Had we selected the 150 most important men in the power structure of each country, we would have had difficulty in finding 150 equivalent women in the same organizations, not to mention the difficulties we would have had in polling them randomly.

Women are active in the public sphere but in general are not sufficiently aware of being so. The ideology is that of the dominant sex. Those women who try to follow the traditionally male path of political activity inevitably find themselves blocked on the way to the top.

The temptation to keep aloof from politics is necessarily strong not only for women but also for all strata of the population who see that access to leadership is barred to them and that politics in practice is dramatically blind to the common good. Yet, women must not withdraw. By expanding their participation, they can change the functioning of parties and governmental structures. At the same time, they need an organization of their own to create a network to traverse the various parties and governmental structures and to mobilize people of both sexes around issues that concern women directly.

While women should assert their rights and experiences as women, it would be stupid and immoral if they conceived of themselves as a race apart. As previously noted, we do not know in which ways the natures of men and women diverge, and it is certainly important to do more research in that direction. However, the vast majority of men share the same goal as almost all women: to give priority in politics to the principles of nurture and respect for human dignity rather than to power itself, whether economic, political or ideological.

The most far-reaching transformation in the whole history of mankind is taking place under our eyes. This research documents not only the transformation but also the fact that people are not yet fully aware of it.

Nobody knows how long this process will take nor how much more of a struggle that it will entail, nor how many more changes that it will produce at all levels of society. Indeed, nobody knows whether a counter-reaction will burst forth. The future of the process depends not only on women but also on men, on their broad-mindedness, and on their readiness to become aware of and to eradicate the most ancient and deeply ingrained discrimination that has characterized human history until today.

Notes

1 Another hypothesis, kindly suggested by Judith Buber Agassi, is that there may be a counterbalancing influence to the usually more egalitarian influence of higher education, which originates in the occupational culture of the middle-class jobs that more educated people tend to secure.

2 The failure of socialism to achieve gender parity does not necessarily lead to taking a stand against socialism. The socialist feminists, in fact, tried to show the need to merge the two approaches, presenting them as complementary to each other (Kuhn and Wolpe, 1978; Eisenstein, 1979a).

3 It is necessary, though, to emphasize that the slogan 'The personal is political' was not intended by all feminists as advocating the abolition of the family. Very often the slogan was used to call attention to the fact that certain crucial experiences of women, such as wife battering, sexual harassment, child molesting, lack of sexual satisfaction, and non-availability of contraceptives or abortion, which were all considered private matters, are and should be political issues.

GENERAL
APPENDICES

APPENDIX A

BASIC INFORMATION CONCERNING WOMEN IN THE FOUR COUNTRIES

1 Canada

1.1 *Background*

In spite of its immense territory, more than 82% of the population lives in urban centres. The tertiary is the largest economic sector and women are mainly employed in it.

Although gender parity was officially decreed after World War II, a 1970 report (*Report of the Royal Commission on the Status of Women*) stigmatized the existence of several forms of discrimination against women, especially in the government.

1.2 *Family Structure*

The multi-family household is in clear decline (1951: 6.7%; 1978: 1.2%), while the non-family households (mainly widows and divorcees) have more than doubled (1951: 11%; 1978: 24.8%).

It is interesting to note the consistent growth of one-parent families (1976: 9.8%; 1981: 11.3%). The vast majority of them (83%) are composed of women. The phenomenon is better understood if we compare the situation in 1971 (477,525 cases) and in 1976 (559,330): an increment of 17%, while the traditional nuclear family increased in the same period by 13%.

Since 1965 a decline in married women and an increase in widowed and divorced women has taken place. This is owing not only to women's greater life expectancy but also to a growing reluctance to remarry (although about one-fifth of all marriages are re-marriages). The divorces in 1978 (57,155) were 2.5 per thousand marriages. Before the *Divorce Act* of 1968, the only ground for divorce was adultery. The new Act recognizes not only mental and physical cruelty, rape, alcoholism, and drug addiction but also marriage breakdown. In 1978 twice as many divorces were granted to female as to male petitioners: 66% v. 34%. With age, the number of female petitioners contracts: this not only reflects the decline in chances for older women to remarry but also shows their dependence on the husbands.

The fertility rate, which following the 1940-50 baby boom has been declining since 1961, is of 15.5 births per thousand. The number of children per family has changed from 1.9 in 1961 to 1.5 in 1981. Childless marriages are increasing in numbers.

An impressive phenomenon is the increment in unwed mothers, who more than doubled between 1960 (20,413; 4.3% of total births) and 1979 (42,311; 11.9% of the total births).

The largest increase in female labour has been observed among young mothers (the percentage of employed mothers with children under 5 increased from 34.7% in 1975 to 47.2% in 1981, and with children aged 6 to 15 from 48% to 61%) but the number of day-care centres is inadequate. They grew from 700 in 1971 to 2,000 in 1971, catering for 81,000 children (about 5% of the children under 3, 16% of the children between 3 and 5, less than 1% of the children over 6).

Contraception is legal as is abortion, although this is not easily obtainable, especially in the smaller centres. In 1980, 65,053 abortions took place (16.2 per thousand women aged 15-44), of which 28.3% were on women under 20.

1.3 *Education*

The number of university students more than doubled in 1977 (367,000 = 12% of the population aged 18 to 24) with respect to 1960. Women, who passed from 26% of undergraduates in 1961 to 46% in 1980, remained a minority at the graduate level (36% in 1980), although their percentage had more than doubled since 1961 (16%).

But the gender difference becomes evident when we examine the areas in which women enrol. Their numbers are very high in the "expressive" faculties and in the caring professions but the gap is narrowing, especially in veterinary fields, optometry, agriculture, commerce and forestry.

The socialization that is received at home and in school as to sex roles is traditional. Such stereotypes are perpetuated by the mass-media and religion.

1.4 *Labour*

The seventies witnessed an impressive growth of the labour force (3.4 million units; 39%), compared to an increase of 12.9% of the total population. Such a growth was caused by the baby boom and by women. In 1979, 6.7 million men and 4.2 million women were employed. The proportion of women increased tremendously (1951: 24.1%; 1979:

48.9%), especially for women aged over 25 but also for the group below that age (the opposite trend occurs for men).

Even more important is the fact that the increase among women was especially high for married women between 25 and 44. In the same decade, their number doubled (from 900,000 to 1,800,000) and their participation rate jumped from 40% to 62%! It was 10% in 1931.

It is the mothers aged 35 to 44 with children under 6 (!) who share the largest increase in participation, followed by the mothers aged under 34 with children under 6.

Female labour force participation is strongly influenced by educational attainment: 70.7% of women with a university degree are employed (1979), followed by 52.2% with a high school degree, while below high school the rate drops to 26.4%.

In 1979, 8.8% (386,000) women were unemployed as against 6.6% of men. One-third of them are re-entrants into the labour force. Of the 138,000 women who resumed working in 1979, almost 46% had been out of it for more than 1 year.

From the quantitative point of view the Canadian picture may be satisfactory for women but a different conclusion must be reached when we examine the occupational structure. As in pre-war times, women concentrate in the jobs of low prestige and poor self-realization: in 1980, 63.1% of all employed women were to be found in the clerical, service and sale sectors.

If we inspect more closely the clerical workers (78.2% of whom are women), we discover that women concentrate in the "weak" fields (such as agriculture, trade, hospitals, shops, banks). In the utility sector (construction, transport, processing), where jobs are more interesting and better paid, the majority is male.

Almost all managers, also in firms which employ mostly women, are men.

In each occupation, women's wages are lower. Even if education, occupation, number of hours worked per year, career continuity and skills are held under control, women's wages amount to less than 70% of men's (1967: 55%; 1979: 63%).

In 1979, about a quarter of the work done by women is part-time. For men, it represents barely 6%. Of all women with a part-time job, 63.4% cite personal and/or family reasons for it; less than 1% of all men with a part-time job give such reasons. On the contrary, 56.1% of all *married* men allege school as a reason for it; 1.3% of women give such a reason. The difference is astounding.

One consequence for women of being in the lower occupational layers is that they receive lower fringe benefits. Private pension-plans are rarer for them. For instance, in commerce 41.4% of all employees are women but only 11% of them (v. 15% of men) are covered by a pension scheme. In the service sector (60.3% women), only 22% can look forward to a pension-plan. Private pension-plans are common in well-paid industries, such as oil and manufacturing, where almost no woman is found. This also shows the unions' lack of concern for women.

In any case, women, even if they are covered by a pension-plan, are paid less and so receive less than men when they retire.

It is superfluous to say that pensions do not cover women's contributions to the household and to children, either in the positive or negative sense. (If women give up extra-domestic work to take care of the family, they receive a lower pension.)

1.5 *Public Organizations*

While the Canadian picture in general presents indisputable signs of deep changes in favour of women, the plight of women in public life is still traditional.

The number of employees in the public administration amounts (1980) to 885,000 (7.6% of the total labour force). Women represent 34.7% of them, concentrated mostly at the federal level (145,000). A closer look reveals that they are found mainly in the support occupations, with very few at the higher levels of hierarchy. The consequences, in terms of salary and fringe benefits, are the same as we have seen for the private sector.

In 1978, 3.3 million Canadians were trade-union members (31.3% of the labour force). Of them, only a quarter (835,263) were women (19.7% of the female labour force v. 37.7% of the male labour force). But, in spite of concentrating in sectors with a short history of union activity (services, trade, public administration), women's membership is growing faster than men's (in the last decade, 160% v. 40%). Nevertheless, women are poorly represented at the top. In 1970, 9.8% of the unions' executive boards were women, in 1978, 17.5%. The gap between the two increments is beyond any comment.

In politics also, women (52% of the voters) are heavily absent. In 1979, they represented 4.6% of all members of Parliament, which is little enough but still better than ten years earlier, when they did not amount to 1%. The picture looks a little less grim at the lower (provincial, local) levels.

Although it is often said that the "feminist movement" has been very active in the last two decades, it is far from clear what that expression means. In reality, it is a mosaic of groups of different and often divergent inspiration, which moreover must fight with ethical and regional issues. Two streams may be recognized: a reformist one that identifies (1972) with the National Action Committee, which was born in the wake of the above-mentioned *Report of the Royal Commission* and gathered around itself 172 groups; and a cluster of groups dealing with specific issues such as rape, day-care centres, and wife battering. In 1972 a movement (Women Unite!) for revolutionary action was formed and in 1979 the Feminist Party was created, both of them doomed to failure.

1.6 *Conclusion*

Gender equality in Canada is still a remote goal. The strong increment in women in the labour force and in higher learning, which is certainly a relevant step forward, has not produced a radical change in their status. As a matter of fact, it is possible to argue that it has furthered their oppression, inasmuch as it has merely generalized the double role for them. Their absence in the public sphere of decision-making corroborates this conclusion.

2 Italy

2.1 *Background*

The post-war Italian economy witnessed an unprecedented growth, second only to that of Western Germany. Between 1949 and 1969, industrial production increased five times.

The definitive entrance of Italy among the industrialized countries, which started to take shape in that period, was the result of an intensive exploitation of the "weak" layers of the population, in the first place of women and southerners.

Such a process was made possible by the existence of capital in the north and a high rate of unemployment in the south, which in 1961 still amounted to 1,500,000 units, in spite of the massive stream of emigrants, northwards or abroad, in the decade 1951-61 (1,780,000).

The economy expanded in response to a growing international demand. Such expansion could not directly benefit the average population, which did not possess a buying power adequate for that kind of production. The so-called "Italian miracle" was more apparent than real.

The gap between wealthy and poor people and north and south increased. The economic structure became dualistic: on one side, the export economy, with an advanced technology, which resulted in a small increase in employment; on the other, the economy geared to the internal market, with a relatively backward technology, which absorbed a great deal of available labour, but at low wages.

The standard of living remained generally rather modest, because the increment in the consumption of durable goods, which was restricted to the upper-middle classes, was not matched by an equivalent increase in the consumption of goods of a more basic nature and by the expansion of public expenditure (low throughout the 1960s).

Investments concentrated in the already developed north-west. Cheap labour from the south, especially from rural areas, flowed in in large numbers (about one million in 1961-71). This was made up mainly of unskilled male family heads, who were leaving behind wife and children in the hope of coming back and buying some land.

In 1950, more than 50% of the labour force in the South was employed in agriculture, a backward sector because of a poor commercialization network and a lack of entrepreneurship. The departure of men left it largely in the hands of women.

A consequence of the intensive industrialization was the growth of urban centres. In 1971, 23,000,000 people were living in 32 metropolitan areas, with an increase of about 7,000,000 units in comparison with 1951: i.e. the entire demographic increment. These cities were largely deprived of social services and were often surrounded by slums.

Women were forced into their traditional tasks. This explains why they did not enter the labour market as massively as elsewhere.

The situation worsened in the 1960s because of the lack of competitiveness of Italian industry. Unemployment rose, but the unions' strength prevented the employers from benefiting from it. The restructuring of production took place largely in the direction of cottage industries. The 1970s witnessed a tremendous increase, especially in north-east and central Italy, of small units employing a large quantity of poorly paid and unprotected female labour.

In line with the philosophy of the Catholic Church, politically embodied in the ruling Christian Democratic Party, the role of housewife emerged reinforced. Some important victories for women, such as the new family law, divorce, and abortion, did not radically alter their traditional status in society.

2.2 *Family Structure*

The size of the family has decreased from 3.97 in 1951 to 3.0 in 1981.

Extended, mainly rural, families have drastically decreased (from 22.5% in 1951 to 2.6% in 1981). Nuclear families have also decreased from 55.6% in 1951 to 52.5% in 1981, while childless families passed from 11.3% in 1951 to 17% in 1981.

The number of marriages decreased (1971: 403,406; 1978: 336,417), while that of separation increased (1971: 17,023; 1978-79: 35,992).

The number of re-marriages dwindled: from 18,510 in 1974 to 12,803 in 1978. Since the new family law (1975) removed any practical difference between married and non-married couples (concerning children also) many people, after the first marriage, do not care to marry again. This may also explain why the number of divorces is tending to decline, while that of separations is increasing (more on the initiative of women than men).

Fertility rates have decreased. At the time of our research, married women had an average of about 2 children in comparison with 3.3 in the mid-40s.

The number of unwed mothers was 25,689.

Domestic labour in 1976 amounted to 929,555 units, who were covered by social security, and at least 200,000 illegal individuals, most of whom came from Third World countries.

The number of day-care centres for children under 3 is low. In 1975 there were 970, of which 855 were public, and accommodated 74,174 children.

Kindergartens for children between 3 and 5 exist more in the north (16,359 for 1,099,103 pupils) than in the south (13,600 for 753,322 pupils). In 1978-79 693,796 children attended public, and 1,160,423 children attended private, kindergartens (75% of all children in that age group). The majority of kindergartens (71.9% of the public and 89.3% of the private) supply meals. Most of the private kindergartens are run by religious orders.

Contraception and abortion are free. In 1978 727 family centres were in operation, 72% of which were in north and central Italy.

2.3 *Education*

The level is in general low. In 1981, 3.8% of women (2.6% over 55) and 2.2% of men (1.4% over 55) were illiterate, and 20% of women (8% over 55) and 16.2% of men (5.2% over 55) had not completed elementary education. If we add those who completed elementary education, we reach the figure of 65.9% of women and 57.9% of men having such a poor background. University graduates represent 3.5% of men and 2% of women, who concentrate mainly in the faculties that give access to teaching. Agriculture and veterinary posts, which we saw expanding in Canada, do not attract even 1% of women in Italy but there is an increase in women in medicine and law. All in all, the picture demonstrates the persistence of gender discrimination.

The fact that high school and especially elementary school teachers are mostly women perpetuates the stereotype that there are jobs for men and jobs for women. Traditional socialization is reinforced by the instructional material, especially at elementary school level, which tends to present women as being endowed with integrative traits and men with instrumental traits. However, the influence of political parties and other organizations with an ideological impact is rather strong among teachers. This fact, coupled with the diffusion of progressive textbooks especially for secondary high schools, counterbalances to some extent the traditional push.

2.4 *Labour*

In 1978, the official male labour force amounted to 75.5% of the total force (22,372,000; 39.9% of the population).

The female labour force increased in industry (1951: 5,803,000; 1978: 7,520,000) and the tertiary sector (1951: 5,250,000; 1978: 9,764,000) but decreased markedly in agriculture (1951: 8,640,000; 1978: 2,919,000), mainly because many small family farms underwent a crisis which in 1979 expelled 1,159,000 women from employment.

Female labour force participation contracts at about 30 years of age. Children make a difference: 37% of active women are childless wives. "Family reasons" as a cause for not working is alleged by 1% of men and 56% of women. The percentage of married women employed in agriculture (84.9%) is much higher than in industry (61.9%), while this is less true for men (79.1% v. 74.7%).

The percentage of women who work for a pay at home is high. (The official figure is 17.9% of all female labour, i.e. 1,270,000 units, but the real figure is estimated at about 3,500,000.) However, such a form of segregation depends not so much on family reasons but on the kind of labour supply. A high percentage of men (12.1% of all male labour = 1,703,801 units) also work at home, but they are professionals or craftsmen.

Women's wages (manual and non-manual workers) are about 80% of men's. The gap is larger for non-manual workers, especially in the chemical, textile, leather goods, wooden furniture, and paper industries. This is owing not only to lower seniority, less overtime, and a higher rate of absenteeism but also to the fact that women hold fewer qualified jobs.

In all sectors, but especially in agriculture and the tertiary sector, occasional or seasonal work is more common among women (12.1%) than men (6%). The same is true for part-time work.

2.5 *Public Organizations*

The picture concerning women's participation in public life is slightly better in Italy than in Canada with regard to politics, but similar as to the rest.

Compared with 5,319 male officials in public administration, there are only 285 women. In elementary schools, where women make up 77.34% of all employees, only 28.12% of principals are female. In the judiciary, there are 399 women compared with 7,331 men.

Women represent 14.75% of entrepreneurs or managers (but in banking female managers make up 0.04% and in commerce 3%).

Women form 11% of journalists but none of them is the editor of a newspaper or a weekly (except fashion and entertainment periodicals).

In the national broadcasting system, 26% of the employees are women, but 95.8% of the executive positions are held by men.

In higher education, there are 7,558 women teachers compared with 15,958 male teachers, but women concentrate at the lower levels of the academic hierarchy.

In the political parties there is a solid presence of women (a little below 50% of the 2,400,000 affiliated men, with the exception of youth organizations, where the percentage of women is about two-thirds that of men), but it is rare to find women at the top.

Very few women among those elected in the Parliament (9%) or the Senate (4%) play a significant role in the government.

The percentage of women who are affiliated to a union is higher in the left-wing Confederazione Generale Italiana del Lavoro (1,500,000 women v. 4,500,000 men) than in the other federations. Although it is possible to find women on the boards of single unions, it is rare to find them in the central organizations.

The feminist movement has been very active. As in Canada, it is a mosaic of groups, many of which campaigned for specific issues, while others carried on consciousness-raising activities. It is important to realize that the Italian feminist movement operates in a highly politicized milieu. It must take into account the powerful feminine organizations that exist within the main parties, especially the Communist and the Christian Democratic parties.

2.6 *Conclusion*

As in Canada, formal equality disguises a discriminatory situation for women in Italy. This should not conceal the fact, however, that deep changes have taken place in all spheres of life, politics included.

3 Poland

3.1 *Background*

The present situation of Poland was determined by the outcome of World War II. The generation that grew up before 1918 lived under foreign occupation. Two generations lived between 1918 and 1945 in a country which, from the socio-political point of view, was a mixture of classes partly anchored to feudal times and of conflicting political forces; from the economic point of view, it was mainly agricultural (1931: 72.6% of the population was living in the countryside). The generations born after 1945 witnessed the complex process of reconstruction along totally new principles. From the last generation there sprang up, in the year after the data for our research had been collected, the movement known as Solidarity.

Two main forces have dominated the Polish scene: the class tradition of both the aristocracy and the workers, on one side, and the Catholic Church, on the other. The intelligentsia, unlike in the West, emanated from the aristocracy and preserved its models. The Catholic Church provided a bulwark for national identity. These two facts explain why Poland has been tendentially close to the ferments that sprouted in Europe in the wake of the intellectual, political and economic revolutions of the eighteenth and nineteenth centuries .

In the struggle to preserve national identity, women played a specific role: while fathers and brothers were fighting, imprisoned or exiled, women acted as vehicles to transmit Polish culture to the newer generations.

Extra-domestic work is not a novelty for them. Even before socialism, the majority worked out in the fields or as domestic helpers and, indeed, the percentage in the industrial sector was not irrelevant (1931: 33.6% of all industrial workers).

After World War II, which modified the country territorially and led to ethnic homogeneity, Poland underwent a quick process of industrialization under the leadership of the Polish United Workers' Party and some minor allied political forces. As a consequence, in 20 years (1950-70) the urban population increased by more than 91%.

Agriculture became largely a female occupation: about one-third of all farms ended up under the management of women, large numbers of whom had been left behind in the countryside.

Equality has been stressed in all spheres of life. Gender equality, not only in work and education, as a premise to complete equality, but also in social and political life, has been almost constantly propagandized, but with varying emphasis. The creation of national systems of education, health care, and social services has also been presented as a support for it.

3.2 *Family Structure*

In 1975, 56% of families lived in urban centres. Urban families are much smaller than rural families, averaging in 1970 about 3 members. Yet, in that same year, 15% of them were still extended. In fact, 55% of people over 65 were living with their children (compared with 75% in the countryside). The percentage of one-parent families is 12% in the urban centres, 8% in the rural centres (1974).

In 1972, one-child families were 23.1%; two-child families, 35.9%; three, 19.2%; four and more, 15.9%. The difference between the urban centres and the countryside is impressive: families with four or more children make up 25.4% of rural and only 8.5% of urban families.

In 1970, of the total of single mothers (widows, divorcees) with a child under 16, the percentage of unwed mothers was 12%. It is realistic to assume that only a negligible minority of unwed mothers had a child as the result of a deliberate choice.

In 1976, 1.6 men and 2.6 women per thousand were divorced. The divorce rate is much smaller than in the West, because divorce is discouraged by the combined efforts of the Church and the government. However, it increased between 1946 and 1978 from 0.3 to 1.02 per thousand. The difference between the urban centres and the countryside is again impressive: 1.7 v. 0.4.

The fertility rate shows strong variations: 1962: 82.8 per thousand; 1969: 63; 1979: 75.6. The difference between countryside and urban centres is marked (1979: 81.6 v. 71.6).

The birth rate fell drastically for married women: in 1931 it was 6.93 per thousand; in 1972, 2.62.

Domestic help does not exist as a full-time occupation. It is done mostly as a second job, and no figures are available.

Day-care centres for children are scarce, contrary to what one might expect in a socialist country. In 1960 2.6% of children under 3 used them;

in 1979, 5.4%. The picture looks better for kindergartens: in that same year, 34% of children between 3 and 6 had access to them.

Contraception and abortion are free, but the exact relevance of them is unknown. Graduate and urban women have recourse to them more than others.

3.3 *Education*

A successful effort has been made to curtail the discrimination against women, especially in higher education: the percentage of women at university increased between 1950-51 and 1973-74, by 12.5%, and they slightly exceeded men in 1979.

The overall picture in 1979 presents 49.3% female pupils, with fewer women in vocational schools.

At university level, women concentrate in faculties that give access to teaching, but also in medicine and economics.

Government policy as to sex role socialization has varied a great deal. Immediately after the war, it stressed, for both men and women, involvement in the new political system; in the period 1949-57, the emphasis fell on the need to industrialize the country, leaving to infrastructures the traditional functions of women; in the years 1957-61, with the recession, women were requested to be primarily wives and mothers; in the period 1961-74, with the industrial growth of the country, the accent was placed on the need to buy consumer goods, and the family was exalted as a pillar of the economy. After 1974, career and family were presented by official propaganda as equally important for women.

The traditional stereotype that a woman's place is in the home has been prevalent, nevertheless, in the daily life and cultural patterns of Polish people. It can be found in printed matter, ranging from comics for children to textbooks.

3.4 *Labour*

In 1935 women represented 33.5% of the labour force (domestic helpers included). Thanks to the five-year plan, the increment of women in the labour force grew conspicuously (in 1975, 42%; in 1979, 43.2%), much more so than that of men: in the period 1955-74, the number of women increased by 235.8%, men by 152.3%.

In that same period, together with an improvement in educational level which was especially tangible for women, the occupational structure changed profoundly: new forms of work organization were introduced and the tertiary sector expanded. The number of female blue-collar workers declined and that of female white-collar workers increased, while among men the percentage of blue-collar workers was still growing, albeit marginally.

In 1979 women predominated in financial and insurance institutions, health and social welfare, education, trade, and public administration.

The number of married women with children increased: 1956, 30.3% of all women employed; 1967, a little more than 70%; 1975, 75%.

Women are beginning to enter traditionally male occupations with relative ease, although they still stay away from technical occupations in industry. One obstacle is represented by the preference shown by managers for men.

In fact, openings are reported more often for men than for women. However, the picture is changing: in the late 1960s, the jobs offered to women represented 14.65% of the declared vacancies; in 1979, 28.7%.

In general, women concentrate in the low-paid occupations, at the bottom of the hierarchical ladder. About two-thirds of the gender difference in wages is owing to the "pure advantage" of men's income over that of women. These two-thirds correspond to 38% of women's monthly wages and can be equated with a difference of 7 years in schooling before beginning work or a difference in seniority of about 30 years!

3.5 *Public Organizations*

The role of women in public administration and government is moderate. In 1977, out of 12 cabinet members only one was a woman. The number of women Members of Parliament increased from 4.1% in 1957-61 to 23% in 1965. Their presence is a little higher at the provincial and local levels.

In other branches of public administration, such as the judiciary and diplomacy, few women are found.

In higher learning too, their presence concentrates in the lower positions. In 1975, for instance, 7 women v. 77 men were appointed full professors; in 1979, 8 women v. 134 men. In 1979, 17.2% of associate professors were women. In that same year, the percentage of PhDs that were granted to women was 31.5%.

In the Academy of Sciences, out of 235 members only 8 are women.

Female membership in the Polish United Workers' Party amounted (1979) to 26.2%. Similar percentages were found in the other two minor parties, the United Peasants' Party and the Democratic Party, which are controlled by the main party. No woman is in a leadership position.

As far as trade unions are concerned, in the mid-1970s women comprised 39% of the members at factory level, 31.9% of the shop stewards, and 26% of the members of the national boards of the various unions. But when we look at the Praesidium of the Central Committee of the trade unions, we discover only 3 women out of 33 members.

It is appropriate to recall that in the socialist countries union membership is more of a formality than an act of affiliation to an organization ready to fight for workers' rights. The case of Poland in the months following our research is a good illustration of this point.

No feminist movement exists in Poland (1980). The Women's League coordinates, under the supervision of the party, 346 women's centres throughout the country, which deal mainly with family life and professional issues. There is also another organization, "Circles of Peasant Women", dealing with similar problems in the countryside.

3.6 *Conclusion*

The status of women in Poland has greatly changed in the post-war period, more as a function of the profound transformation that the country has undergone than as the result of concrete measures that are aimed at attaining gender parity. From this specific point of view, it seems that traditional stereotypes about the role of women tend to survive in the mass of the population and even influence to some extent the government's policy and the official propaganda.

4 Romania

4.1 *Background*

This paragraph suffers from lack of information. For instance, the last data concerning the family appeared in 1966.

The overall picture is characterized by the undisputed rule of the Romanian Communist Party, defined in the 1965 Constitution as "the unique leader of the state and society". Its impact is felt in all areas of life, but the role it plays in the economic field is overwhelming. In 1981, it owned directly 76.4% of all industrial companies, covering 90.6% of employees in the secondary sector; 51.8% of all commercial firms, covering 81% of employees in that sector; 30.6% of the agricultural enterprises.

The state also supervises the cooperatives which manage 60% of agricultural enterprises, 48% of commercial firms, and 24% of industrial companies.

The goal of the regime has been to build up of socialism through industrialization. In the 30 years to 1980 heavy industry increased 44-fold, light industry 17-fold.

The implementation of this goal, together with the abolition of the private ownership of land, caused an impressive flow of migrants to the urban centres. The size of the labour force employed in agriculture decreased by 55% between 1960 and 1970, while that in industry increased by 150%. The urban population passed, as a consequence, from 32% of the total population in 1960 to 50% in 1980.

Equality is stressed in all aspects of life. The sacrifices that the population has to meet in order to industrialize the country are presented as a necessary step to achieve that goal. Gender equality is exhibited as one of the areas where progress has been attained.

The rate of capital accumulation has been kept at an impressive pace: from 17% in the period 1950-60 to 26% in the next decade, to 34% in the following five years, to 36% in the period 1975-80. In the four years 1976-79 it amounted to the total wages that were paid to labour in 1978-79.

Consumption, consequently, has been kept at low levels.

4.2 *Family Structure*

The demographic policy too is subordinated to the goal of industrialization. As we will see, it sways conspicuously in the course of time.

However, the size of the family has declined (1930: 4.3; 1966: 3.2), the decline being stronger in the urban centres than in the countryside (1966: 2.9 v. 3.5). The number of one-person households increased from 5.6% in 1930 to 14.2% in 1966 and that of two-person households from 16.1% to 23.4%.

In 1966, 93% of families were nuclear. The survival of extended families is more tangible in the countryside.

Household heads were 41.9% blue-collar workers, 34.4% cooperative farmers, 14.2% white-collar workers, 4.6% independent farmers, and 2.6% cooperative craftsmen. Independent farmers and cooperative craftsmen had the highest average household size (respectively 3.5 and 3.4) and white-collar workers the lowest (2.8).

The divorce rate is much higher in the cities than in the countryside (2.4 v. 0.76 per thousand), with almost no gender difference.

The percentage of divorcees who remarry has decreased in Romania during the last two decades and such a trend is more consistent for women (1960: men, 12.5%, women, 10.4%; 1981: men, 11.2%, women, 5.5%).

Since 1966, the government's policy has been to discourage divorce. Marriage breakdown is no valid cause for divorce, which can be granted only on a fault basis. The procedure is long and costly. The rate fell from 1.94 per thousand in 1965 to 1.50 in 1981. No information is supplied about who petitions for divorce.

The fluctuations in the fertility rate are even more impressive: 1956, 89 per thousand; 1966, 55; 1967, 105; 1981, 71. They are the result of the demographic policy pursued by the government.

Although in the period 1930-48 the Romanian population increased from 14,141,000 to 15,893,000, in spite of the war and a high infant mortality, the live birth rate decreased in that same period from 34.1 to 23.9 per thousand. In the following years the tendency continued. Especially after 1957, with the liberalization of abortion (which led to the highest percentage of abortions in the world), the live birth rate dropped to very low levels (1956: 24.2 per thousand; 1966: 14.3). Such a result in a decade was the equivalent of the contraction that was observed in the 27 years preceding the liberalization of abortion. Its impact was very impressive especially in the rural areas, where the live birth rate dropped from 36.9 per thousand in 1930 to 16.1 in 1966.

We have already mentioned the strong urbanization that took place in the post-war era. In the period 1956-70, more than two million rural workers, most of them young people, moved to the towns, but the number of apartments in the urban centres was not enough. In spite of this, after 1966 the government started a pro-natalist policy that brought the live birth rate to 27.4 per thousand in the following year (although the lack of buildings forced it to decline again to 17 per thousand in 1981). The increment was impressive for all age groups (it almost doubled for the age group 40-44). Taking 1966 = 100, in 1981 it was 62.5 for the group under 19, 135.9 for the group aged 20-24, 123.8 for the group aged 25-29, 105.6 for the group aged 35-39, and 75.9 for the group aged 40-44.

The same year, 1967, witnessed a dramatic increase in still birth rates and infant mortality (respectively, 136.8% and 93%).

No data about unwed mothers are available.

No data about domestic helpers are available.

Day-care centres are few for children under 3. In 1981 only 80 per thousand (93,688) of 1,172,978 children in that age group had the opportunity of using them. The rate for children between 3 and 6 is higher, but still far from satisfactory (379 per thousand, 458,662 out of 1,208,469).

4.3 *Education*

The growth of the educational system since the end of the war has been impressive: the number of schools increased by 55%, that of teachers three times, pupils more than doubled (4,453,902 in 1981), and university students quadrupled.

In 1981-82, 70.1% of males aged 6-24 and 78% of females in the same age group were attending school. A closer inspection shows that the percentage of women decreases on moving up the educational ladder. At university level we find, for instance, 4.5% of men and 3.4% of women. However, a conspicuous progress towards gender parity in education has taken place, especially if we compare the picture in pre-war times with that of the present.

4.4 *Labour*

In 1965 the percentage of female labour employed in agriculture was higher than that of male labour; in 1978 it was about equal to that of men in the tertiary sector and amounted to 32% in industry. An active campaign to mobilize women to work has been constantly waged by official propaganda, with tangible success in all sectors. Women are also tending to move towards occupations that are considered traditionally masculine.

From the point of view of wages, women concentrate in those fields where wages are low. The gap is especially marked if we compare manual and non-manual employees. Women fall mostly in the manual category.

4.5 *Public Organizations*

The rate of women employed in public administration is 37.3% (22,900 units).

The number of women in the top positions at the head of the economic plan is low.

In Parliament women comprise 33%. The percentage increases in lower level elected bodies; 19% of all mayors are women.

In the judiciary (1977), 39.3% are women.

Women form 14.4% of managers: 2,150 are at the top in industry, 345 in cooperative farms.

In the mass-media the percentage of women is 40.9%. The number of female managers is unknown.

At university level (1981), 30.6% of the teaching staff are women (4,399). At the higher levels of the academic hierarchy their percentage shrinks. For instance, out of 919 deans only 67 are women.

In 1982 women made up 30.59% of the party membership. At the local and provincial levels they held about 33% of leadership positions. No data are known concerning their presence in the central organs. However, a hint may come from the fact that, at the National Congress of the party in 1982, out of 99 members of 11 commissions only 9 were women.

In the unions about one-third of the offices are held by women.

No women's organization exists outside of the party.

4.6 *Conclusion*

As in Poland, the profound changes that affected women's status in the post-war period in Romania are mainly a function of the radical transformations that the country has undergone. However, the issue of women's emancipation, if not explicitly of gender parity, has been dealt with more earnestly and pervasively by the Romanian regime, which boasts the progress that it has accomplished in this field as one of its most tangible social conquests.

APPENDIX B

MULTIVARIATE STATISTICAL ANALYSIS OF THE DETERMINANTS OF MEN'S AND WOMEN'S PUBLIC PARTICIPATION

1 Introduction

The results obtained in chapter 5 are based on a detailed analysis of the relationships between sex, various concomitant variables, and different aspects of power and participation. This interactive analysis is carried out with reference to the different countries and social categories considered in our investigation. This approach allowed us to formulate some relevant hypotheses on the mechanisms that account for gender (in)equalities concerning public participation and power. However, the statistical support of these hypotheses is weakened by the separate consideration of many different aspects of power and participation, and of various groups of explanatory and concomitant variables. Often the findings of different analyses seem to conflict with each other, owing to the effect of higher order interactions which are not controlled in this methodological approach.

Thus there is a need for a simultaneous analysis of the complex relationship linking the various explanatory, concomitant and response variables examined in this survey. In particular, it seems necessary to provide, within this framework, a global measure of power and participation which takes into account the many aspects that may identify this elusive social phenomenon.

In this appendix we first try to set up a multivariate statistical model of socio-political participation and power in the countries under examination. In this framework, we then single out the role of the "sex" variable. Here, by a "statistical model" we mean essentially a "statistical key" to the appraisal of the information conveyed by the data matrix constituting the object of our analysis. To this end we utilize, in a non-traditional fashion, well-known techniques of multivariate analysis (1).

In order to clarify the above considerations and, more specifically, the notion of combining different multivariate techniques, we should illustrate in detail the statistical object on (and through) which we wish to set up the above-mentioned "model": the data matrix, which we denote by D. This matrix has 4,125 rows (corresponding to the interviewed individuals) and m columns (corresponding to the variables concerning the various items in the questionnaire). Among the variables that were considered in the questionnaire we selected those most relevant to the subject of this appendix, according to prior knowledge and to the empirical results described in other chapters of this book. After this selection, our matrix D consisted of 146 variables.

Before analysing the contents of D, it may be useful to recall the essential features characterizing the survey which gave rise to D.

From a statistical viewpoint this survey may be defined as (a) cross-sectional; (b) observational as to the contents but "quasi-experimental" as to sample-design; (c) partially retrospective (for some of the investigated items).

These characteristics will condition, as we shall see later, both the strategy of analysis and the way of interpreting the results.

As to the rows, D can obviously be partitioned into 39 blocks (corresponding to the combination of sex, country, and sample category). Several aggregations of these blocks can be considered for special purposes (e.g. the same partition in the four countries, or the dichotomous classification opposing the individuals with power and the remaining people).

As to column partitioning, we may envisage the blocks of variables listed below. Note that in the following pages we will use the term "variable" to indicate both the statistical attribute (or "character") as a whole (e.g. sex, or country) and its "levels" or "categories" (e.g. male, female; or Poland, Italy, etc.). In the latter case, an appropriate "indicator variable" will correspond to each level of an attribute.

(a) Stratification variables (sex, country, sample category) denoted by the matrix notation S;
(b) Variables concerning power and socio-political participation (past and present offices in party, trade unions, governmental organizations, other associations, at different territorial levels); we shall denote this block by Y;
(c) Socio-demographic variables (age, education, religion, etc.), denoted by W;
(d) Attitude and opinion variables concerning various aspects of socio-political participation (economic and political information, opinion on sex equality with respect to work, etc.), denoted by Z;
(e) Behavioural variables concerning family managing, denoted by V;
(f) Other behavioural and opinion variables, which we shall denote by U.

Since the central task of this appendix is to study "political participation" and "power", we need to begin with block Y, as holding "objective" information on this phenomenon. At a subsequent stage it will be possible to connect, within a general framework, the remaining blocks (in particular S) to Y.

When using such terms as "power" or "participation", we actually refer to countless aspects of the individual life as related to community. This implies, from a statistical viewpoint, the immeasurability (by a "direct" way) of these phenomena. In other words, we are arguing about intrinsically multivariate phenomena, which can only be defined by means of a block of variables (such as Y) concerning different facets of social life. The main issue, in this connection, consists of finding appropriate methods for the appraisal and the utilization of this information in order to establish its relationship with other phenomenological areas, such as those illustrated by the various blocks of D.

It is convenient, for this purpose, to summarize Y, without losing essential information while reducing the dimensions of this block. The use of Correspondence Analysis (CoA) as a tool for retaining the essential information in Y and for achieving a suitable summary for further analysis is justified, in our case, by the mixed nature of the considered variables (continuous, categorical with ordered and unordered levels) and by other useful theoretical and practical properties (see par. 2 and *Methodological Note*). The vertical partition of D into 39 blocks suggests two different approaches of CoA: the first aimed at the study of Y as a nonpartitional matrix (4,125 rows), the second applied to Y viewed as a collapsed matrix consisting of 39 rows, one for each block. In the former case the statistical units coincide with the real individuals and we shall apply the technique of Multiple Correspondence Analysis (MCoA). In the latter case the statistical units are defined by the "treatments" provided by the combination of sex, country and sample category; in this context we shall adopt the technique of Simple Correspondence Analysis (SCoA) as applied to a set of two-way tables.

A common objective is to describe the joint behaviour of statistical units and variables by looking for a low-dimensional space, which provides an "optimal" synthesis of the overall variation in Y. The coordinate axes of this space establish a new set of variables (which cannot be observed directly), for use in further analyses which aim at the examination of relationships with the remaining blocks of D.

Nevertheless, CoA does not limit itself to this factorial interpretation. It will be clear when commenting upon the results of this technique (see par. 2) that these will constitute by themselves a first step towards setting up the statistical model which we mentioned at the beginning of this chapter.

Therefore, the strategy of analysis at this stage is twofold. On one side we shall exploit the results of CoA as a descriptive contribution to the "model" for power and participation (to this end we shall utilize, among others, the technique of "supplementary points", to be illustrated later on). On the other side, we shall use the factor scorings obtained by CoA (in particular by MCoA) in order to set up more extensive "models" which will account for the information contained in the remaining parts of D.

We should underline, at this point, that this strategy of analysis emphasizes the role of the variables considered in this research. This is consistent with the traditional approach to the analysis of sociological data. The technique of CoA modifies this asymmetry between rows and columns of D, by assigning the same importance to both elements (individuals and variables).

Therefore, our strategy of analysis goes back to the original matrix D, towards a more detailed analysis of statistical units (individuals or "treatments") by means of classification techniques (see par. 3.3).

This in turn will allow us to verify the basic hypotheses put forward for explaining gender differences in public participation.

2 The Study of the Variables concerning Power and Participation (Y), by Means of Correspondence Analysis

2.1 *Introduction*

Our first objective, at this stage of analysis, is to determine an overall measure of the phenomenon underlying the characters contained in Y. This measure is not directly observable, as it is defined by a combination of a large set of variables (set J) which refer to each individual, concerning the extent of participation and commitment in political and non-political associations, and the offices held in these organizations (see par. 2.2). We shall determine the mentioned measure by means of CoA. The choice of this technique is illustrated in the *Methodological Note* at the end of this appendix. Using CoA will allow us to draw a picture of the relationships among the variables in Y and between these variables and other characters in D. This information will be matched, and to a certain extent integrated, with the results obtained by means of modelling (par. 3.2) and of typological analysis (par. 3.3).

We shall proceed in two ways:

1 Analyse Y in its original form, with reference to 4,125 individuals, after having introduced the indicator variables that correspond to each item of the initial characters. This leads us to using MCoA, which provides, among other results, individual factor scores.

2 Analyse a collapsed version of *Y*, presenting 39 rows. For each combination of sex, country, and category, the frequency of each item of the variables in *Y* is recorded. This amounts to considering a set of two-way contingency tables cross-classifying the compound variables "sex × country × category" with each variable in the original matrix *Y* (after transformation of the quantitative characters into categorical variables). The principles of SCoA, as applied to this set-up, are illustrated in the *Methodological Note*.

In both types of analysis we can utilize other variables belonging to *D* (and not to *Y*) as supplementary aids for the interpretation of the results. This can be done by projecting the vectors representing these variables on to the factorial space determined by the (active) variables in *Y*, and by assessing the positions taken by these projections in the factorial space. (Further details are given in the application later on, and in the *Methodological Note*.)

2.2 *Description of the Variables in* Y

The set of characters in *Y* can be classified in the following way:

(a) Offices held in non-governmental organizations. (For the labels assigned to categories, see Table 1 which refers only to the variables illustrated in the figures which follow.)
(b) Offices held in governmental organizations. Both kinds of offices, (a) and (b), are classified according to type of admission (candidacy, appointment, election) and territorial level (within city, city, region, nation).
(c) Offices held in political organizations (party, unions) and non-political associations (women's groups, voluntary associations). These offices are classified into past and present, besides the distinctions mentioned for (a) and (b). It should be noted that the information concerning participation in more than one voluntary group has been summarized by a unique variable, taking into account the number of groups for which an office is held.
(d) Some measures of the extent of participation in the various types of organizations mentioned in (a), (b), and (c), such as number of hours spent in group activity, taking the floor in group meetings, and seniority in the organization.

* * *

Table 1 Key to Labels used in Figures in Appendix B

Part A: Active variables

Participation variables	Party	Trade unions	Women's org.	Volunt. assoc.	Other volunt. assoc.
Number of years in ...					
1-4 years	PY01	UY01	WY01	VY01	OY01
5-10 years	PY05	UY05	WY05	VY05	OY05
11-14 (or more†) years	PY10	UY10	WY10	VY10	OY10
15-19 years	PY15	UY15	---	---	---
20 or more years	PY20	UY20	---	---	---
No answer	PYMR	UYMR	WYMR	VYMR	OYMR
Not applicable	PY00	UY00	WY00	VY00	OY00
Speaks at ... meeting					
Often	PW01	UW01	WW01	VW01	OW01
At times	PW02	UW02	WW02	VW02	OW02
Seldom	PW03	UW03	WW03	VW03	OW03
Never	PW04	UW04	WW04	VW04	OW04
Voluntary work					
Yes	PV01	UV01	WV01	VV01	OV01
No	PV02	UV02	WV02	VV02	OV02
Number of hours for ...					
0 hours	PH00	UH00	WH00	VH00	OH00
1-5 hours	PH01	UH01	WH01	VH01	OH01
6-15 hours	PH06	UH06	WH06	VH06	OH06
16-50 (or more†) hours	PH16	UH16	WH16	VH16	OH16
50 or more hours	PH51	UH51	---	---	---

Office variables		Party	Trade unions	Women's org.	Volunt. assoc. or other volunt. assoc.
Offices within city	[W]				
One time		PNW1	UNW1	WNW1	VO11
Two or more times		PNW2	UNW2	WNW2	VO12
Offices city	[C]				
One time		PNC1	UNC1	WNC1	VO21
Two or more times		PNC2	UNC2	WNC2	VO22
Offices intermediate	[R]				
One time		PNR1	UNR1	WNR1	VO31
Two or more times		PNR2	UNR2	WNR2	VO32
Offices national	[N]				
One time		PNN1	UNN1	WNN1	VO41
Two or more times		PNN2	UNN2	WNN2	VO42

† Applies only to women's organizations and voluntary associations

Table 1 Key to Labels used in Figures in Appendix B

Governmental/ [G] Non-gov offices [N]	Within City (W)	City Low (G C/NL)	Intermed. Medium (G R/NM)	National High (G N/NH)
Candidate [C]				
Never candidate	GCW0	GCC0/NLC0	GCR0/NMC0	GCN0/NHC0
One time	GCW1	GCC1/NLC1	GCR1/NMC1	GCN1/NHC1
Two or three times	GCW2	GCC2/NLC2	GCR2/NMC2	GCN2/NHC2
Four	GCW4	GCC4/NLC4	GCR4/NMC4	GCN4/NHC4
No answer	GCWM	GCCM/NLCM	GCRM/NMCM	GCNM/NHCM
Elected [E]				
Never candidate	GEW0	GEC0/NLE0	GER0/NME0	GEN0/NHE0
One time	GEW1	GEC1/NLE1	GER1/NME1	GEN1/NHE1
Two or three times	GEW2	GEC2/NLE2	GER2/NME2	GEN2/NHE2
Four	GEW4	GEC4/NLE4	GER4/NME4	GEN4/NHE4
No answer	GEWM	GECM/NLEM	GERM/NMEM	GENM/NHEM
Appointed [A]				
Never candidate	GAW0	GAC0/NLA0	GAR0/NMA0	GAN0/NHA0
One time	GAW1	GAC1/NLA1	GAR1/NMA1	GAN1/NHA1
Two or three times	GAW2	GAC2/NLA2	GAR2/NMA2	GAN2/NHA2
Four	GAW4	GAC4/NLA4	GAR4/NMA4	GAN4/NHA4
No answer	GAWM	GACM/NLAM	GARM/NMAM	GANM/NHAM
Appointed or elected [S]				
Never candidate	GSW0	GSC0 ---	GSR0 ---	GSN0 ---
One time	GSW1	GSC1 ---	GSR1 ---	GSN1 ---
Two or three times	GSW2	GSC2 ---	GSR2 ---	GSN2 ---
Four	GSW4	GSC4 ---	GSR4 ---	GSN4 ---
No answer	GSWM	GSCM ---	GSRM ---	GSNM ---

Some of the variables in the above list were not considered in the analysis either because of their redundancy with respect to the remaining characters or because of the very low frequencies of the items within them. These variables, however, are retained in the study as supplementary variables. Altogether, we have 57 "active" variables (giving rise to 268 indicator variables, set J) and 55 "supplementary" variables (317 indicator variables, set J^+) which are partly reported in Table 1, part B. We ought to underline that some redundancies still exist within the set J^+ , owing mainly to the categories concerning "no participation" or "no power". A large number of the sampled individuals fall into these categories, showing in their statistical "profile" numerous responses "not applicable". On the other hand, we observe a certain number of missing values (no answer) for particular subsets of J. In both cases we end up with a large group of similar profiles which provide the same information (or lack of information) and, consequently, obtain the same scores. Even the definition of the factors is affected by this group. We shall see that in MCoA one

Table 1 Key to Labels used in Figures in Appendix B

Part B: Supplementary variables

Country		Sex	
Canada	CAN	Male	MMM
Italy	ITA	Female	FFF
Poland	POL		
Romania	ROM		

Category	
Blue-collar worker	BCOL
White-collar worker	WCOL
Teacher	TEAC
Housewife	HOUW
Out of work	OUTW
Decision-maker	DEMA

Sex x Category x Country
(C)an (I)ta (P)ol (R)om

Male blue-collar worker	MBC ()
Female blue-collar worker	FBC ()
Male white-collar worker	MWC()
Female white-collar worker	FWC ()
Male teacher	MTE ()
Female teacher	FTE ()
Housewife	FHW ()
Man out of work	MOW()
Male decision-maker	MDM()
Female decision-maker	FDM ()

Age		
Over 65	years	AGE1
56-65	years	AGE2
46-55	years	AGE3
36-45	years	AGE4
26-35	years	AGE5
Under 25	years	AGE6
No answer		AGMV

Number of working years		
< 1	year	WOR1
1-2	years	WOR2
3-5	years	WOR5
6-10	years	WO10
11-15	years	WO15
16-20	years	WO20
> 20	years	WO + +
Not applicable		WYNO

Education	
Some compulsory	EDU1
Compulsory	EDU2
Some high school	EDU3
High school	EDU4
College/university	EDU5
Graduate school	EDU6
No answer	EDMV

Father's Occupation	
Upper level manager	FOEM
Professional	FOPR
Middle level manager	FOMM
Small businessman	FOSB
White-collar worker	FOWC
Blue-collar worker	FOBC
Blue-collar w. unskilled	FOBU
Small farmer	FOFA
No answer	FOMV

Politics: male business ?	
Total disagreement	PMB1
Partial disagreement	PMB2
Partial agreement	PMB3
Total agreement	PMB4

Perception of social inequality	
+ + +	SIQ1
+ +	SIQ2
+	SIQ3
-	SIQ4
--	SIQ5
---	SIQ6

Political socialization	
+ +	POS1
+	POS2
-	POS3
--	POS4
no answer	POS5

Information on politics	
+ + +	INP1
+ +	INP2
+	INP3
-	INP4
--	INP5
---	INP6
----	INP7

of the factors is entirely a result of this group of individuals. In SCoA it will be possible to eliminate this redundancy as we shall explain later on.

2.3 *Results of the Multiple Correspondence Analysis on* Y

2.3.1 *Interpretation of Factors 1 and 2*

It seems convenient to focus our attention on the first three factorial dimensions which result from the MCoA (2). The clouds of the points N(I) and N(J) (3) are visualized in that subspace through the planes 1-2 and 2-3. As the number of points is very high, we have preferred to illustrate the above-mentioned planes by means of areas rather than to reconstruct in an aggregate way the latent meaning that is expressed by the factorial dimensions.

If we consider (Fig. 1) the cloud N(J), superimposing the cloud N(I) (respectively: F_1 = horizontal axis, F_2 = vertical axis), it is possible to outline it through the prevailing positioning of the main blocks of variables (Table 1) in some specific areas of the plane.

The shape of these clouds stretches out along a direction which crosses the quadrants II and IV of the plane 1-2. The intensity of the phenomenon "participation and power" grows as it moves towards quadrant II. From now on, we shall therefore call "advanced" (or "withdrawn") every positioning with major (or minor) coordinates according to the positive side of that direction.

We have preferred to illustrate immediately in detail the course of the supplementary variables (Fig.s 2 and 3) in order to qualify better the areas of the plane that are described in Fig.1.

We can observe in Figure 3a (4) that the "natural" order of the variable category (decision-maker, teacher, white-collar worker, blue-collar worker, man out of work, housewife) is mainly reflected in the shape, with a systematic "disadvantage" for women versus men (which is shown, anyway, in the mostly "withdrawn" positioning of women (F) in quadrant IV of Fig. 2a).

We have found particular situations for each country for the different categories. For example, looking at Fig. 2a, we can make the following remarks.

1 Considering the decision-makers:
   (a) on the whole, Poland and Canada hold a more advanced position than Romania and Italy;
   (b) in Canada and Italy the female decision-makers even surpass the male decision-makers;

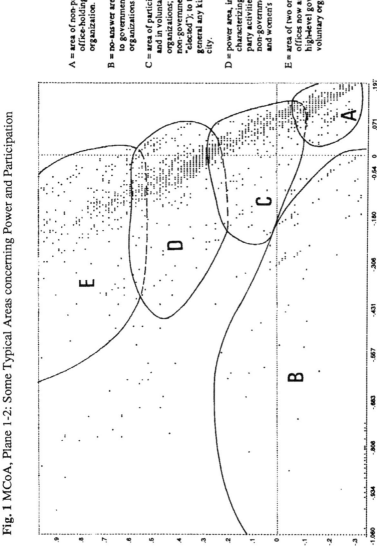

Fig. 1 MCoA, Plane 1-2: Some Typical Areas concerning Power and Participation

A = area of non-participation and non-office-holding in any kind of organization.

B = no-answer area, with special reference to governmental offices and voluntary organizations.

C = area of participation in trade unions and in voluntary and women's organizations; area of trade union and non-governmental offices (especially "elected"); to this area belong in general any kind of offices within the city.

D = power area, inclusive of the items characterizing participation in party activities, governmental and non-governmental offices, voluntary and women's organizations.

E = area of two or more offices and/or offices now and in the past in party, high-level governmental organizations, voluntary organizations.

Fig. 2 MCoA, Plane (F_1, F_2): Display of Items pertaining to
    "Supplementary" Variables of Matrix D

(a) Sex by Country by Category †

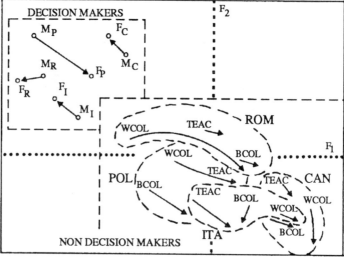

† Within each area pertaining to a country, the letter identifying the
country is omitted in the single labels; the arrow represents the oriented
vectors from male to female

(b) Socio-Demographic Variables

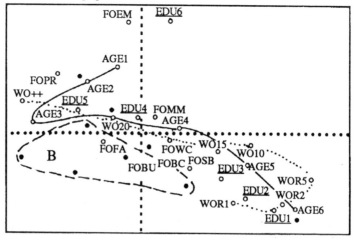

Fig. 3 MCoA, Plane (F_1, F_2): Display of Items pertaining to Participation and Category, Country and Local Offices

(a) Participation

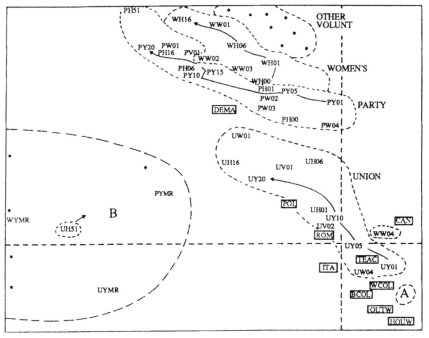

(b) Local Offices

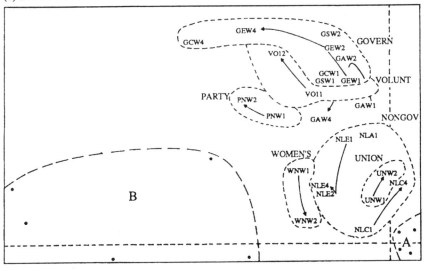

(c) in Poland we find the biggest gender difference, in favour of the males.

The above considerations are well documented by the directior and length of the arrows in the display.

2 Considering the non-decision-makers:

(a) the women systematically hold a less advanced position with respect to men (see the direction of the arrows in quadrant IV of the display);

(b) teachers, white-collar workers and blue-collar workers hold a more advanced position in Romania than in Poland. In addition, the above categories, when considered globally in the socialist countries, precede the corresponding categories in Canada and Italy;

(c) in Romania and Poland the gender difference concerning teachers and blue-collar workers is less marked than that concerning the white-collar workers. Exactly the opposite finding is recorded in Italy;

(d) the greatest homogeneity is observed for housewives, no matter which country is considered.

All in all, we may conclude that a larger group in between decision-makers and non-decision-makers is observed in the capitalist countries than in the socialist countries.

In Fig. 2b, the situation of the variables of block W (socio-demographic) is described. On the whole, as the positionings along the shape grow, we find items that are relative to a longer work seniority (WO) (along, of course, with increasing age), to a better education (EDU) and to a better social level (FO).

As far as the variables of block Z are concerned, we go gradually from the opinion that participation is useless and from lack of political information (INP7) and lack of political socialization (POS5) --- the family is considered as an obstacle too --- to having political information (INP1) and earning more than the spouse.

We can now begin the systematic analysis of the single factorial dimensions of the plane 1-2.

The first factor F_1 (explaining 6.6% of total variation) turns out to be linked essentially to the groups of responses "Not applicable" and "No answer", as we anticipated in the previous section (5). In fact, these categories account for 86% of the "inertia" pertaining to the first factorial axis (if we sum up the "absolute contributions" of all such categories; see *Methodological Note*).

The left side of this axis has a slight characterization in terms of the variables that pertain to participation and power: party seniority (PY), voluntary work in unions (UV), taking the floor in a party (PW), present offices at a national level in a party (PNN), hours of party activity (PH) (see Fig. 3a).

The above remarks would exclude the first factor as a reliable measure of participation and power. However, this factor suggests some fundamental distinctions: the opposition between participation in party life and "no participation" owing to objective or subjective reasons; moreover, the opposition between decision-makers and most of the remaining categories (Fig. 2a and 2b). The similarity of location (left side) of decision-makers, party members and missing values is not to be overlooked. In this connection, we observe that 52% of the individuals who do not answer the set of items concerning governmental offices are in fact decision-makers, while we should expect only 24.8% of individuals belonging to this category to be among the missing values, if the distribution were random.

Roughly speaking, the first factor represents a general attitude towards "non-responding", with some emphasis on the individuals with power. In other words, by means of this factor, we measure a component of the attitude towards non-responding which is more closely linked with a dimension of power.

The second factor F_2 (explaining 4.9% of total variation) may represent, on the contrary, a good measure of participation and power, because of its clear correlation with being active and with holding offices in the various organizations.

As a matter of fact, in correspondence with the negative coordinates of F_2, we find items of non-participation in any organization, of non-office-holding (see area A in Fig. 1) and of no-answers relative to governmental offices (see area B); in correspondence with the positive coordinates of F_2, we observe a progressive stratification of items relative to the commitment and office-holding in a union, to non-governmental offices, to the commitment in voluntary associations and offices in female organizations, and to party-life participation (expressed in terms of hours, PH, of seniority, PY, and taking the floor, PW).

Thus, in correspondence with higher coordinates on F_2, we find items that are relevant to government offices as well as to offices in party and other voluntary organizations.

This progressive scaling on F_2 can be well evaluated, if we observe the scheme of Fig. 4 which reports the range on F_2 of the coordinates for each block of items.

We can observe in Fig. 4 that the scorings referring to the offices held in the various organizations are higher than those concerning a simple participation in the same organization. We may argue that F_2 gives more weight to the offices than to participation as such.

Fig. 4 Ranges of Coordinates on F_2 (blocks of items).

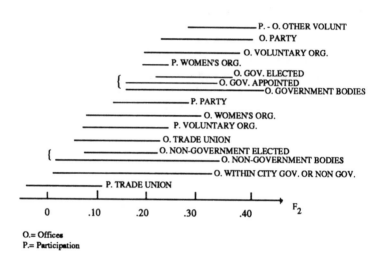

O.= Offices
P.= Participation

The unions and the women's organizations show different patterns in terms of coordinates. With regard to the unions, which represent the most frequent form of participation, we note generally low scores (in any case, lower than the corresponding scores in the party). However, the items concerning participation in women's organizations usually have top scores on F_2. This can be partially explained by the fact that these items refer only to women, with a particular emphasis on Canadian women (for which a higher frequency of group membership is recorded)(6). In order to gain a more detailed illustration of this constellation of positions, we refer to Fig. 3a.

We can observe finally that F_2 is a function of both the frequency with which an office has been held (with the exception of the non-governmental offices that are held more than twice) and the degree of importance of the office. In fact local offices (within city) generally score lower than the corresponding national offices (see Fig. 3b). We cannot say the same as to the ways in which offices are obtained (candidate, appointed, elected), which, as we shall see, are better represented on F_3.

Moreover, the spreading of the items on participation and power, approximately along the bisection of the axes, clearly shows a progressive intensity of the (latent) measure as the distance from the origin increases.

Therefore, we may consider this factor (F_2) as a starting-point for further refinements, before introducing explicit "models" for describing the relationship with other variables in *D*.

2.3.2 *Interpretation of Factor 3 on Plane 2-3*

The study of the third factor offers the chance to complete the analysis of matrix *Y* in the three-dimensional subspace.

F_3 represents a further point of view from which we may observe some fundamental differentiations on the just defined continuum of participation and power. As a matter of fact, F_3 (4.5% of total variation) turns out to be the factor that mostly discriminates each of the four countries. We report in Figs. 5 and 6 the blocks of the supplementary and active variables on plane 2-3.

In Fig. 5a we observe the contrast, with regard to F_3, between Romania, Poland, Canada and Italy. In this connection we can talk, because of these positionings, of the Romanian side and the Canadian side.

Observing in Fig. 6 the various groups of items belonging to the active variables, we infer as follows:

(a) On the *Romanian side* (quadrant I), there are those items that are inherent to participation in party (Fig. 6a) and union (Fig. 6b); there are also the offices of every level in the union (Fig. 6b) and the local offices (within city) of the party (Fig. 6a) and of governmental and non-governmental organizations (Fig. 6e and 6f). As far as these organizations are concerned, we observe, in particular, that whatever the relationship is between the respondents and the offices (candidate, elected, appointed), all types of offices belong to this side, provided that they are local offices (within city) and, as far as non-governmental organizations are concerned, that they are intermediate (non-high-level), "elected type" offices too.

(b) On the *Canadian side* (quadrant IV), generally there are, instead, the non-local (i.e. city, region, nation) offices of the party (Fig. 6a), and the offices of the non-governmental (Fig. 6f) and governmental (Fig. 6e) organizations. In particular, there are all of the "appointed type" offices and those that are held more than twice (with the exception of the local ones). Still on this side, but in intermediate positioning (and therefore with lower coordinates on F_3), we find the items of partic-

Fig. 5 MCoA, Plane (F_1, F_2): Display of Items pertaining
to "Supplementary" Variables of Matrix *D*

(a) Sex, Category, Country, Sex by Category

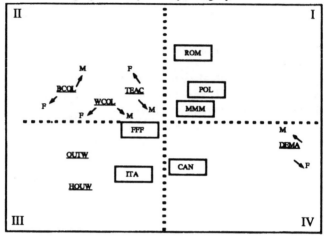

(b) Socio-Demographic Variables

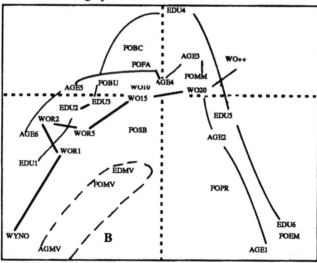

Fig. 6 MCoA, Plane (F_2, F_3): Display of Items pertaining to
"Active" Variables in Six Blocks of Matrix Y

(a) Party

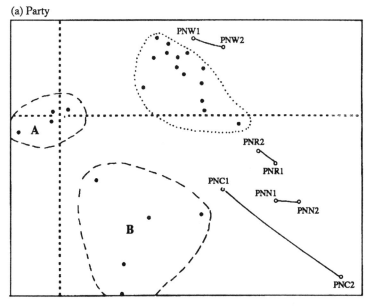

(b) Trade Union

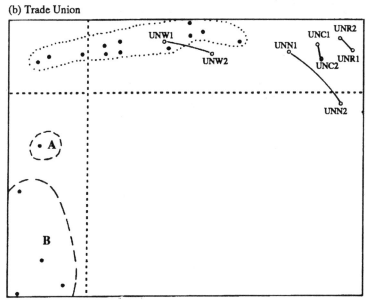

Fig. 6 MCoA, Plane (F_2, F_3): Display of Items pertaining to "Active" Variables in Six Blocks of Matrix Y

(c) Women's Organizations

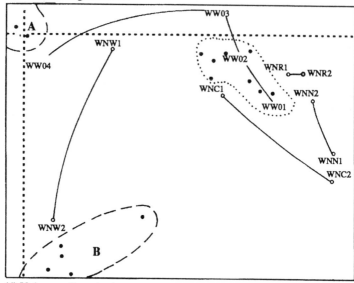

(d) Voluntary Organizations

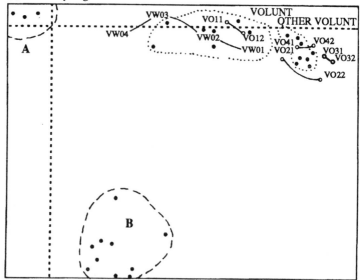

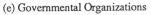

Fig. 6 MCoA, Plane (F_2, F_3): Display of Items pertaining to "Active" Variables in Six Blocks of Matrix *Y*

(e) Governmental Organizations

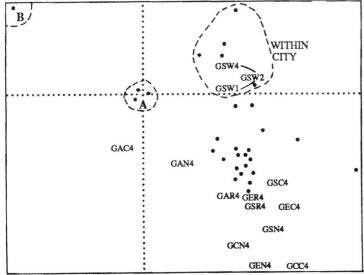

(f) Non-Governmental Organizations

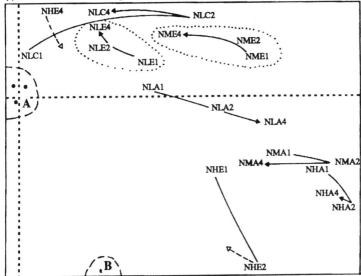

ipation in women's associations (Fig. 6c) and voluntary associations (Fig. 6d) as well as their relevant offices.

We can note, in Fig. 6, the differentiated positioning of the sets of "no answer", almost always with positive coordinates on F_2, with the exceptions of the union (on the Romanian side) and the governmental offices (on the Canadian side).

Regarding the supplementary variables of the W and Z blocks, we can observe on the Canadian side the items corresponding to older people (> 55 years), with very high education, a very high father's occupation (FOPR, FOEM), and well off, and to people who do not believe that politics is only a man's business.

On the Romanian side, we find the items with better political information and socialization and with economic equality in men's and women's income; moreover, we find the people with maximum work seniority (WO + +) and with their father's occupation of an intermediate level (FOMM) (see Fig. 5b).

From this set of information we can deduce that in the two political-cultural systems there is a different tendency in terms of the modes of participation. In reality there is.

(a) In the Romanian model there is a prevalence of offices at the city level and of decentralization (stronger participation of non-decision-makers), of involvement in unions and parties, and of offices obtained in the "elected" way;

(b) in the Canadian model there is an increase in persistence of office-holding, correlated to a higher seniority and to a stronger social stratification; a prevalence of involvement in voluntary women's associations; and a stronger characterization of power through governmental and non-governmental offices of a medium and high level.

Therefore, the third factor consists of a continuum along which offices are arranged by importance (from local to national) and by frequency of repetition; where, moreover, the local character of the office, typical of the Romanian model, prevails on the type and the mode of obtaining it, whilst the "appointed" mode, typical of the Canadian model, prevails on the level of the office.

It is not difficult to realize that the similarity between Canada and Poland is mainly owing to office-holding in voluntary associations, while that between Canada and Italy is to be attributed chiefly to repeated office-holding.

On the other hand, the closeness between Poland and Romania depends on their analogous behaviour concerning offices in the unions and in non-governmental organizations.

In addition, from the plane 2-3 we can point to the "intermediate" position of Poland between Romania and Canada, with a strict correspondence between the voluntary and women's associations, and to the "marginal" position of Italy, which is placed in quadrant III where there are large sections of non-decision-makers and of no-answers (Fig. 6b and 5a) and, for instance, scarce political information.

2.4 *Results of Simple Correspondence Analysis on the Collapsed* Y

To study further the differences between countries, it is useful to take into consideration all the information that is relative to the D matrix, classified according to the 39 categories of the sample. These are taken as analysis units which are still defined by the 57 "active" variables already examined in MCoA. In such a way, the information is organized in 57 two-way contingency tables which can be studied by means of SCoA (Leclerc, 1976). By this procedure we can eliminate that part of the redundant information that results from the repeated occurrence of profiles which have missing values or are not applicable, with regard to the various groups of variables related to the various organizations.

The different form of the data matrix does not allow us to expect the same factors as in MCoA. In particular, we cannot obtain a factor that is analogous to F_1, because redundancy has been eliminated. Moreover, since the "quality" of representation of the corresponding factorial spaces is usually higher in SCoA than in MCoA, we should not be surprised to find relevant differences from this point of view (see *Methodological Note*). Table 2 shows the quality of representation of the first six factors of SCoA and confirms what we said before.

We take into consideration the first two factors which seem to be the most significant and which lend themselves to a useful interpretation within the framework of the results already obtained in MCoA. However, we should underline that the fourth factor, which by itself is of very modest relevance, does represent an important contribution from the point of view of our research. In fact, it shows the poor impact that sex exerts on the variables under examination (7).

Table 2 Quality of Representation of the First Six Factors in SCoA

Factor	Eigenvalue	Percentage of explanation with respect to total variation	Cumulative percentage of explanation
$F_{(1)}$	0.148	35.07	35.07
$F_{(2)}$	0.095	22.56	57.63
$F_{(3)}$	0.063	14.84	72.47
$F_{(4)}$	0.021	5.05	77.52
$F_{(5)}$	0.020	4.94	82.46
$F_{(6)}$	0.014	3.24	85.70

We denote by $F_{(i)}$ ($i = 1...6$) the various factors in SCoA to distinguish them from the factors in MCoA.

2.4.1 *Interpretation of Factors*

The first factor, $F_{(1)}$ can be studied by referring to Fig. 7. Do not confuse $F_{(1)}$ for F_1 : see par. 2.3.1. In Fig. 7 the horizontal axis (representing $F_{(1)}$) contrasts the decision-makers of the various countries (on the left side) with the other categories. This supplies a dimension of power/no power. (Since the power positions are on the left side of the axis, a higher power is represented by negative scores. In what follows we shall omit reference to the negative sign and speak simply of high or low scores on power and participation).

Along this dimension only Poland shows different behaviour according to sex (men in a better position than women), whereas Italy reveals a slightly more favourable position of women, in agreement with what has been already obtained in MCoA (see Fig. 2a).

On the opposite side of $F_{(1)}$, the different locations of the various categories within and between the countries correspond to different tendencies towards power.

In Fig. 8 we can find indications for a more complete interpretation of $F_{(1)}$. The shape of the points in the plane ($F_{(1)}$, $F_{(2)}$) is parabolic with concavity turning towards the positive side of $F_{(2)}$. Thus, there exists a continuous ordering along the first axis. The most relevant items, in this dimension $F_{(1)}$, are: governmental and non-governmental offices, followed by the offices held in voluntary groups and in the party and, finally, to a lesser extent, the offices held in the unions and in women's organizations.

We also notice a concordance among the scores on $F_{(1)}$, as far as the categories pertaining to voluntary work are concerned, in all types of organizations. On the opposite side, we find all of the categories concerning non-participation.

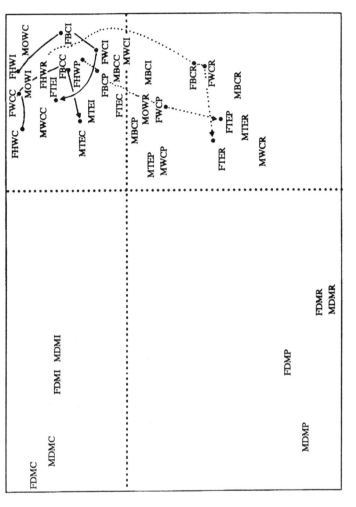

Fig. 7 SCoA, Plane (F$_1$, F$_2$): Display of 39 Categories

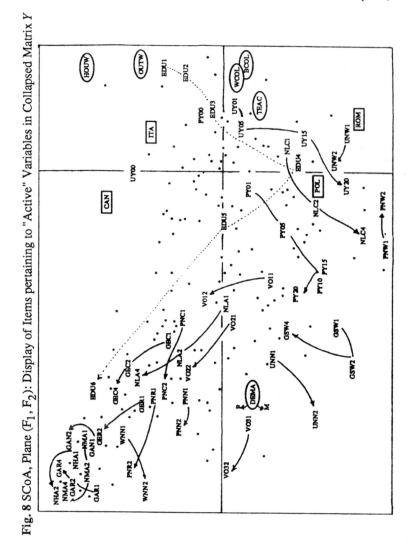

Fig. 8 SCoA, Plane (F_1, F_2): Display of Items pertaining to "Active" Variables in Collapsed Matrix Y

On the whole, $F_{(1)}$ shows many similarities to $F_{(2)}$ (defined in MCoA), though it also represents some aspects of F_1 (see par. 2.3.1).

Let us now discuss $F_{(2)}$, while continuing our inspection of Fig. 7 and Fig. 8. This factor allows us to make some distinctions between groups of individuals with similar scores on $F_{(1)}$. Thus, looking at the left side of the first axis in Fig. 8, we find in quadrant II (upper left) the correspondence between decision-makers of Canada and Italy and in quadrant III (lower left) the correspondence between decision-makers of Poland and Romania. This distinction does not pertain only to the decision-makers.

In fact, on the plane $(F_{(1)}, F_{(2)})$ (Fig. 7), the broken lines reproduce, for each country and both sexes, the "natural" order among the non-decision-makers (from men out of work and housewives to teachers). These lines are somewhat different from each other. Nevertheless, we can single out two typical patterns: that pertaining to Canada and that pertaining to Romania. The former is correlated with the positive values of $F_{(2)}$, the latter with negative values of the same factor. This is a striking result which confirms what we have already seen in par. 2.3.2.

Looking at these patterns in more detail, we can make the following remarks:

1 Romanian female teachers (Fig. 7) are clearly apart from the female blue-collar workers of the same country. They are closer to the centre of gravity (showing a "less marked lack of power", if we can use this expression). In this respect, their position is better than that pertaining to the corresponding males.
2 Polish females show a pattern which is very close to the overall pattern of Romania. However, in terms of power, they are always "backward" with respect to the corresponding males.
3 Italian females follow a pattern similar to that of Romania. It should be noticed that they score "worse" than all of the remaining groups on factor $F_{(1)}$.
4 Canadian females have different positions on the plane, according to whether they are white-collar workers (upward trend: "Canadian pattern") or teachers (downward trend: "Romanian pattern").
5 The male non-decision-makers generally show a "less marked lack of power" and are more homogeneous in the Romanian pattern (this holds also for the Polish sample), whereas they are heterogeneous in the Canadian pattern.

We see that the Canadian and Italian blue-collar workers and Italian white-collar workers have the lowest scores, whereas the teachers have better scores. It is noticeable that the Italian teachers are located close to Canadian white-collar workers.

$F_{(2)}$ can be interpreted as expressing a second dimension of power, linked to a distinction among the countries. Further support for this interpretation is provided by an inspection of Fig. 8. Here we see, in quadrant II (decision-makers of Canada and Italy), the governmental and non-governmental offices (by nomination, and/or election at the regional and national level). In quadrant III (decision-makers of Poland and Romania), we find either governmental offices at the local level or non-governmental offices at any level by election or candidacy, and finally, offices held in voluntary organizations and in the unions. Thus, the two types of offices seem to characterize the two socio-political systems (capitalist v. socialist) (8).

3 Statistical Models for the Analysis of Power and Participation

3.1 *Search for a Factor of Power and Participation*

3.1.1 *The Analysis of Factor* F_2

The "objective" information concerning power and political participation, which is contained in sub-matrix Y, can be summarized by means of the factors obtained by the application of CoA. We shall focus our attention on F_2 (in MCoA), because this provides us with individual scores which can be interpreted as coordinates along a latent axis representing participation and power, as we showed in par. 2.3.1. However, before setting up specific models which relate F_2 to other variables (especially those in blocks S, W, Z), it is necessary to cast some more light on the meaning and properties of F_2. First of all, we shall examine its distribution in our sample as a whole and in appropriately selected sub-samples. F_2 has a mean equal to zero (because factors in CoA are centred), its standard deviation is 0.42 and the range is equal to 3.2. The distribution of F_2 is illustrated in Fig. 9a.

We notice the asymmetry of the total sample (58% of individuals falling in the interval $-.33/+.22$, with a larger variation in the right tail: 1.4% of units below -2 v. 4.8 of units beyond $+2$). The maximum observed value of F_2 is 1.87, but only 100 people take on a value > 1 (36 persons a value < -1). People in the upper part of the distribution have, seemingly, accumulated during their life the greatest number of offices and/or the most extensive commitment to associations and decisional bodies. As to the shape of the distribution, consideration of its modes and of the partial distributions that are relative to the categories in the sample and concomitant variables (see comments later on in this section), suggests the hypothesis of a mixture between two basic distributions (see Fig. 9a). These components are substantially linked with two different groups of individuals (decision-makers and the others). This remark will have some implications in the subsequent analysis.

Fig. 9 Distribution of 4,125 Individuals on F_2 and F_2^*

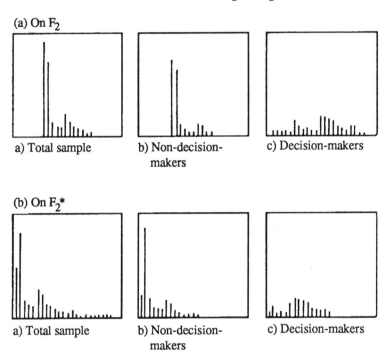

(a) On F_2

a) Total sample

b) Non-decision-makers

c) Decision-makers

(b) On F_2^*

a) Total sample

b) Non-decision-makers

c) Decision-makers

The interpretation of F_2 can be further enriched by the analysis of its partial means, given the stratification characters (sex, country, and category). These are reported in Table 3 (figures without brackets). We note that the decision-makers are the only category taking positive mean values of F_2 (.38 for the females, .40 for the males). The remaining categories have negative means, ranging from values close to zero (teachers and white-collar workers) down to the lowest scorings for men out of work and housewives. Women have generally lower means than men, the average differences being .06 (smaller than the mean differences between categories).

Regarding country, we obtain the following ranking: Italy (-.09), Canada and Romania (near zero), Poland (.08). Also in this case we find

Table 3 Partial Means of Factor F_2 Relative to Sex, Country and Category in the Sample (Within brackets the corresponding Means for Factor $F_2^{\bullet}$)

	Blue-collar	White-collar	Teacher	House-wife	Men out of work	Decision-maker	Male	Female	Total
Canada	-.19 (-.50)	-.20 (-.54)	-.10 (-.34)	-.18 (-.51)	-.25 (-.65)	.52 (.95)	.03 (-.09)	.02 (-.10)	0.2 (-.10)
Italy	-.18 (-.43)	-.18 (-.50)	-.18 (-.35)	-.31 (-.70)	-.27 (-.46)	.22 (.74)	-.07 (-.10)	-.10 (-.17)	-.09 (-.14)
Poland	-.15 (-.20)	-.05 (-.11)	-.01 (-.06)	-.02 (-.60)	— (0.00)	.45 (1.16)	.16 (.46)	.01 (.00)	.08 (.21)
Romania	-.03 (-.15)	-.02 (-.03)	.07 (-.07)	-.26 (-.63)	-.09 (-.23)	.36 (1.20)	.05 (.15)	-.02 (-.05)	.01 (.05)
Male	-.11 (-.25)	-.07 (-.17)	-.03 (-.11)		-.20 (-.45)	.40 (1.00)			
Female	-.17 (-.39)	-.15 (-.42)	-.08 (-.23)	-.24 (-.61)		.38 (0.96)			
Total	-.14 (-.32)	-.11 (-.29)	-.06 (-.17)	-.24 (-.61)	-.20 (-.45)	.39 (.98)	.04 (.08)	-.02 (-.08)	0.00 (0.00)

a weak interaction with sex: the gender differences are in favour of the males, but range from .15 in Poland to .01 in Canada (to be compared with the mean difference .06).

The interaction between country and category ranges Canada and Poland (with a marked difference between decision-makers and others) opposite Italy and Romania (with a more uniform distribution). Romania, in particular, shows the highest values for blue- and white-collar workers and for teachers.

These findings confirm what has emerged in the previous analysis, and especially the ranking of the countries (see Fig. 3).

If we take into account the sampling design, we realize that some of the above-mentioned features might result from in-built relationships connected with the choice of the different categories. It is therefore interesting to check whether at least the general trend we observe in Table 3 is confirmed as far as non-decision-makers are concerned.

The main modification occurs in the ranking of the countries: Canada and Italy have the lowest means, while Romania takes first place (.04), surpassing Poland (.09). We may conclude that the structure of the distribution of F_2, relative to the variables in block S (stratification characters), is sufficiently stable, whether or not we retain the decision-makers in the analysis. This finding reinforces the interpretation of F_2 as a latent measure of participation and power. However, in order to gain a better insight into the nature of this factor, we carried out an analysis of the dependence of F_2 on the variables which have contributed to its definition (in MCoA).

The variables have been used as explanatory variables in a sequence of linear models having F_2 as response variable and sex and country as stratification variables appearing explicitly in the model. Several analyses of variance have been carried out for this reason, considering main effects and first order interactions. The results are briefly described in what follows.

The first group of models relates F_2 to office-holding in governmental and non-governmental organizations. All the implied variables show a significant effect on F_2. More specifically, people who hold offices in governmental organizations have a mean value of F_2 greater than that attained by people with offices in non-governmental organizations (.55 v. .33, but .64 for those holding both types of offices). The score increases for the individuals with repeated offices at the city and intermediate levels by election or nomination (.80 to .90). This group attains scores up to 1.27 in Poland and 1.08 in Canada, whereas in Italy the top values are reached by the candidates (.85 to .90). The interaction with sex reveals a higher score for women who hold offices as compared with the corresponding men. This is a startling result. The opposite is true for people not holding offices. However it should be underlined that the explanatory variables considered so far account for only 30% of the total variation in F_2. This percentage increases dramatically if we add the variables concerning membership and participation in political and cultural organizations (party, unions, women's organizations, voluntary associations). The multiple correlation coefficient attains the value .8, with a strong contribution provided by party membership. This variable seems to act as a "filter" or a "key" to power and participation. This appears to be a very realistic result which encourages us to trust the indications collected with our instruments. Conversely, union membership and seniority turn out to be non-significant, thus appearing to be linked generally to personal or corporate interests rather than to the assumption of a decisional role in society. This is emphasized by the fact that the highest mean values of F_2 pertain to the group of people with maximun seniority in the party (1.38) and this holds true uniformly for both sexes and each country. In fact, if we drop sex and country out of the model, the index R^2 does not substantially decrease. Moreover, if we restrict the analysis to the non-decision-makers (3,101 individuals), we get approximately the same fitting as in the whole sample ($R^2 = .780$ v. $R^2 = .796$). This finding gives further support to the adequacy of F_2 in our analysis of participation and power. In particular, as a result of the application of the above-mentioned linear models, we may define F_2 as being a "measure of participation in social and political life" rather than a measure of power in the restricted sense of office-holding.

Obviously, there exists a "natural" link between these two facets of social life, but what we consider here is the "weight" of such variables as party membership, seniority, voluntary work, and taking the floor, in the determination of F_2.

3.1.2 *The Determination of a Rotated Factor*

In order to obtain a better fit of the cloud of points that are represented in the first factorial plane (F_1, F_2), we used the technique of oblique rotation called "Oblimin". We obtained two new factors $\overset{.}{F_1}$ and $\overset{.}{F_2}$ (9). The main effect of this rotation concerns the "missing values". These are now more related to $\overset{.}{F_2}$ than to $\overset{.}{F_1}$.

The group of individuals with missing values referring to office-holding have negative or negligible coordinates on $\overset{.}{F_2}$. This adjustment is likely to produce a modification in the meaning of this factor, which we shall comment upon in what follows.

A technique for testing the nature of $F_2^\bullet$ consists of modelling it by means of the same variables and models we utilized for F_2. In this way we shall be able to single out the analogies and the differences between the two dependence structures. The results of this analysis make clear that $F_2^\bullet$ is affected to a larger extent, as we might have expected, by office-holding in various organizations (specifically in governmental bodies and, more generally, in national offices by election/nomination). In the group of items related to participation, party again plays the main role, whereas participation, in the union's activities confirms its weak weight on the factor. It should be underlined that the influence of sex is negligible. In other words, the structure of $F_2^\bullet$ is not affected by gender differences.

It is interesting to compare directly $F_2^\bullet$ with F_2 in particular sub-samples. If we consider the individuals having $F_2^\bullet > .6$ (403 units), the correlation coefficient is $r = .89$ (v. $r = .71$ in the total sample). Evidently, beyond a certain threshold, these two factors provide a measure of the same phenomenon.

However, they differ to a given extent with respect to the individuals having intermediate scorings on $F_2^\bullet$ (from -.6 to .6). In this group the correlation coefficient is $r = .40$. We may say that, for these individuals, "power" means something different from "participation". Another remark in this connection concerns the opposition between Canada (where we obtain $r = .94$) and the remaining countries (where $r < .55$). This emphasizes a different structure of power in the North American country.

Following the same procedure that we adopted when analysing F_2, we shall now gain some insight into the distributional properties of $F_2^\bullet$.

Fig. 9b illustrates the distribution of $F_2^\bullet$. In the total sample, we notice a high concentration of units on the negative side and an approximately semi-normal shape on the positive side of $F_2^\bullet$. The distribution of $F_2^\bullet$ in the group of decision-makers here shows a roughly Gaussian shape. The centre of Fig. 9b depicts the situation for non-decision-makers. We notice a large concentration for low values of $F_2^\bullet$, followed by an exponentially decreasing trend.

The above considerations suggest the following interpretation. The overall distribution of $F_2^\bullet$ has three components which can be referred to three sub-populations.

1 People with no power in any sense (these constitute nearly 33% of our sample, with $F_2^\bullet < -.6$). We find here the individuals who do not participate in political life *and* do not hold offices of any type. It is useful to remark that, after rotation, the frequency pertaining to this band of the factor has decreased from 61% to 33% (this may be interpreted

as the effect of the greater precision in measuring power obtained by $F_2^{\bullet}$).

2 People who keep up a more complex relationship with society, though they do not belong to the group of decision-makers. They participate in the life of some organizations: sometimes they hold offices in them (mainly at a local level). Whereas the individuals of group 1 are almost uniformly distributed on the negative range of $F_2^{\bullet}$, those belonging to group 2 are scattered along the central range of factor scorings, following an approximately normal distribution.

3 Decision-makers. These individuals are normally distributed (10) with a mean value near to 1. According to our sampling design, the great majority of them have been selected purposely (they account for about 20% of the sample).

The overall distribution of $F_2^{\bullet}$ depends on the weights assigned to groups 1, 2, and 3 respectively. The sampling design does not allow us to estimate these weights in the parent population (constituted by all adults living in the four countries). We must, therefore, argue on the basis of the weights realized in our sample. This does not prevent us from inferring the relationship between $F_2^{\bullet}$ and the variables in other blocks of our original data matrix. This can be done along the lines already illustrated in the analysis of F_2 (see par. 3.1.1).

We start from the stratification variables. In Table 3 we report, within brackets, the means of $F_2^{\bullet}$ relating to sex, country and category. We notice that $F_2^{\bullet}$ introduces a more marked discrimination among different groups of individuals than the corresponding discrimination obtained by F_2. Thus the general trend is unmodified, while the differences are enhanced. In particular, regarding the categories, we obtain a mean value of .98 for the decision-makers, compared to -.16 for teachers, -.29 for white-collar workers, and -.61 for housewives. Italy and Canada show lower values than Poland and Romania for all categories. The position of white-collar workers and teachers in Poland and, more markedly, in Romania is higher than in the other two countries. The gender difference is negligible among the decision-makers (.998 for the female, .964 for the males). However, it is remarkable in the other categories (particularly among the white-collar workers who have -.17 for the males and -.42 for the females).

If we consider the variable "seniority in work", in this case also the differences are more marked in $F_2^{\bullet}$ than in F_2. Seniority in work has a greater influence in Poland and Romania, with respect to Italy and Canada, but it is negligible in the group of decision-makers. This finding supports the hypothesis that the pathway to power is almost independent of the career in working life (this may be linked with the scarce weight of activity in the union in terms of power).

If we consider age, instead of "seniority in work", the greatest difference is found in Poland, and the lowest in Italy. With the exception of a fraction of decision-makers (about one hundred), the individuals below 35 years obtain very low mean scores in terms of $F_2^{\cdot}$.

As far as the influence of education is concerned, besides that of the stratification variables, positive mean values are recorded only in the groups with the highest levels of education (university and graduate studies). This is true everywhere, except in Poland. The remaining groups have negative values approximately inversely proportional to the number of years of schooling. The gender difference is constant (in favour of males) in all these groups, except in the highest level of education where we observe .30 for males and .33 for females.

It is interesting to note the difference between socialist and capitalist countries in connection with the group of people with high school education. In this group we observe: .50 in Poland, -.08 in Romania, -.36 in Canada, and -.37 in Italy.

If we analyse, finally, the influence of "father's occupation", we discover that the main feature is provided by the interaction with country. Canada seems to be the most "conservative" country in this respect: only the sons of managers and professionals have positive mean values (remarkably higher than the corresponding values in the other countries). On the opposite side, Poland presents positive values for all the occupations (except for managers, with a value -.02, but there are only five people in this position). Romania shows an analogous, though less enhanced, behaviour. Italy is similar to Canada but, again, in a reduced scale. The women everywhere have lower scores than men, with the exception of the top class (managers) who score equally with or better than men.

It is interesting to see that, among decision-makers, the highest mean values pertain to people with modest origins (1.29 for the sons of countrymen v. .80 for the sons of professionals and managers). This seems to support the original socio-economic conditions. The role of subjective factors must not be neglected (as we shall see in the following sections). On the contrary, the link between fathers and sons appears much stronger in the group of non-decision-makers.

3.2 *Linear Models for the Rotated Factor* F_2^*

3.2.1 *The Role of Stratification and Demographic Variables*

We start with a basic model containing the stratification variables, and add to it different blocks of variables, taking into account the indications that were provided by the results obtained in the previous section. We refer to the total sample, but we have also verified some of the conclusions by repeating the analysis on the sub-sample of non-decision-makers. Regarding the variables in block Z (opinions and attitudes), we do not utilize them individually, but only as an overall indicator of attitudes obtained by means of MCoA applied to this group of variables. This application is described in detail in par. 3.2.2. Here we use this factor according to the interpretation illustrated in that section.

We limit ourselves to reporting the main features of the results obtained by the above procedure.

1   The strong influence of category is confirmed, with the usual "scaling": decision-makers --- teachers and white-collar workers --- blue-collar workers --- men out of work and housewives.
2   There is a difference between the two socio-economic systems: Poland and Romania have higher scores than Canada and Italy. It is important to note that this difference is greater when we consider models containing more variables (age, education, father's occupation, etc.). This means that we are dealing with a structural difference resulting from the system rather than from specific co-variates.
3   The gender difference is significant, though its effect is smaller than those of the system and category. It should also be noted that the effect of gender is perceptible only among the non-decision-makers (owing to the way this latter group has been selected). Moreover an interaction does not seem to exist between sex and country, seniority in work, and father's occupation.
4   Seniority in work has a slight effect, but it strongly interacts with country. It has the greatest influence in Poland, followed by Canada and Romania, and has no influence at all in Italy. Similarly, the father's occupation is significant in Canada and Poland, but not so in Italy and Romania.
5   The indicator of attitudes towards politics and social matters (factor G, see par. 3.2.2) always has a significant effect on F_2^*. The correlation between these two variables is .72. (Had we considered F_2 instead of F_2^*, this correlation would have been only .32.) Since we used this indicator as a co-variate in our models, our aim being that of controlling its influence on F_2^*, we shall not dwell here on its relationship with F_2^*

(see par. 3.2.2). A consideration of this indicator (which appears to play a role in F_2) in the linear models that relate F_2 to other structural variables allows us to interpret the effects of these variables as being adjusted for the influence of opinions and attitudes.

6 Age has a significant influence on F_2, though the correlation coefficient is always very low.

7 In terms of goodness of fit, the various models explain no more than 40% of the variation in F_2. However, this percentage should be considered as good, in a situation like ours, and typical of social research. In fact, the response variable under examination is likely to be affected by numerous factors. Since we have our models on no more than six variables at a time (for the reasons already explained), we should not expect a better fit than that we actually obtained on our data. In this respect, it should be underlined that our aim is to cast light on the mechanisms that underlie power rather than to predict individual scores on the basis of a particular set of variables. Along these lines it is interesting to verify the above-mentioned mechanisms in the sub-sample of non-decision-makers. We have fitted the same models as in the total sample. Though we do not report the corresponding tables here, we make some comments on the results obtained. On the whole, the structure we found previously is confirmed, even if the goodness of fit of the various models decreases $(.20 < R^2 < .30)$. This is because the variable "category" was dropped out of these models. As to the remaining variables, we notice a lesser influence of the indicator of attitudes $(r = .203$ v. $r = .719$ in the total sample) and a greater weight of sex, country and their interaction. In fact, the gender difference increases (from .06 to .18) ranging from .09 in Canada, .19 in Italy, .25 in Romania, to .26 in Poland, which again appears to be the country with the largest difference (in favour of males). It should be underlined that the exaggeration of the differences when considering the sub-sample is because of the "masking effect" of decision-makers who are more homogeneous with respect to F_2.

3.2.2 *The Role of Opinions and Attitudes*

We have already noted the importance of subjective factors as contributing to F_2 scores. To reach this conclusion, we have taken into consideration several items in the questionnaire, which refer to the attitudes towards social participation, to the perception of social differences, to the opinions about the gender role in political life, and so on. We have discarded the idea of analysing these variables individually for statistical reasons (related to the different nature and importance of

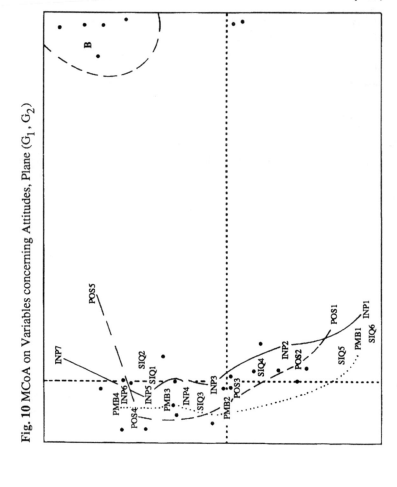

Fig. 10 MCoA on Variables concerning Attitudes, Plane (G_1, G_2)

each character, to the different incidence of missing values, and to the difficulty of inserting these variables as such in a single model).

Instead, we adopted a factorial approach and applied MCoA to the set of 48 items that pertain to the above-mentioned variables. Fig. 10 displays the projections of these items on to the first factorial plane (G_1, G_2).

Factor G_1 is essentially linked with the missing values. Therefore, it represents a measure of the will to collaborate in the interview by providing or not providing appropriate answers to the proposed questions. Factor G_2 is directly connected with the latent dimensions we are looking for, namely a scale of attitudes summarizing the way a person looks at social and political activities. In fact, we find on the positive side of the G_2 axis all types of items which describe a sort of "lack of confidence" in politics and social life: "participation is useless", "politics is a male business", no political information, family not interested in politics, opposition to women's participation.

On the left side of G_2 we observe all the opposite items which illustrate an open attitude towards participation and a substantial confidence in politics. We can state that G_2 is a suitable measure of attitudes towards political and social matters, scaling the individuals from progressive or liberal to conservative. For our purposes it would be more useful to have the inverse scaling. This can easily be achieved by reversing the sign of G_2.

Figure 10, where we have projected several supplementary variables belonging to different blocks of the data matrix D, provides further information about G. The inverse correlation with age is displayed, whereas a clear positive correlation with education is shown. The position of "non-religious people" (.43) as opposed to religious persons (.0) should be noted. The same type of opposition is found between "divorced people" (.22) and the remaining items of marital status (in particular, married people and widows, with negative coordinates).

All in all, the role of subjective factors, as summarized by the variable G, is particularly important in the association structure among the variables connected to power and participation. It is more evident in specific groups of individuals (Canadians, decision-makers, etc.). On the other hand, our measure of attitudes shows a significant correlation with many other variables, such as marital status, education, and religion. This reinforces the reliability of the latent dimension, represented by G, as an adequate synthesis of the attitudes concerning socio-political matters.

3.3 *A Typological Analysis of Power*

3.3.1 *A Description of Subgroups with Respect to* $F_2^\bullet$

In this section we try to characterize the different groups of individuals according to their scorings on $F_2^\bullet$. From the results of the previous analysis we may state that the most significant classes are constituted by people with $F_2^\bullet > 0.6$ and people with $F_2^\bullet < -.6$. The former score identifies persons who have attained significant positions in public life. It is, therefore, very useful to investigate the main characteristics of these distinguished people, with the aim of discovering the "determinants" of power. This procedure is typical of retrospective studies where we have "cases" (people with power) and "controls". In our context, the total sample may act as a control group. It is well known that inferences that are drawn in this way cannot be qualified as "casual inferences". Nonetheless, they may provide us with suitable indications about the mechanisms that underlie power, which can be matched with those that were obtained in the previous analysis. Very roughly, we may express these two ways of tackling the same problem by means of the following scheme:

(a) $(S, W, Z)\text{-------} > F_2^\bullet$

(b) $F_2^\bullet \text{ sub} \text{------} > (S, W, Z)$

Procedure (a) is based on the linear model previously described (the arrow indicates the direction of the relationship); procedure (b) is essentially based on a comparison between the partial distributions of S, W, Z, relative to $F_2^\bullet$, and their marginal distribution (the arrow indicates that we start from the groups individuated by $F_2^\bullet$).

We shall dwell, in particular, on the analysis of the results obtained by procedure (b), as applied to the sub-sample presenting $F_2^\bullet > .6$. We shall comment first on the partial distributions of sex, country, category, education, and father's occupation. In Table 4 we report the relative frequencies pertaining to stratification variables in the sub-sample and in the total sample (data concerning education and father's occupation not shown in the table).

We can appreciate both the striking incidence of decision-makers and the ranking of the remaining categories which reflects the order to which we have been accustomed in all of the previous analyses. We also notice a prevalence of males and of Polish people (with a lower presence of Romanians and Italians). There exists, in this class, an overwhelming number of graduates and of individuals with high school education. We

Table 4 Distribution of the Stratification Variables in the Sub-sample of Individuals with $F_2^* > .6$ and in the Total Sample

| | $F_2^* > .6$ | | Total Sample | |
	N	%	N	%
Country				
Canada	239	(25.3)	1,099	(26.64)
Italy	203	(21.5)	1,100	(26.67)
Poland	295	(31.3)	1,000	(24.24)
Romania	206	(21.8)	926	(22.45)
Total	943	(100.0)	4,125	(100.00)
Sex				
Male	512	(54.3)	2,013	(48.80)
Female	431	(45.7)	2,112	(51.20)
Total	943	(100.0)	4,125	(100.00)
Category				
Blue-collar worker	62	(6.6)	798	(19.35)
White-collar worker	92	(9.8)	805	(19.52)
Teacher	112	(11.9)	799	(19.37)
Housewife	12	(1.3)	400	(9.70)
Man out of work	16	(1.7)	299	(7.25)
Decision-maker	649	(68.8)	1,024	(24.82)
Total	943	(100.0)	4,125	(100.00)

record also a higher frequency of people with upper-class background (30% v. 20% in the total sample).

The partial bivariate distributions cast light on the interactions among the variables that were analysed in Table 3.

The main findings can be summarized as follows:

1 The incidence of decision-makers in our sub-sample varies dramatically according to the social system. In the capitalist countries we have 83.3% of people who belong to this category, whereas the analogous percentages in the socialist countries are 66.8% in Poland and only 43.2% in Romania. The latter country appears to be the most "open" in the field of participation and power, if we consider the greatest diffusion of these attributes among categories which have not been selected a priori on the basis of their power. (Incidentally, it should be noted that the same pattern is shown with respect to F_2, which is, as we said, a better indicator of participation.)

2 Another finding which confirms the above considerations is the significant presence, in our sub-sample, of white- and blue-collar workers belonging to socialist countries (80% v. 20% living in capitalistic countries). In this respect, it is useful to recall the point

about "seniority in work" being more associated with power in the socialist system than in the capitalist.

3 A further confirmation of what was said in 1 and 2 is provided by a consideration of father's occupation. The incidence of the upper-class categories (managers and professionals) is 52% in Canada, 35.5% in Italy and only 18% and 16% respectively in Poland and Romania.

4 The interaction between sex and category is particularly significant. The incidence of decision-makers among the females belonging to our sub-sample is greater than that of males (75.6% v. 63.1%). Conversely, the related frequency of white- and blue-collar workers is higher for men than for women (21.5% v. 10.2%).

In this connection we may describe in the following way the pattern of gender differences:

(a) Women with power are very similar to the corresponding males as to both their background and the individual pathways to power. We should remark that this finding is not in-built in the sampling design, since we are considering an indicator of power which has been constructed a posteriori.

(b) Housewives and men out of work show analogous behaviour with respect to participation and power.

(c) The gender differences are more marked in the "intermediate" groups (teachers, white-collar workers, blue-collar workers). In these groups we also find significant interactions with other variables, with country being placed first.

3.3.2 *Cluster Analysis of the First Three Factors of MCoA*

When modelling the relationship among the variables, we take into account the overall pattern of the observed characters, with reference to the entire sample of individuals. None the less, it often happens that such global (or average) "laws" are contradicted by the existence of different patterns in particular sub-samples. Therefore, it seems useful to apply appropriate techniques of analysis aimed at detecting the possible occurrence of these cases. This is particularly important if the group of individuals who show this behaviour can be characterized in some relevant way, according to sociological considerations (in other words, if the group defines a "type" in the framework of our research).

For this reason, classification of the individuals according to the first three factors of MCoA was considered. This yields a cloud of points in a three-dimensional space, which has been analysed by means of cluster analysis (Diday, 1982). The first outcome provides 15 clusters which can be further pooled into 6 clusters, whose single groups will be characterized in terms of both the variables concerning power and participation (block *Y*) and the variables of the remaining blocks.

The reader can immediately see (Fig. 11) the difference between the positioning of the groups on planes F_2 , F_3 and $\overset{\bullet}{F_2} F_3$. Note that the improvement concerns group 5 in relation to its representation on the power axis ($\overset{\bullet}{F_2}$).

There follows a brief description of the classes thus obtained.

Group 1 (N = 1,432; 34.7%)

It is a group of individuals who are clearly "alien" to politics and consequently to participation and power as we have defined them in this research. This group is essentially characterized by the considerable weight, within it, of housewives and men out of work (almost 80% of these belong to this group) and with an incidence of women, old people and youngsters and low education levels which is far greater than average.

As evidence of this, we find here not only 75% of those who state that their spouse earns all of their income but also a large number of no-answers to the questions on power, which have to be interpreted as "non-pertinent".

As regards country, Canada and Italy characterize the group with 72% of the individuals; with respect to status we find 10% of people classified a priori as "decision-makers". They belong, evidently, to that subgroup of the latter who do not hold public offices or who, more likely, did not want to state it during the interview.

Group 2 (N = 1,326; 32.1%)

This is a group of individuals who are still "distant" from power, understood in terms of public offices and in terms of participation, either in politics or party life. Instead, this group is strongly characterized by participation in activities that derive directly from the work environment: most people who are registered in a union belong to this group, particularly those with a long active service in the trade unions (73% of the total) and who dedicate most time to these organizations.

Sex does not play any role (in the sense that the male and female presence is totally balanced) nor do education and father's occupation. The group can be described as composed of young people, workers, teachers from all countries, with a prevalence of those from Romania.

Fig. 11 Display of the Centres of Gravity of Six
Groups on Planes (F_2, F_3) and (F_2^*, F_3)

(a) Plane (F_2, F_3)

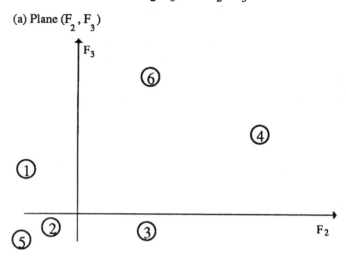

(b) Plane (F_2^*, F_3)

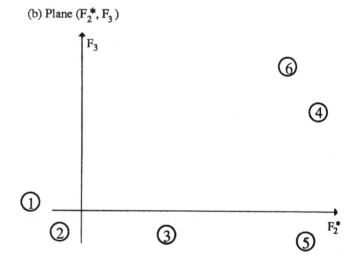

Group 3 (N = 856; 20.8%)

This is a group of individuals who are directly involved in the management of power, here meaning mainly that they participate in party life and hold governmental offices to a significant extent. It is characterized moreover by a high educational level, by a larger presence of males as opposed to females, and by Poles and Romanians (who represent almost 75% of the group). Unlike the other groups, we have for these individuals a positive influence of the factor "attitude" (for instance, religion at the lower levels, and political information at the higher).

Finally, 45% of the subjects of this group, belong to the subgroup of decision-makers (37.1% of the total).

Group 4 (N = 323; 7.8%)

This group gains a strong qualitative importance within our research on typologies with respect to power. As a matter of fact, besides high involvement in party life and the acquisition of governmental offices, this group is noticeably characterized by "negative" values for trade unions (such as no enrolment) and by positive values, such as for feminist associations and voluntary organizations. The group is again positively defined by the influence of the environment as well as by social birth privileges (managers' families, high education, long seniority at work, etc.). As far as country is concerned, the group is mainly formed by Canadians (57%) and Italians (26%), and as regards category, by decision-makers (28%).

Since we do not find sex differences here (unlike in group 3), we can formulate the hypothesis that in the group of people with the highest social and political power (therefore with greater familial and environmental opportunities to succeed), the gender differences tend to disappear. The hypothesis is confirmed by other findings in this research.

Group 5 (N = 77; 1.96%)

This group of individuals is mainly characterized by two features as far as the information available to us is concerned: they certainly belong to privileged classes (decision-makers, college education) but they consistently gave a "no answer" reply to a whole series of questions (those on governmental offices). As regards country, only Canada is scarcely represented (5% of the total). As regards sex, this group is mostly composed of males.

Group 6 (N = 111; 2.7%)

The classification of the people of this group can be accounted for mainly by the third factor which is, indeed, linked to power but is understood in terms of acquisition of local offices. It is interesting to note the occurrence of a large presence of Poles and Italians, and of a high percentage of Catholics and church-goers. The "attitude" factor is not, on average, very influential. (Apart from the "negative" effect of the combination religion/religious practice, there are, in fact, progressive attitudes towards participation in general, but especially towards female participation.)

The large presence of workers and of party members hints at particular phenomena of participation from the floor (consider Federazione Lavoratori Metalmeccanici in Italy, for instance, and Solidarity in Poland as well as a strong presence in the two countries of voluntary associations).

* * *

Within the framework of the results obtained by means of cluster analysis, we may try to single out the role played by gender differences. In this connection, we should recall that our stratified sample is not representative of the reference populations in terms of sex. Therefore, the results under examination must be interpreted as an attempt to define "typologies", irrespective of the numeric weight that they may happen to have in each of the investigated countries. Each typology is characterized by specific interactions among sex, power and other concomitant variables, which cast light on the mechanisms of gender (in)equalities.

Following this premise, we can say that the gender differences mainly operate at two different levels of power and participation.

The first level concerns the majority of the interviewed people, namely those who are positioned near the centre of gravity in the factorial space (F_1, F_2, F_3). These account for 66% of the people sample and give rise to groups G_1 and G_2 of cluster analysis, which turned out to be very consistent in the successive allocation to ten as well as six classes. These people are mostly alien to both power management and party involvement. The simultaneous analysis of the two groups gives substance to the hypothesis that the gender differences are nullified (passing from G_1 to G_2) essentially because of the effect of the "work" variable. It is interesting to note that G_1 is mainly formed by Italians and Canadians, while Poles and Romanians prevail in G_2 where the equalizing effect of "work" takes place.

The second level concerns people who score high on power and participation. These people constitute groups G_3 and G_4. Again, the comparative analysis of these two groups allows us to single out the factors that affect the gender difference, at this level of power. In fact, group G_3 shows an overall gap between males and females, owing to the fact that, unlike women, males follow an individual trend towards power, supported by high scores on factor G (political information, opinions and attitudes) and by "appropriate" choices as to their personal curriculum (education, party membership, etc.). Conversely, group G_4 does not show any gender difference as to power and participation and is characterized by persons belonging to a social "elite". In this context, males and females do not differ as to their social background and personal curriculum. Thus, the variables that are connected with these last aspects seem to account for the gender (in)equalities, at the highest level of power and participation. We observe that group G_2 is more characteristic for Poles and Romanians and G_4 for Canadians and Italians.

4 Conclusion

The application of the various multivariate methods described in this appendix allowed us to achieve three main results:

1 We obtained a global but detailed appraisal of power and public participation as a common sociological phenomenon in the four countries under investigation;
2 With reference to this synthetic measure of power and participation, we have been able to single out the explanatory and concomitant variables that exert the main influence on the individual's relationship with social and political life;
3 We succeeded in better understanding the specific status of gender differences in the framework of the above-mentioned relationships.

There follows a brief description of the results, referring to each of the above three points.

1 By means of the factorial score of power and participation, we obtained:
(a) a gradient of the institutions related to power, starting from the unions and proceeding through women's organizations, the party, and voluntary associations (see Fig. 1);
(b) an insight into the role in the party within the above sequence, which is not "linear" in the sense that membership in the party seems

to act as a "filter" towards getting the most important offices and, consequently, the highest scores on the power factor;

(c) a ranking of the most relevant positions that can be held along the factorial dimension of power and participation: lack of economic independence; membership in some association; taking the floor, seniority, holding one office, holding several offices in that association.

2 With reference to the relationship between power and other variables, we realized that:

(a) among the variables that identify the social background of a person, the most relevant are those involved in defining factor G (opinions, attitudes, information) rather than the traditional explanatory variables such as father's occupation, social class, etc.;

(b) the individual path in society (education, occupation, seniority in work and in associations) affects to a great extent the positioning of a person along the dimension of power and participation.

3 Independently of the remaining variables, a gender difference in favour of males has been systematically ascertained, particularly among the non-decision-makers. When considering the interaction with country, we realized that this difference shows up only in the group of decision-makers, with the females who belong to the capitalist countries overtaking the respective males while exactly the reverse phenomenon occurs in the socialist countries. This finding pushed us towards probing into the factor that accounts for the above-mentioned difference. The typologies which were obtained by means of cluster analysis clarified this point by casting light on the mechanism of the barrier that may prevent women from achieving equal conditions, with respect to men, regarding power and participation. In fact, referring first to those who have the highest scores on power, we found that in group 4, where factor G and the individual paths in society do not differentiate females from males, no gender differences are observed (rather a slight superiority of women, specifically in the capitalist countries). However, when looking at people who score low on power and participation, we realized that it is the factor "work" which tends to equalize the sexes (this phenomenon is more evident in the socialist countries).

Notes

1 We use the denomination 'non-traditional' to refer to the way of combining the various techniques rather than to the application of each single technique.

2 The first three factors account for 16% of the total variation in our matrix. This should be considered a sufficiently satisfactory result, taking into account the size of the matrix and the properties of MCoA.

3 N(I) and N(J) indicate respectively the clouds of the individual points and of the item (or category) points of matrix D.

4 In general, figures carry single labels pertaining only to significant points. Those remaining are either reported without any specific label or have a common label identifying a certain group (e.g. A or B, with the same meaning as in Fig. 1).

5 We see in Fig. 3b that the 'No answer' lies on the left side of the axis, whereas the categories 'not applicable' are on the right side (broken lines in Fig.3).

6 This remark should be borne in mind when interpreting the position of Canada in terms of power and participation with respect to other countries.

7 Reporting the absolute and relative contributions of the 39 categories (pertaining to the compound variable) to the first four factors.

8 However a more careful study would help the reader to interpret these factors. We omit them for the sake of brevity. emphasizes some differences between countries belonging to the same system. For instance, if we refer to the decision-makers, we observe that Canada accounts for 47% of the inertia of $F_{(1)}$, whereas the corresponding percentage for Italy is only 10% (in both cases a larger part of the percentage is owing to women rather than to men). On the other hand, Poland accounts for 16.5% (nearly 13% owing to men and the rest to women), Romania for only 2%. A different ranking of contributions is observed for $F_{(2)}$. Poland accounts for 23% of the inertia of this factor, followed by Romania, Canada and Italy with, respectively, 16.5%, 13.4% and 4%.

9 We note that the new factors, though providing a better fit in the plane, are no longer the best *individual* dimensions in terms of the amount of total inertia accounted for. This property rests uniquely with F_1 and F_2. Instead, the percentage of inertia pertaining to the plane remains unchanged.

10 It should be underlined that the assumption of normality (in homogeneous sub-populations) may be justified on the grounds of the way in which $\overset{\bullet}{F_2}$ (or F_2) is constructed. This variable results from the combination of a very large number of contributions (the quantified categories of each of the original variables that was considered in MCoA). These contributions act as a set of small and approximately independent random effects on the total score. This, in turn, is the classical rationale behind the Gaussian approximation.

METHODOLOGICAL NOTE

The purpose of this note is to provide the reader who lacks an advanced statistical background, but nevertheless has a statistical background above the average, with the rudiments of Correspondence Analysis. Consequently, we have deliberately skipped many technical details which the interested reader may find in the texts quoted at the end of the References.

1 Correspondence Analysis

Correspondence Analysis is a technique of factor analysis which is particularly suitable for qualitative variables. There are several ways of presenting this technique from a mathematical viewpoint (reciprocal averages, dual scaling, principal component analysis, etc.; see Tenenhaus and Young (1985), for a detailed discussion). Greenacre (1984) and Lebart et al. (1984) provide a thorough description of this method, supported by illustrations of numerous applications. In what follows, we shall limit ourselves to emphasizing the features that are relevant for understanding the way we processed our data in this appendix.

Correspondence Analysis can be applied to several types of data tables, giving rise to different specifications of the same basic technique. We shall illustrate here the specific methods we utilized, namely Multiple Correspondence Analysis (MCoA) and Simple Correspondence Analysis (SCoA) as applied to a set of two-way contingency tables with one common margin.

1.1 *Multiple Correspondence Analysis*

A population of n individuals is described by a set of p qualitative variables $V_1...V_p$ with $m_1...m_p$ categories (items). The total number of items is $m = \Sigma m_j$. We define $j\ell$ as item ℓ of variable j. For each individual i ($i = 1,...,n$), we define:

$$x_{ij\ell} = \begin{cases} 1 \text{ if individual i is in category } \ell \text{ of the variable j} \\ 0 \text{ otherwise} \end{cases}$$

These quantities are the element of an n-element binary indicator vector $x_{j\ell}$ which is associated with item ℓ of variable j:

$$x'_{j\ell} = \{x_{1j\ell},..., x_{nj\ell}\}$$

($x'_{j\ell}$ denotes the vector $x_{j\ell}$ transposed. Since $x_{j\ell}$ is always considered as a column vector, $x'_{j\ell}$ is a row vector.)

Together, the m_j vectors for variable V_j form an (n by m_j) binary indicator matrix : X_j .

Finally, for all p variables, we obtain the (n by m) binary indicator matrix X by horizontally adjoining the X_{js} :

$$X = \{X_1,..., X_p\}$$

MCoA may be viewed as a method of simultaneously quantifying the individuals and the items of several qualitative variables. In fact, a sequence of different quantifications can be determined from the analysis of X, in decreasing order of importance according to the amount of "variation" explained at each stage, h, of the analysis (h = 1,2...). In exactly the same way, the well-known technique of Principal Component Analysis (PCA), for quantitative variables, allows us to single out the sequence of latent dimensions which are associated with successive (decreasing) parts of the total variations that are measured on the original data. Indeed, MCoA consists of a PCA of the binary indicator matrix X, after having weighted each individual by $1/n$ and each item $j\ell$ by the "relative" frequency $n_{j\ell}/np$, where $n_{j\ell}$ is the number of individuals who present item ℓ of variable j.

At stage h of the analysis, we obtain the individuals' scores: $s_1^h,..., s_i^h,..., s_n^h$, and the scores of the items: $v_{11}^h,..., v_{j\ell}^h,..., v_{pm_p}^h$

As in PCA, the individuals' scores are linear combinations of the indicator variables:

$$(1) \qquad s_i^h = \sum_{j=1}^{p} \sum_{\ell=1}^{m_j} \alpha_{j\ell}^h x_{ij\ell} , \ (i = 1,..., n)$$

where $\alpha_{j\ell}$ is a number associated with item ℓ of variable j (at stage h). The coefficient $\alpha_{j\ell}$ measures the importance of item ℓ of variable j, in defining the h-th factorial dimension.

Analogously, the scores of the items are provided by the following linear combinations:

$$(2) \qquad V_{j\ell}^h = \sum_{i=1}^{n} \beta_i^h x_{ij\ell} , \ (j = 1,..., p; \ \ell = 1,..., m_j)$$

where β_i^h is a number associated with individual i (at stage h), which measures the importance of this individual in defining the h-th factorial dimension.

The individuals and the items can be simultaneously represented on each factorial axis, by means of their scores. A justification for this simultaneous representation is provided by the "transition formulae":

(3)
$$s_i^h = c_h \frac{1}{p} \sum_{j=1}^{p} \sum_{\ell=1}^{m_j} x_{ij\ell} \, v_{j\ell}^h$$

$$v_{j\ell}^h = c_h \frac{1}{n_{j\ell}} \sum_{i=1}^{n} x_{ij\ell} \, s_i^h$$

where c_h is a constant (depending only on h). The relationship (3) states that the point representing each individual on the h-th axis is approximately located at the centre of gravity of the points representing the items that pertain to that individual. Analogously, each item is approximately located at the centre of gravity of the individuals presenting that item. Therefore, the items characterizing a particular individual are close to that individual and, vice versa, the individuals presenting one particular item are closer to that item than are the remaining individuals. On the other hand, the proximity between two individuals (on the h-th axis) is a geometrical translation of their similarity with respect to what the h-th axis represents in terms of the items that are associated with it (see "absolute contributions" below).

An analogous interpretation is to be given to the proximity between two items, which underlines their association (with respect to the latent dimension that is represented by the h-th axis). In general, not all possible factorial axes are retained in the analysis. As in PCA, the most significant factors are associated with the largest eigenvalues of the square matrix (which we do not show here) whose spectral analysis provides the scores (1) and (2). Each eigenvalue λ_h (h = 1,2,...,H) measures (in decreasing order) the amount of variation accounted for by the h-th axis. As an index of the explanatory power of the h-th factor, the following ratio can be used:

$$\pi = \lambda_h / \sum_h \lambda_h$$

In MCoA, for technical reasons, which cannot be dealt with here, this index provides, in general, very low values, thereby systematically undervaluing the power of each factor.

More specific measures of the representational quality of factor h are given by the so-called "relative contributions" (RC) of each individual and item:

$$RC_h(i) = (s_i^h)^2 / \sum_{h=1}^{H} (s_i^h)^2$$

(4)

$$RC_h(j\ell) = (v_{j\ell}^h)^2 / \sum_{h=1}^{H} (v_{j\ell}^h)^2$$

The individuals who have a good representation on the h-th axis are those who show a high value of RC_h. The same holds true for the items. In order to obtain a statistical interpretation of function h, the so-called "absolute contributions" (AC) of each individual and item are to be considered:

$$AC_h(i) = (s_i^h)^2 / n\lambda_n$$

(5)

$$AC_h(j\ell) = n_{j\ell} (v_{j\ell}^h)^2 / n\lambda_n$$

The indices (5) measure the fraction of the total variation that is accounted for by the factor h, which is due to that particular individual (i) or to item (jℓ). Obviously, factor h is mainly characterized by the individuals and items whose AC are largest. However, the way in which each individual or item is linked with factor h is more specifically expressed by the scores s_i^h, $v_{j\ell}^h$ whose algebraic signs show the direction of this link.

In MCoA, as well as in PCA, it is common practice to devote special attention to the first factors, providing a graphical representation of individuals and items in the planes (1,2) (1,3) (2,3), etc.

It can be shown (Greenacre, 1984; Lebart et al., 1984) that this representation on low-dimensional spaces corresponds to a projection on to the above-mentioned planes of the vectors representing the individuals (in R^m) and the items (in R^n). This property can be exploited in order to represent, for instance, a "new" item (not yet considered in the analysis) in the already determined factorial planes. In fact, provided that this item is observed in the same individuals of the original data matrix X (belonging, therefore, to the space R^n), it can be projected on to the factorial plane under consideration. Its location in this plane can be interpreted according to the meaning that we have already attached to the area in which it falls (on the basis of the interpretative rules previously recalled). An analogous representation can be provided for a "new" individual, provided that the same p variables as in matrix X have been observed in this individual. From this point of view, the elements (individuals, items) in X are called "active" elements, whereas the "new" elements, which are projected on to the factorial planes after the analysis has been carried out, are determined as "supplementary" elements.

1.2 *Simple Correspondence Analysis as Applied to Two-way Contingency Tables*

It may be shown (e.g. Greenacre, 1984) that SCoA is a particular case of MCoA, when p = 2. In this case the data matrix can be represented as a two-way contingency table which cross-classifies the individuals according to the qualitative variables V_1, V_2 . We denote by n_{rc} the frequency of individuals presenting item r of V_1 and item c of V_2, and by N_{12} the (m_1 by m_2) matrix whose elements in row r and column c is n_{rc}. The marginal distributions of Y are respectively denoted by $n_{r.}$ and $n_{.c}$ (r = 1 ,..., m_1; c = 1 ,..., m_2), where

(6)
$$n_r = \sum_{r=1}^{m_2} n_{rc}$$
$$n_c = \sum_{r=1}^{m_1} n_{rc}$$

Two new matrices can be derived from N_{12}, which are respectively called the "row-profile" matrix P_{12}^r and the "column-profile" matrix P_{12}^c, whose elements are obtained from N_{12} , by dividing each n_{rc} respectively by $n_{r.}$ or $n_{.c}$. It can be shown that SCoA is a PCA of P_{12}^r or, equivalently, of P_{12}^r having introduced an appropriate Euclidean distance between two row-profiles or two column-profiles. Considering, for instance, the PCA of P_{12}^r, we obtain scores for the rows (items of V_1) and columns (items of V_2) in a way which is analogous to that already described for the data matrix X in MCoA.

The same rules of graphical representation and interpretation apply also in this case, if we replace only the (individual by item) array X with the (item by item) array P_{12}^r. In the latter case we realize a "correspondence" (in the factorial planes) between items belonging to two different variables (V_1 and V_2), whereas in the former case we had a correspondence between individuals and items belonging to a set of variables. On the grounds of the equivalence between MCoA, as applied to V_1 and V_2, and the PCA of P_{12}^r , we may also represent the individuals beside the items of V_1 and V_2 in the same factorial planes, thus fully exploiting the information that is contained in the original data.

Leclerc (1976) takes into consideration a more complicated data matrix, which is obtained by adjoining a set of two-way contingency tables with one common margin. Let us suppose, for instance, that we are willing to analyse the association between V_1 and each of the remaining variables: V_2,..., V_3,..., V_p. To this end we may consider {m_1 by

$(m_2 + ... + m_p)\}$ matrix $N = (N_{12}, N_{13},..., N_{1p})$ whose rows refer to the items of V_1 and whose successive columns to the items of V_2, V_3...V_p. Formally, a row-profile matrix P^r can be derived from N if we divide each frequency n_{rc} by the sum of the marginal frequencies n_r for each sub-table N_{12}, N_{13},... etc. SCoA, as applied to N, is equivalent to a PCA of P^r. A simultaneous representation of the items of V_1, on one hand, and the items of V_2, V_3 etc., on the other, can be obtained in the factorial planes that are yielded by SCoA of N.

In this case, the transition formulae (3) refer to the set of items of V_1, on one side, and to the set of items of *all* the remaining variables, on the other. The interpretation is carried out in terms of the pairwise associations between V_1 and each of the remaining variables.

Of course, the variable that defines the common margin of the two-way tables (namely the rows of N) can be chosen as a given partition of the population of n individuals. We did this in our application. In fact, in our case, we defined a compound variable, resulting from the combination of sex, country, and category, which acts as a partition of the population into 39 categories. The cross-classification of this partition with each of the variables pertaining to power and participation defines, in our case, the data matrix N to which SCoA has been applied. The results of this analysis cast light on the association structure that links the 39 categories with the several variables which measure different aspects of power and participation.

2 Linear Models

In this section we could have reported a few tables concerning the analysis of the relationship between factors F_2 and $\dot{F}_2$, and a group of explanatory variables. We decided not to reproduce them here is because they make dull reading.

APPENDIX C

THE SAMPLE DEMOGRAPHIC STRUCTURE

The principles upon which the sample was constructed have been described in the Introduction. Here our purpose is to present the sample comparing the respondents in Canada, Italy, Poland and Romania in order to show the similarities and differences that exist among them. We again remind the reader that this is not a representative sample; only for the sake of brevity do we speak of Canada, Italy, Poland and Romania.

1 Sex

It is one of the main assumptions of the project that there should be an equal number of men and women in all of the categories making up the sample.

2 Age

The categories show some differences as far as age is concerned (Table 1). On the whole, blue- and white-collar workers are relatively younger than members of the other categories. However, this is not always the case. In some countries, such as Italy, male blue-collar workers are among the oldest respondents. On the other hand, decision-makers of either sex are clearly older than the other respondents, with the mean age of female decision-makers ranging between 45 (Poland) and 48 (Canada) and that of male decision-makers between 47 (Poland) and 50 (Italy).

An analysis of age differences between men and women within each category shows that there are no statistically significant differences in Canada, while in Italy male white-collar workers, in Poland male teachers and in Romania male decision-makers are older than their female counterparts.

A comparison between categories of the same sex within each country shows that, apart from decision-makers, no common pattern emerges in the countries of our study. Statistically significant differences appear in more cases in Romania and Poland than in Italy and Canada.

Table 1 Age Distribution, 1980 (number with percentage in brackets)

Age range	Blue-collar workers		White-collar workers		Teachers	
	Male	Female	Male	Female	Male	Female
			Canada			
≤ 29	32 (32)	19 (19.2)	37 (37)	56 (56)	10 (10)	23 (23)
30-39	35 (35)	33 (33.3)	35 (35)	22 (22)	71 (71)	46 (46)
40-49	14 (14)	24 (24.2)	14 (14)	9 (9)	15 (15)	21 (21)
≥ 50	19 (19)	23 (23.2)	14 (14)	13 (13)	4 (4)	10 (10)
Average	37	41	36	33	36	38
			Italy			
≤ 29	8 (8)	46 (46.5)	5 (5)	20 (20)	16 (16.2)	19 (19)
30-39	11 (11)	29 (29.3)	14 (13.9)	30 (30)	26 (26.3)	29 (29)
40-49	30 (30)	17 (17.2)	31 (30.7)	27 (27)	27 (27.3)	21 (21)
≥ 50	51 (51)	7 (7.1)	51 (50.5)	23 (23)	30 (30.3)	31 (31)
Average	48	34	49	41	44	43
			Poland			
≤ 29	50 (50.5)	51 (50.5)	44 (43.6)	44 (42.3)	34 (34.3)	9 (9)
30-39	19 (19.2)	16 (15.8)	20 (19.8)	25 (24)	26 (26.3)	12 (12)
40-49	23 (23.2)	18 (17.8)	27 (26.7)	25 (24)	23 (23.2)	74 (74)
≥ 50	7 (7.1)	16 (15.8)	10 (9.9)	10 (9.6)	16 (16.2)	5 (5)
Average	35	35	36	36	38	43
			Romania			
≤ 29	38 (38)	51 (51.5)	20 (20)	21 (21.2)	20 (20)	14 (14)
30-39	32 (32)	17 (17.2)	19 (19)	32 (32.3)	31 (31)	29 (29)
40-49	23 (23)	19 (19.2)	36 (36)	29 (29.3)	23 (23)	35 (35)
≥ 50	7 (7)	12 (12.1)	25 (25)	17 (17.2)	26 (26)	22 (22)
Average	35	35	43	40	42	42

An international comparison, on the other hand, shows that there are no significant differences among, respectively, blue- and white-collar workers in the four countries. Among the other categories, the significant differences show that the Italian and Romanian members tend to be older. In Poland decision-makers of both sexes are younger than their colleagues in the other countries.

3 Education

It was obvious from the start that the categories selected for inclusion in the sample would differ in terms of their average level of education

Table 1 Age Distribution, 1980 (number with percentage in brackets)

	People out of work		Decision-makers	
	Male	Female	Male	Female
Age range				
		Canada		
≤ 29	38 (38)	22 (22)	2 (1.3)	4 (2.7)
30-39	31 (31)	54 (54)	30 (20)	45 (30)
40-49	13 (13)	16 (16)	46 (30.7)	32 (21.3)
≥ 50	18 (18)	8 (8)	72 (48)	69 (46)
Average	37	37	50	48
		Italy		
≤ 29	68 (68)	9 (9.1)	6 (4)	4 (2.7)
30-39	16 (16)	23 (23.2)	15 (10)	33 (22)
40-49	12 (12)	32 (32.3)	56 (37.3)	53 (35.3)
≥ 50	4 (4)	35 (35.4)	73 (48.7)	60 (40)
Average	46	29	50	47
		Poland		
≤ 29	---	39 (39)	5 (3.3)	9 (6.2)
30-39	---	42 (42)	31 (20.5)	37 (25.5)
40-49	---	11 (11)	50 (33.1)	56 (38.6)
≥ 50	---	8 (8)	65 (43)	43 (29.7)
Average	---	35	47	45
		Romania		
≤ 29	3 (3.1)	18 (18)	2 (3.2)	0
30-39	10 (10.2)	25 (25)	1 (1.6)	3 (4.6)
40-49	26 (26.5)	27 (27)	25 (39.7)	44 (67.7)
≥ 50	59 (60.2)	30 (30)	35 (55.6)	18 (27.7)
Average	43	50	50	48

(Table 2). The open question was whether men and women from the same category would have the same standards of education.

Italians are relatively less educated than respondents from the other countries. In general, decision-makers have had most advanced education, though teachers come a close second and in Canada they are educated as highly as decision-makers. Blue-collar workers, particularly female, are everywhere a group with a very low education, almost on the same level with housewives, who in Italy and Romania are less educated than all other female categories.

Only rarely can statistically significant differences be found between men and women from the same category: in Canada male blue-collar workers are better educated than female blue-collar workers, in Poland

Table 2 Levels of Education (average number of years completed)

	Canada	Italy	Poland	Romania
Male blue-collar workers	11.1	7.0	11.2	10.3
Female blue-collar workers	10.2	7.9	9.6	9.1
Male white-collar workers	14.0	11.3	13.2	13.4
Female white-collar workers	13.0	11.8	12.5	12.7
Male teachers	17.0	14.7	16.2	16.0
Female teachers	16.6	14.1	14.9	15.1
Men out of work	10.2	11.2	-	8.6
Housewives	11.3	6.3	10.7	7.5
Male decision-makers	17.5	16.6	16.9	17.6
Female decision-makers	16.3	15.6	16.0	16.6

male teachers and decision-makers, and in Romania male decision-makers.

Statistically significant differences (p < .001) can, however, be found when members of different categories are compared. Polish women stand out here, because in this country statistically significant differences can be found only between female decision-makers and members of all other female categories.

A cross-country comparison revealed that there are no significant differences (p < .001) in the level of education among the men out of work from the three countries. In all other categories the comparison shows that the Italians are the least and the Canadians the most educated.

4 Marital Status

Married respondents are a majority in all countries, ranging from 67.2% in Canada to 77.2% in Romania. Next come the respondents who never married (from 13% in Romania to 20% in Canada), followed by divorced or separated people (from 4% in Italy to 10.7% in Canada). Widowed respondents are in a clear minority (from 2% in Canada to 4.3% in Italy).

The various categories in the sample have a different composition in terms of their members' marital status. By far the lowest proportion of married people can be found among men out of work in Canada and Italy (not more than one-third); among the Romanian men out of work, on the other hand, that proportion is twice as high. Of course, the highest proportion of married people can be found, almost by definition, among housewives. In Canada, Romania and Poland, all housewives are married, while in Italy a small proportion is not. Next, obviously, because of their age, come male decision-makers, ranging from 84.6% in Italy to

90.3% in Romania. Practically the reverse is true for female decision-makers, who present the lowest (or, as in Romania, one of the lowest) proportions of married women in comparison with men and women in all of the other categories. When it comes to divorced or separated people, their proportion among female decision-makers is relatively higher than in the other categories in Italy, Poland and Romania. In Canada, female decision-makers have among them the largest proportion of widows.

5 Household Composition

The types of household composition existing among the respondents are described in Table 3.

Two types of households predominate: the "nuclear" family and the "large" family. In Poland, Romania and particularly Canada, the "nuclear" family is clearly prevalent, while in Italy the "large" family predominates. Some regularities were found to exist. Relatively more male decision-makers and female teachers live in "large" family households than do members of the other categories.

More female decision-makers than male decision-makers live alone. This is more true for this category than for all of the others, male or female, with only one exception (Canadian men out of work).

The respondents' households do not always include children. In many categories, the average number of children per household is smaller than 1. Such is the case in all countries, except Italy, among male white-collar workers, teachers, and men out of work (in the latter case also including Italy). The same is true of the households of female blue- and white-collar workers in all countries, except Italy, as well as those of female teachers in Canada and Romania. The mean number of children in the families of men and women belonging to the same categories is rather similar, with female respondents usually having fewer children than the males, save Polish female teachers who have more children than male teachers. In all of countries under consideration, housewives, again almost by definition, have the largest number of children, or one of the largest. In Poland, though, female teachers come first in this respect.

The t test shows that statistically significant differences concerning the number of children in the male respondents' households can be found relatively more often in Canada. In this country, male white-collar workers and male decision-makers have significantly ($p < .01$) more children than women in the same categories. In Italy, a similar difference exists between male and female decision-makers, while in Romania no differences were found (1).

Table 3 Household Composition (number with percentage in brackets)

	Blue-collar workers		White-collar workers		Teachers	
	Male	Female	Male	Female	Male	Female
Canada						
Alone	4 (4)	16 (12.6)	15 (15)	16 (16)	12 (12)	19 (19)
Nuclear family	54 (54)	45 (45.5)	37 (37)	44 (44)	59 (59)	56 (56)
Relatives	14 (14)	14 (14.1)	26 (26)	23 (23)	17 (17)	8 (8)
Nuclear family and others	28 (28)	24 (24.2)	22 (22)	17 (17)	12 (12)	17 (17)
Italy						
Alone	4 (4)	2 (2)	4 (4)	7 (7)	6 (6)	6 (6)
Nuclear family	33 (36)	47 (47.5)	43 (42.6)	47 (47)	48 (48)	33 (33)
Relatives	5 (5)	23 (23.2)	6 (5.9)	16 (16)	14 (14)	14 (14)
Nuclear family and others	55 (55)	27 (27.3)	48 (47.5)	30 (30)	32 (32)	47 (47)
Poland						
Alone	12 (12.1)	12 (11.9)	9 (8.9)	11 (10.6)	4 (4)	1 (1)
Nuclear family	38 (38.4)	31 (30.7)	43 (42.6)	38 (36.5)	50 (50.5)	47 (47)
Relatives	21 (21.2)	40 (39.6)	20 (19.8)	21 (20.2)	19 (19.2)	9 (9)
Nuclear family and others	28 (28.3)	18 (17.8)	29 (28.7)	34 (32.7)	26 (26.3)	43 (43)
Romania						
Alone	3 (3)	8 (8)	6 (6)	7 (7.1)	12 (12)	1 (1)
Nuclear family	56 (56)	43 (43)	46 (46)	38 (38.4)	49 (49)	42 (42)
Relatives	17 (17)	24 (24)	16 (16)	18 (18.2)	13 (13)	18 (18)
Nuclear family and others	24 (24)	25 (25)	32 (32)	36 (36.4)	26 (26)	39 (39)

The "nuclear family" includes a couple with or without children. "Relatives" refers to a situation where the respondent lives with his/her parents-in-law, other relatives, or live-in domestic help. "Nuclear family and others" corresponds to the "large" family, e.g. a household combining the features of the two previous types.

Cross-country comparisons show that there are no statistically significant differences between male and female blue-collar workers, men out of work, and housewives from all countries. As for other categories, the significant differences found show that Italians tend to have more children in all of them, especially in comparison with Poland and Romania.

Table 3 Household Composition (number with percentage in brackets)

	People out of work		Decision-makers	
	Male	Female	Male	Female
Canada				
Alone	51 (51)	0	13 (8.7)	41 (27.3)
Nuclear family	24 (24)	74(74)	81 (54)	34 (22.7)
Relatives	14 (14)	0	6 (4)	19 (12.7)
Nuclear family and others	11 (11)	26(26)	50 (33.3)	56 (37.3)
Italy				
Alone	9 (9)	3 (3)	14 (9.3)	25 (16.7)
Nuclear family	17 (17)	36 (36)	58 (38.7)	30 (20)
Relatives	54 (54)	10 (10)	7 (4.7)	39 (26)
Nuclear family and others	20 (20)	51 (51)	71 (47.3)	56 (37.3)
Poland				
Alone	-	0	9 (6)	18 (12.4)
Nuclear family	-	60 (60)	74 (49)	57 (39.3)
Relatives	-	2 (2)	9 (6)	21 (14.5)
Nuclear family and others	-	38 (38)	59 (39.1)	49 (33.8)
Romania				
Alone	9 (9.1)	2 (2)	4 (6.3)	5 (7.7)
Nuclear family	33 (33.1)	64 (64)	27 (42.9)	20 (30.8)
Relatives	13 (13.1)	0	1 (1.6)	5 (7.7)
Nuclear family and others	44 (44.4)	34 (34)	31 (49.2)	35 (53.8)

6 Social Background

The different social and political structures of the countries included in the study makes it obvious that the transfer of parental social status to children will be more frequent in Italian and Canadian societies than in Polish and Romanian.

The findings are especially interesting because they show up the differences in social background among decision-makers.

6.1 *Father's Occupation*

In Italy and Canada a large segment of female and male decision-makers have fathers who are (or were) professionals or managers of middle level. This is true in Italy for 52.2% of female decision-makers and 42.2% of male decision-makers; in Canada for respectively 43.6% and 52.4%. In Poland and Romania the portion is much lower. In Poland, it is true only for 22% of male and 25% of female decision-makers, in Romania for respectively 22.2% and 15.8%. In the latter countries many decision-makers have fathers who are (or were) farmers or skilled blue-collar workers. In Poland, this is true for 44% of male and 34% of female decision-makers, in Romania for respectively 46% and 34.9%. In Italy only 9.6% of male and 10.9% of female decision-makers have fathers who are (or were) farmers or blue-collar skilled workers. In Canada the percentage of decision-makers who possess such a social background is higher than in Italy (25.5% and 15% respectively). We can say that the countries in our study clearly differ in the "social roots" of their decision-makers, to the point that they might be classified in two different groups.

An analysis of the social background of the respondents in the other categories of our sample shows similar patterns of differences among the four countries.

Having a father who is a small businessman almost never occurs among our Polish and Romanian respondents, contrary to what we find among Italian and, especially, Canadian respondents. The latter mention having a father who is a small businessman almost twice as often as they do a father who is a farmer. However, in Canada respondents with skilled blue-collar fathers represent almost 40% of respondents in all categories, with the exception of almost all teachers and a quarter of skilled blue-collar workers whose fathers are middle-level managers. In Italy, almost half of the blue- and white-collar workers have fathers who are skilled and unskilled blue-collar workers. In this country not only respondents but also their fathers are less educated than in Canada and Romania. In Italy, only among housewives does a relatively large percentage (a quarter) have fathers who are farmers.

A different pattern is found in Poland. The respondents' fathers who are skilled or unskilled blue-collar workers and also farmers constitute a majority (70-80%) in all categories, with the exception of male teachers and decision-makers of both sexes. Respondents who have a father who is a farmer constitute the largest portion among female blue-collar workers and teachers, housewives, and male decision-makers (about a quarter in each of those categories).

In Romania and in Canada respondents whose fathers are skilled blue-collar workers are a majority among male and female blue-collar workers. They also constitute about 40% of white-collar workers, housewives, and men out of work. Among the two last groups, however, a large segment of respondents (about 40%) has fathers who are farmers. It is also worth pointing out that about 30% of white-collar workers and teachers have fathers who are middle-level managers or, less frequently, professionals.

6.2 *Mother's Occupation*

A comparison of mothers' occupations shows that in all countries an overwhelming majority of mothers are housewives, but there are some differences among the countries. The highest number of housewives among the mothers of our respondents is in Italy: it ranges from 73.5% to 95.6%, depending on the category. Canada is second in this respect, with a proportion of housewives ranging from 59% to 81.2%. Third comes Romania, where the percentage of respondents' mothers who are housewives ranges from 48.5% to 66.7%. In Poland, where the percentage is lowest, it ranges from 46.9% to 60%.

In Canada and Italy, slightly more men than women in all categories have mothers who are housewives. This pattern is not so consistent in Poland and Romania, but in these countries male decision-makers more often than female decision-makers have (or had) mothers who are (or were) housewives.

In the case of Italian and Canadian decision-makers of both sexes, the next largest occupational group among the respondents' mothers are middle-level managers: they represent about 10% in each of these countries.

In all countries, but especially in Poland and Romania, mothers of female decision-makers are more educated than mothers of male decision-makers. In these countries the number of respondents whose mothers are middle-level managers is almost twice as low as in the other two. Female decision-makers whose mothers are white-collar workers, middle-level managers, and professionals constitute 27.8% in Poland and 19.3% in Romania, while the figures for male decision-makers are 19.3% and 3.2%. Compared with the other countries, the figures for female decision-makers in Canada are 24.2%, in Italy 16.3%; for male decision-makers in both Canada and Italy, 14.1%.

Another category of respondents whose mothers are occupationally active in professions which demand relatively higher education are school teachers and white-collar workers of both sexes in all countries, with the exception of Italy where almost all mothers of those respondents are housewives.

In Poland and Romania, however, some number of respondents of these same categories have mothers who are blue-collar workers, and, in Poland, also farmers and unskilled blue-collar workers. This almost never occurs in Canada and Italy.

6.3 *Spouse's Occupation*

Everywhere the occupational structure of the spouse is clearly different in the case of male and female respondents. The husbands of our respondents are very rarely not active, while a quite large number of wives of our respondents, especially in Canada and in Italy, are housewives. In Poland and Romania, wives who are just housewives are a minority; in both countries they constitute about 5%, with the exception of male decision-makers whose wives more often stay at home (their percentage is up to 15%). The same pattern --- a higher number of housewives among wives of decision-makers than in the other categories --- is found in Canada: here they constitute 68.9%. In Italy, where housewives constitute a majority (from 51.7% to 87.6%) the opposite pattern emerges: decision-makers' wives more often than wives of other respondents tend to be active (about half of them).

A comparison of the social status of husbands and wives (in other words, who is married to whom) shows to some extent a consistent pattern among countries.

Wives of blue-collar workers in Canada and Poland, if they are not housewives, are most often white-collar workers (over 30%) or skilled blue-collar workers (about 20%). In Poland, wives who are unskilled blue-collar workers constitute another rather large group (also about 20%). In Romania also, working wives of blue-collar workers belong mainly to the same occupational groups, but the majority of them are skilled blue-collar workers. In Italy almost all wives of blue-collar workers are housewives. We can say that male blue-collar workers tend to marry into the same or a higher social status than their own.

An analysis of the social status of the spouses of female blue-collar workers shows a different pattern. Their husbands are mainly skilled blue-collar workers: in Romania 83.1% were found to be married to skilled blue-collar workers (in Poland 52.7%, in Canada 54.4%) or to white-collar workers (about one-fifth in Canada) or to unskilled blue-collar workers (about one-fifth in Poland). Italian female blue-collar workers differ from all other respondents belonging to the same female category. They split into two groups: those married to white-collar workers and those to unskilled blue-collar workers.

A comparison of male and female white-collar workers shows a different, but fairly consistent pattern among countries. Women more often than men have spouses with higher status (middle-level managers or professionals), although many are married to people who are also white-collar workers or skilled blue-collar workers (the last group is almost absent in Italy).

A similar pattern of differences in spouses social status exists among male and female school teachers (less pronounced in Poland). Only in this country does a relatively high number of female teachers have skilled blue-collar workers for husbands (a quarter). But in all countries, almost half of the respondents of either sex are married to middle-managers or professionals. In Romania the tendency is even stronger, especially among female teachers whose husbands almost exclusively (80%) belong to these socio-occupational groups.

Housewives included in our study are married to men belonging to different socio-occupational groups, except in Romania, where over 90% of housewives are married to male blue-collar workers. In Poland and Canada it is the same for more than a half, in Italy for one-third. Husbands of Polish housewives are mainly white-collar workers (a quarter) and unskilled blue-collar workers (almost half). In Canada almost one-fifth of housewives are married to white-collar workers and a few to middle managers and small businessmen, besides those who are married to blue-collar workers. Italian housewives are more differentiated in this respect. The same number of housewives are married to white- as to blue-collar workers, and a number to small businessmen, unskilled blue-collar workers, middle managers, and professionals.

The socio-occupational structure of the wives of men out of work varies to some extent. In Canada and Italy, about 60% of them are housewives, in Romania only one-fifth. Other wives in Canada represent all possible socio-occupational groups (with the exception of executive managers and professionals). In Italy they are mainly white-collar workers, in Romania mainly skilled and unskilled blue-collar workers. Men out of work were not included in the Polish sample.

As in many other studies, spouses of male decision-makers, if they work at all, have a socio-occupational status lower than the spouses of female decision-makers, who are mainly professionals (over 50%), with the exception of Romania where they are mainly middle-level managers. This tendency is especially strong in Canada. In other countries, some number of decision-makers of both sexes are married to white-collar workers (the highest portion is found in Italy among male decision-makers and in Poland among female decision-makers, in each case about a quarter).

7 Religion and Religiosity

The nations covered by the study differ deeply as far as religion is concerned. Italy and Poland are strongly Catholic, a fact reflected in the composition of the sample: 97.6% of Italian and 95.5% of Polish respondents described themselves as Catholics. People from other faiths appear in negligible numbers in the Italian and Polish samples ; 2% of the Italians and 4% of the Poles say they are non-believers. In Italy, this last group consists almost solely of male and female decision-makers: in Poland there is a somewhat higher proportion of male and female white-collar workers and male teachers who proclaim themselves non-believers.

In Canada, Protestants make up the largest group of respondents (55.1%), followed by Catholics (28.5%). Other faiths are represented in small numbers: Jews account for 3.8% of the sample and non-believers for 6.3%. In Canada, there are more Catholics among blue- and white-collar workers and men out of work, while Protestants make up a large proportion of male and female teachers as well as male decision-makers (over 60% in both categories). Non-believers were usually found among men out of work and housewives (some 9% in each case).

In Romania, an overwhelming majority of respondents belongs to the Greek Orthodox Church. Catholics (3.8%) and non-believers (5.6%) form small groups. One-third of all non-believers are decision-makers of either sex.

As far as religious practice is concerned, some differences of intensity were found, especially between Romania and the other three countries. Of Romanian respondents, 65.2% said that they do not practise their religion at all; 1.2% do so very much. In the other three countries, people who do not practise their religion at all account for about one-third of the sample. Some 10% of Polish and Canadian and some 6% of Italian respondents say they practise very much.

There are only sporadic statistically significant differences between men and women belonging to the same categories (2).

Generally speaking, people at the bottom of the social structure practise their religion more. In Poland, the main dividing line runs between decision-makers of either sex and the other categories.

Cross-country comparisons show that statistically significant (p < .001) differences, as regards the intensity of religious practice, appear between all categories in Romania and the corresponding categories in the other three countries. Moreover, Polish male blue-collar workers and housewives practise their religion more often than do their Italian counterparts, while Polish decision-makers do so less often than Italian and Canadian decision-makers.

Notes

1 In Canada, there is also a statistically significant (p < .001) difference between male decision-makers and virtually all other male categories, as well as between men out of work, on one side, and male blue-collar workers and white-collar workers, on the other, in the sense that male blue- and white-collar workers have more children. Among Canadian women, the differences are not so pronounced: white-collar workers have significantly fewer children than decision-makers and housewives, blue-collar workers fewer than housewives. These are the only significant differences found in Canada among women. In Italy, among male respondents, only teachers have significantly fewer children than men out of work, on the one hand, and decision-makers, on the other. Among Italian women, a statistically significant difference was found only between decision-makers and blue-collar workers, the latter having more children. In Poland, statistically significant differences (p < .001) concerning the number of children in the household were found only among female respondents: housewives have more children than blue- and white-collar workers, and teachers have more children than decision-makers. In Romania, statistically significant differences (p < .001) appear between male blue-collar workers and teachers, the latter having fewer children. As for Romanian women, housewives have relatively more children than women from the other categories, and decision-makers have more children than teachers.

2 There are no clear-cut regularities in Italy and Canada. In Romania, men out of work and male blue-collar workers clearly practise their religion more often than do men from the other categories.

SPECIFIC APPENDICES

Appendix 1 - Index of Social Class (or of Socio-economic Opportunities)

The construction of this index consists of two phases.

In the first phase, a variable called "educational level" was created. This variable expresses homogeneously the different situations existing in each country as far as number of years of education and titles of studies are concerned. The combination of these two factors yields for each country some stable groupings (with minimal variance) that correspond to the following six levels:

1 some compulsory school;
2 compulsory school, completed;
3 some high school;
4 high school, completed;
5 college or university, some or completed;
6 post-graduate, some or completed (only in Canada).

Of course, in each country the limits of the classes corresponding to the six levels vary a great deal.

In the second phase, following the logic of multi-dimensional positioning, we applied the correspondence analysis to the two variables: level of study and occupational level of the father. The factor scores on the first factor, which resulted for the categories of the two variables, are shown in Table A.

Table A Factor Scores on the First Factor for the Categories of the Two Variables

Occupational level of father	Canada	Italy	Poland	Romania	Total	Frequencies
1 Upper-level manager	-1.43	-1.24	-.42	.49	-1.64	60
2 Professional level	-1.33	-1.38	-1.54	-1.16	-1.10	326
3 Middle manager	-.62	-.88	-1.29	-1.53	-.40	517
4 Small business	-.23	.10	-1.11	-.39	-.29	281
5 White-collar worker	-.22	-.33	-.59	-.91	.43	686
6 Skilled blue-collar worker	.82	.78	.07	.43	1.19	1,041
7 Unskilled blue-collar worker	.13	1.17	1.35	.57	.71	390
8 Farmer	1.07	1.10	.32	.81	1.36	586
No answer						238
Level of education						
Some compulsory school	1.58	1.42	1.98	1.35	1.37	405
Completed compulsory school	1.16	.89	.59	1.20	.94	467
Some high school	.50	.36	.55	.49	.63	564
Completed high school	.40	-.09	-.62	.24	.09	1,160
College/university	-.52	-.92	-.82	-.98	-.97	1,240
Post-graduate	-1.19	-	-	-	-1.72	126
No answer	-	-	-	-	-	163
N = 4,125						

The reader will immediately realize that the scale concerning the level of study is strictly coherent, while the scale concerning the father's occupation presents an incoherence as far as unskilled blue-collar workers are concerned. We put forward, as an explanation, the hypothesis that this may be owing to the greater drive towards social climbing and economic self-improvement that can be found in that class.

The factor scores of the categories pertaining to the two variables (where $J = 1...M$, where $M = m_1 + m_2$, m_1 are the categories of var. 1 and m_2 the categories of var. 2) generate the scores C_1 for each respondent (where $i = 1...n$, depending on the couple of categories to which the respondent belongs). From this analysis we can draw the relation:

$$c_j^l = \frac{1}{\sqrt{\lambda_1}} \sum_j P_r(i) c^j$$

where λ_1 is the eigenvalue of the first factor and $P_r(i)$ is the row-vector of the matrix of profiles (now inferred from the data matrix considered in complete disjunctive form).

The scores range as follows:

	Minimum	Maximum
Canada	-1.920	1.860
Italy	-1.670	1.510
Poland	-1.890	2.180
Romania	-1.550	1.800

In the course of the analysis we often divided the respondents into three groups, which we called respectively "low", "middle", and "high class", by merely splitting the range in three equal parts. Other ways of grouping the scores were dropped on the basis of the frequency distributions thus obtained, which look unrealistic.

Appendix 2 - Index of Importance of Party Offices

The scores in Table B are factor scores of categories concerning party offices on F_2 (see Appendix B, par. 2.3.1 for a description of F_2) resulting from the global analysis of matrix Y (Appendix B, par. 1).

Table B Factor Scores of Party Offices

	Within City Level	City Level	Intermediate Level	National Level
	Actual			
Once	1.09	1.55	1.80	1.70
Twice or more	1.21	2.74	1.68	1.95
	Past			
Once	1.18	1.51	1.72	1.75
Twice or more	1.25	1.92	1.84	1.89

We adopted this index after comparing it with two others: one built in an intuitive way, another using the betas of regression of actual national offices on the four levels of offices held in the past. The coefficients of correlation between the three indices and the frequency distribution persuaded us to give priority to the index described above. However, we often checked the results of the main analyses, having recourse to the other indices, although for brevity's sake we omitted reference to them in the text.

Appendix 3 - Index of Participation in Party Activities (also called Index of Political Participation)

This index was built on the basis of a Guttman-type scale including the following variables:

1 Party affiliation or involvement;
2 Taking the floor;
3 Voluntary work for party;
4 Actual office holding.

The index varies, consequently, from 0 to 4.
The tests gave the results that are shown in Table C.

Table C Guttman's Tests

Coefficients	Canada	Italy	Poland	Romania
Reproducibility	.9439	.9465	.9941	.9852
Minimum marginal reproducibility	.7928	.7068	.7758	.7278
Percent improvement	.1511	.2396	.2183	.2574
Scalability	.7293	.8174	.9737	.9456

Appendix 4 - Index of Political Commitment of Family of Origin

This index is an average of the scores obtained with these questions:

"When you were an adolescent, how much involved in politics were the following persons:
1 Your mother?
2 Your father?
3 Other people around you?"

The scores were:
1 = "very much"; 2 = "rather"; 3 = "little"; 4 = "not at all".
The reliability of the three items was tested for each category by sex in each country on the basis of the formula:

$$R = \frac{N \times r}{1 + (N - 1)^r}$$

The 39 correlation matrices yielded in all cases highly satisfactory results, which for brevity's sake we cannot report here.

Appendix 5 - Index of Political Commitment of Present Milieu

This index is an average of the scores obtained with the following questions:

"How much are the following persons politically active at the present time:
1 Your spouse?
2 Your parents?
3 Your friends?
4 Your relatives?"

The scores were: 1 = "very much"; 2 = "rather"; 3 = "little"; 4 = "not at all".
The reliability was tested as illustrated in Appendix 4. The 39 results, which are omitted for brevity's sake, were all highly satisfactory.

Appendix 6 - Index of Concern for Political Information (also called Index of Political Interest or of Political Information)

This index is an average of the scores obtained with the following questions:

"Do you regularly follow, through radio and television, political and economic events?"
"Do you read books or articles concerning political and economic matters?"

The scores were: 1 = "very often"; 2 = "at times"; 3 = "seldom"; 4 = "never".
The reliability was tested as in Appendix 4. The 39 results are omitted for brevity's sake. They were, however, all highly satisfactory.

Appendix 7 - Index of Importance of Trade Union Offices

This index has been built using the same procedure that was described in Appendix 2. The weights are shown in Table D.

Table D   Factor Scores of Trade Union Offices

	Within City Level	City Level	Intermediate Level	National Level
		Actual		
Once	.33	1.15	1.30	1.02
Twice or more	.56	0	1.33	1.88
		Past		
Once	.59	1.34	1.30	1.85
Twice or more	.48	1.33	1.49	1.83

As in the case of Appendix 2, we used other indices, built in the way that they are indicated. The empirical validation led us to prefer the measure presented here.

Appendix 8 - Indices of Importance of Governmental and Non-Governmental Offices

This index has been built using the same procedure that is described in Appendix 2. The weights are shown in Table E.
The results for elected and appointed offices have been added in each of the two kinds of offices.

Appendix 9 - Index of Family as an Obstacle

This index was built using the following questions:

"If you do not participate in party, trade union, voluntary association life or your participation is not as much as you would like, why is it so?

1 I have too many family commitments.
....
4 My spouse does not like me to participate."

A "yes" or "no" answer was required. A score of 0 was assigned to those who answered "no" to both questions (or to the first one, in the case of non-married respondents); of 1 if the answer is "yes" in one of the two questions; of 2 if the answer is "yes" in both questions (or to the first one, in the case of non-married respondents).

Table E Factor Scores of Governmental and Non-Governmental Offices

	Within city Level	City Level	Intermediate Level	National Level
Governmental: Elected				
Once	1.13	1.73	1.94	1.59
Twice or more	1.71	1.79	1.74	1.84
More than twice	1.83	2.27	1.82	1.99
Governmental: Appointed				
Once	1.15	1.71	1.45	1.24
Twice or more	1.58	1.33	1.20	1.32
More than twice	1.04	-.30	1.45	.63
Non-Governmental: Elected				
	Low	Intermediate	High	
Once	.73	1.32	1.17	
Twice or more	.41	1.32	2.33	
More than twice	.44	.88	.13	
Non-Governmental: Appointed				
	Low	Intermediate	High	
Once	.72	1.52	1.76	
Twice or more	1.15	1.95	2.01	
More than twice	1.51	1.36	1.81	

Appendix 10 - Index of the Incidence of Children

This index results from the combination of the age and the number of children. It varies from 0 (no child) to 28 (7 or more children, ranging from 1 year to 7 years: that is, in the case of seven strictly consecutive pregnancies). The burden of one child of 1 year (or less) is 5; of two children aged 1 year (or less) and 1-2 years is 9. The burden of one child aged 8 years (or more) is 1.

Appendix 11 - Indices of Involvement in Voluntary Organizations

We included under this heading a variety of indices:
1 An index of participation in voluntary association activities, built on the basis of a Gutt-man-type scale of the kind illustrated in Appendix 3;
2 Several indices measuring the importance of office-holding in voluntary associations.

Appendix 12 - Division in Levels of Political Participation

When necessary, we grouped the Guttman scores as illustrated in Appendix 3, in the following way: Nil = 0; Low = 1, 2; High = 3.

Appendix 13 - Division in Levels of Importance of Party Offices

When necessary, we grouped the scores, as illustrated in Appendix 2, for party offices in the way shown in Table F.

Table F Levels of Importance of Party Office

	Canada	Italy	Poland	Romania
Nil				
Low	1—1.9	1—1.9	1—1.9	1—1.9
Medium	2—3.9	2—4.9	+2	+2
High	+4	+5		

Appendix 14 - Division in Levels of Importance of Governmental Offices

When necessary, we grouped the scores, as illustrated in Appendix 8, for governmental offices in the way that is shown in Table G.

Table G Levels of Importance of Governmental Office

	Canada	Italy	Poland	Romania
Nil				
Low	1—2.9	1—3.9	1—2.9	1—2.9
Medium	3—8.9	4—9.9	+3	+3
High	+9	+10		

Appendix 15 - Index of Trade Union Participation

This index was built on the basis of a Guttman-type scale of the kind that is illustrated in Appendix 3.

Appendix 16 - Index of Organizational Participation

This index aims at giving an overall measure of involvement in various kinds of organizations.

The organizations which are considered are: parties, trade unions, women's organizations, voluntary associations.

The forms of participation considered in each kind of organization are: affiliation, holding and having held offices.

Combining affiliation with the intensity of office-holding, we created an index which varies from 1 (total lack of involvement) to 7 (affiliation with at least two organizations, and office-holding, in the present or the past, in at least two cases).

Appendix 17 - Index of Office-holding in Public Organizations

This index aims at giving an overall measure of office-holding in governmental and/or non-governmental but publicly relevant organizations.

The index takes into consideration whether the respondent has an office in one or both kinds of organizations, and the intensity of the phenomenon.

It varies between 1 (total lack of public offices) and 4 (holding office in at least one kind of organization and at more than one level).

Appendix 18 - Index of Schooling

This index varies between 1 (low) and 3 (high) and is built on the following basis:
1 Below completing high school;
2 High school completed, some years of college or university;
3 College or university completed.

Appendix 19 - Index of Passive v. Active Orientation to Work

This index is built on the basis of three sets of questions.

The first set deals with the "costs" of different kinds of potential promotions: whether male or female respondents would accept a promotion consuming more time than the present job or requiring additional training, etc. The respondents who are ready to accept at least three out of the six kinds of promotions are considered active.

The second set deals with the readiness to protest. The respondents who select at least two out of the five kinds of protest are considered active.

The last one is the question of whether the respondent would like to start working or to continue working, if she/he did not need money.

Appendix 20 - Conception of Ideal Division of Household Chores

This typology is based on the following question:

"If both spouses work, who should in your opinion:
1 Cook?
2 Do the dishes?
3 Do the everyday family shopping?
4 Do the laundry?
5 Clean the house?
6 Look after the children?"

The "radical extremists" are the respondents who stated that the husband should perform always or more often than the wife at least five of the above-listed chores. The "egalitarians" are the respondents who claimed that they should equally be shared by the spouses. The "traditionalists" think that they should be done always or more often by the wife.

Appendix 21 - Index of Attitudes towards Women in Power

This typology is based on the answers to the following questions:

1 "Should women, in your opinion, have the same chance as men to hold leadership positions?
2 Are women better than men in political leadership positions?
3 Do you think that women are as good as men, better than men, worse than men in the work place with respect to:
    (a) Solving conflicts among people?
    (b) Motivating others to do what they have to do?
    (c) Understanding the needs of people?
    (d) Grasping people's thoughts?
    (e) Defending their own ideas even if people oppose them?
    (f) Rewarding and punishing?"

The "radical extremists" are the respondents who agree with at least five out of the eight statements. The "egalitarians" are those who put women on the same footing with men in at least five cases. The "traditionalists" are those who manifest disagreement in at least five out of the eight statements.

Appendix 22 - Index of Appraisal of Gender Inequality in Work-Related Situations

This index (from $0 =$ low to $4 =$ high) is based on the answers, "men tend to be favoured" and "men are strongly favoured", to the following questions:

"Do men and women have the same opportunity to get vocational training?
1 Do men and women have the same opportunity to get a job?
2 In case of a cut in personnel, who is fired first: married men or married women?
3 Do you feel that in this country women are paid as much as men for the same job?"

Appendix 23 - Index of Perceived Sex Inequality

This index is the average of the scores for the following questions:

"In your opinion, do women in your country have the same opportunities as men to:
1 Obtain a professional training?
2 Find a job?
3 Hold a leadership position?"

The scores range from $1 =$ "women are very much favoured" to $5 =$ "men are very much favoured".

Two more indices have been constructed using the same questions with "do" being replaced by "should" (index of Normative Sex Inequality) and by "will have in 5 years" (index of Expected Sex Inequality).

Appendix 24 - Index of Traditional, Egalitarian and Radical Extremist Attitudes towards "Natural" Differences between Female and Male Propensities

The typology is based on the answers to the four items that are quoted in the text. The traditionalists are the respondents who totally agree with at least three of them; the egalitarians the respondents who partially agree or disagree with at least three statements; the radical extremists those who totally disagree with at least three of them.

Appendix 25 - Index of Traditional, Egalitarian and Radical Extremist Attitudes towards the Division of Household Chores

The typology is based on the answers to the six items that are quoted in the text. The traditionalists are the respondents who claim that at least five chores should be done always or more often by the wife; the egalitarians are those who maintain that they should be equally shared; the radical extremists are those who state that at least five of them should be done always or more often by the husband.

REFERENCES †

Ackelsberg, M. and I. Diamond (1987) "Gender and political life: new directions in political science", in Hess, B.B. and M.M.Ferree, pp. 504-525.

Acker, J. (1981) "Toward a theory of gender and class" Arbetslivscentrum (manuscript).

Almond, G.A. and S. Verba (1963) *The Civic Culture*. Princeton University Press.

Almond, G.A. and S. Verba (eds) (1980) *The Civic Culture Revisited*. Little, Brown.

Amsden, A. (1980) *The Economics of Woman and Work*. Penguin.

Ariès, P. (1960) *L'Enfant et la Vie Familiale sous l'Ancien Régime* (Children and Family Life under the Ancien Régime). Plon.

Aronoff, J. and W.D. Crano (1975) "A re-examination of the cross-cultural principles of task segregation and sex differentiation in the family", *American Sociological Review*, 40, pp. 12-20.

Azmon, Y. (1981) "Sex, power and authority", *The British Journal of Sociology*, 32, pp. 547-559.

Balbo, L. (1980) "Riparliamo del Welfare State: la società assistenziale, la società dei servizi, la società della crisi" (Let us talk again about the welfare state: the public assistance society, the public services society, the crisis society), *Inchiesta*, 46-47, pp. 2-19.

Bardwick, J.M. (1971) *Psychology of Women*. Harper and Row.

Baxter, S. and M. Lansing (1983) *Women and Politics: The Visible Majority*. University of Michigan Press.

Beechey, V. (1978) "Women and production: a critical analysis of some sociological theories of women's work", in Kuhn, A. and A.M. Wolpe, pp. 155-157.

Benson, L. (1968) *Fatherhood: A Sociological Perspective*. Random House.

Berk, S.F. (1979) "Husbands at home: organisation of the husband's household day", in Wolk Feinstein, K.

Berk, S.F. (ed.) (1980) *Women and Household Labour*. Sage Publications.

Berkin, C.K. and C.M. Lovett (1980) *Women, War and Revolution*. Holmes and Meier.

Bernard, J. (1975) *Women, Wives, Mothers*. Aldine.

Beynon, H. and R. Blackburn (1984) "Unions: the men's affair?", in Siltanen, J. and M. Stanworth pp. 75-88.

Blanquart, L. (1974) *Femmes: l'Age Politique* (Women: the political epoch). Editions Sociales.

Blasi, J.R. (1983) "Epilogue", in Palzi, M. et al., pp. 305-315.

Blauner, R. (1960) "Work satisfaction and industrial trends in modern society", in Salenson, W. and S. Lipset.

Blauner, R. (1964) *Alienation and Freedom*. University of Chicago Press.

Blood, R.O. and D.M. Wolfe (1960) *Husbands and Wives*. Free Press.

Boals, K. (1975) "The politics of male-female relations: the functions of feminist scholarship", *Signs*, 1, pp. 161-183.

Bodiguel, J.L. (1984) "High level public officials in Eastern and Western European countries: problems encountered in comparative research", in Niessen, M. et al., pp.147-163.

Boneparth, E. (1982a) "A frame-work for policy analysis", in Boneparth, E. pp. 1-14.

Boneparth, E. (ed.) (1982b) *Women, Power and Policy*. Pergamon Press.

Booth, A. (1972) "Sex and social participation", *American Sociological Review*, 37, pp. 183-192.

Bose, C. (1980) "Social status of the homemaker", in Berk, S.F. pp. 69-87.

Boserup, E. (1970) *Women's Role in Economic Development*. Allen and Unwin.

Boulding, E. (1976a) *The Underside of History*. Westview Press.

Boulding, E. (1976b) "Familial constraints in women's work roles", *Signs*, 1, pp. 95-118.

Bourque, S.C. and J. Grossholtz (1974) "Politics an unnatural practice: political science looks at female participation", *Politics and Society*, pp. 225-266.

Bowker, L.H. (1981) "Racism and sexism: hints toward a theory of the casual structure of attitudes towards women", *International Journal of Women's Studies*, 4, pp. 277-287.

Brenner, J. and N. Holmstrom (1983) "Women's self-organisation theory and strategy", *Monthly Review*, pp. 34-46.

Brinkerhoff, M. and E. Lupri (1978) "Theoretical and methodological issues in the use of decision-making as an indicator of conjugal power: some Canadian observations", *Canadian Journal of Sociology*, 3, pp. 1-20.

---

† Specialized statistical literature is separately listed at the end

Brinkerhoff, M. and E. Lupri (1983) "Conjugal power and family relationships: some theoretical and methodological issues" in Ishwaran, K.

Bruegel, I. (1979) "Women as a reserve army of labour: a note on recent British experience", *Feminist Review*, 3.

Buric, O. (1975) "Re-definition of the structure of social power: condition for the social equality of women". *International Workshop on Changing Sex Roles in the Family and Society*, Dubrovnik, 16-21 June 1975 (manuscript).

Buric, O. and A. Zecevic (1967) "Family authority, marital satisfaction, and the social network in Yugoslavia", *Journal of Marriage and the Family*, 29, pp. 325-336.

Burr, W.R. (1973) *Theory Construction and the Sociology of the Family*. Wiley.

Bursche, K. (1973) *Awans robotnikow w zakladzie przemyslowym* (Promotion of Workers in the Work-place).

Burstyn, V. (ed.) (1985) *Women against Censorship*. Salem House.

Caldwell, L. (1978) "Church, state and family: the women's movement in Italy", in Kuhn, A. and A.M. Wolpe, pp. 68-95.

Cantor, M.G. (1987) "Popular culture and the portrayal of women: content and control", in Hess, B.B. and M. M. Ferree, pp. 190-214.

Carchedi, G. (1983) *Problems in Class Analysis*. Routledge and Kegan Paul.

Cartwright D. (ed.) (1959) *Studies in Social Power*. University of Michigan Press.

Centers, R., B.H. Raven, and A. Rodriguez (1971) "Conjugal power structure: a re-examiniation", *American Sociological Review*, 36, pp. 264-78.

Chafe, W.H. (1972) *The American Woman: Her Changing Social Economic and Political Role: 1920-1970*. Oxford University Press.

Chafetz, J. (1984) *Sex and Advantage*. Rowman and Allaheld.

Chesler, P. and E.J. Goodman (1976) *Women, Money and Power*. Marrow.

Chodorow, N. (1974) "Family structure and feminine personality", in Rosaldo, M.Z. and L. Lamphere, pp. 43-66.

Chodorow, N. (1979) "Mothering, male dominance, and capitalism", in Eisenstein, Z.R., pp.83-106.

Christensen, H.T. (1977) "Relationship between differentiation and equality in the sex role structure: conceptual models and suggested research", in Lenero-Otero, L., pp. 205-224.

Christiansen-Ruffman, L. (1982) "Women's political culture and feminist political culture". *World Congress of Sociology*, Mexico City, 16-21 August 16-21, 1982 (manuscript).

Claussen, B. (1978) "Politische Bildung und Frauen-Emanzipation" (Political education and women's emancipation), *Studien zur Politikdidaktik* (1978).

Coin, G.C. (1965) *Married Women in the Labour Force: An Economic Analysis*. University of Chicago Press.

Connelly, P. (1978) *Last Hired, First Fired: Women and the Canadian Work Force*. The Women's Press.

Conseil de l'Europe (1984) *La situation des femmes dans la vie politique* (The situation of women in political life). Direction des droits de l'homme.

Constantini, E. and K.H. Craik (1972) "Women as politicians: the social background, personality and political careers of female party leaders", *Journal of Social Issues*, 28, pp. 217-236.

Cook, A. (1980) "Women in trade-unions", International Institute for Labour Studies, *Women and Industrial Relations*, pp. 3-25.

Cook, B.B. (1985) "Women on supreme courts: a cross-national analysis", *XIII World Congress of the International Political Science Association*, Paris, 15-20 July 1985 (manuscript).

Cook, G.C.A. (ed.)(1976) *Opportunity for Choice. A Goal for Women in Canada*. C.D. Howe Research Institute.

Cott, N. (1977) *The Bonds of Womanhood*. Yale University Press.

CRORA (1987) *Il profilo professionale e personale della donna dirigente in Italia* (The professional and personal profile of the woman manager in Italy), Centro di Ricerca sull'Organizzazione Aziendale, Università L.Bocconi, Milano (mimeo.)

Crosby, F. (1982) *Relative Deprivation and Working Women*. Oxford University Press.

Currell, M. (1974) *Political Women*. Croom Helm.

Czudnowski, M.M. (1975) "Political recruitment", in Greenstein, F.I. and N.W. Polsby, Vol. 2, pp. 155-242.

Darcy, C., J. Syrotuik, and C.M. Siddique (1984) "Perceived job attributes, job satisfaction and psychological distress: a comparison of working men and women", *Human Relations*, pp. 603-611.

Deaux, K. and M.E. Kite (1987) "Thinking about gender", in Hess, B.B. and M.M. Ferree, pp. 92-117.

De Beauvoir, S. (1949) *Le Deuxième Sexe* (The Second Sex). Gallimard.

Deckard, S.B. (1983) *The Women's Movement: Political Socioeconomic and Psychological Issues*. Harper and Row.

Delmar, R. (1976) "Looking again at Engels's 'Origins of the Family, Private Property and the State'", in Mitchell, J. and A. Oakley, pp. 271-287.'

Dogan, M. and D. Pelassy (1984) *How to Compare Nations: Strategies in Comparative Politics*. Chatham House.

Domhoff, G. W. (ed.) (1980) *Power Structure Research*. Sage Publications.

Donati, P.P. (1984) *Risposta alla Crisi dello Stato* (Answers to the crisis of the welfare state). Angeli.

Droppleman, L.F. and E.S. Schaefer (1963) "Boys' and girls' reports on maternal and paternal behaviour", *Journal of Abnormal and Social Psychology*, 67, pp. 648-654.

Eichler, M. (1981) "Power, dependency, love and the sexual division of labour ", *Women's Studies International Quarterly*, 4, pp. 201-219.

Eichler, M. (1983) *Families in Canada Today: Recent Changes and their Policy Consequences*. Gage Publications.

Eichler, M. and A. Thomson (1979) "Women's political participation: a critique". *Round-table on local government of the International Political Science Association*, Kalisz, May-June 1979 (manuscript).

Eisenstein, Z.R. (1979a) "Developing a theory of capitalist patriarchy and socialist feminism", in Eisenstein Z.R., pp. 5-55.

Eisenstein, Z.R. (ed.) (1979b) *Capitalist Patriarchy and the case for Socialist Feminism*. Monthly Review Press.

Elkin, F. and G. Handel (1984) *Transitions*. Academic Press.

Elshtain, J.B. (1979) "Methodological sophistication and conceptual confusion: a critique of mainstream political science", in Sherman, J.A. and E. T. Beck, pp. 229-252.

Elshtain, J.B. (1981) *Public Man, Private Woman*. Princeton University Press.

Engels, F. (1884) *Der Ursprung des Familie, des Privateigensthums und des Staats* (The origin of family, private property and the state). Hottingen.

Epstein, C.F. (1981) "The roles of women in politics in the United States", in Epstein, C.F. and R.L. Coser, pp. 124-146.

Epstein, C. F. (1988) *Deceptive Distinctions: Sex, Gender and the Social Order*. Yale University Press/Russell Sage Foundation.

Epstein, C. F. and R. L. Coser (eds) (1981) *Access to Power: Cross National Studies of Women and Elites*. Allen and Unwin.

Ergas, Y. (1982) "1968-1979: feminism and the Italian party system: women's politics in a decade of turmoil", *Comparative Politics*, pp. 253-279.

Erikson, H. (1964) "Inner and outer space: reflections on womanhood", *Daedalus*, pp. 582-606.

Erikson, J.A., W.L. Yancey and E.P. Ericksen (1979) "The division of family roles", *Journal of Marriage and the Family*, pp. 301-313.

European Federation of Soroptimist Clubs (1972) *La responsabilità della donna nella società contemporanea* (Women's responsibility in contemporary society).

Federici, N. (1984) *Procreazione, Famiglia, Lavoro della Donna* (Procreation, family, woman's work). Loescher.

Feingold, A. (1988) "Cognitive Gender Differences are Disappearing", *American Psychologist*, 43, pp. 95-103.

Feldberg, R.L. and E. N. Glenn (1979) "Male and female: job versus gender models in the sociology of work", *Social Problems*, 26, pp. 524-538.

First-Dilic, R. (1975) "Holistic approach to changing sex roles: theoretical perspective in the case of Yugoslav self-managing socialism". *International Workshop on Changing Sex Roles in the Family and in Society*, Dubrovnik, 1975 (manuscript).

Fischer, L. and J.A. Cheyne (1978) *Sex Roles: Biological and Cultural Interactions as Found in Social Sciences Research and Ontario Educational Media*. Ontario Institute for Studies in Education.

Flora, C.B. (1977) "Working class women's political participation: its potential in developed countries", in Githens, M. and J. Prestage, pp. 75-95.

Flora, C.B. and N.B. Lynn (1974) "Women and political socialization: considerations of the impact of motherhood", in Jacquette, J.S., pp. 37-53.

Fraker, S. (1984) "Why women aren't getting to the top", *Fortune*, 109, pp. 40-45.

Friedan, B. (1982) *The Feminine Mystique*. Penguin.

Galenson, M. (1973) *Women and Work: an International Comparison*. New York State School of Industrial and Labor Relations.

Gamson, W. (1961) "The fluoridation dialogue: is it an ideological conflict?", *Public Opinion Quarterly*, pp. 527-537.

Gardiner, J. (1979) "Women's domestic labor", in Eisenstein, Z.R., pp. 173-189.

Gershuny, J. (1978) *After Industrial Society. The Emerging Self-Service Economy*. Macmillan.

Githens, M. and J. Prestage (eds) (1977) *A Portrait of Marginality: The Political Behaviour of American Women.* McKay.

Glazer, N. (1980) "Everyone needs three hands: doing unpaid and paid work", in Berk, S.F., pp. 249-273.

Glazer, N. and H.Y. Waehrer (eds) (1977) *Woman in a Man-Made World.* Rand McNally.

Glenn, E.N. (1987) "Gender and the family", in Hess, B.B. and M.M. Ferree, pp. 348-380.

Gokalp, C. and H. Leridon (1983) "Incidences de l'activité feminine sur la participation du père à la vie familiale" (Impact of female activity on the father's participation in family life). Colloque de la Société Tocqueville sur "Le travail et la famille en Europe et aux Etats-Unis', *Arc et Senans,* June 1983 (manuscript).

Golden, P.M. and J.B. Reeves (1982) "Male and female patterns of work opportunity structures and life satisfaction", *International Journal of Women's Studies,* 5, pp. 215 - 225.

Goode, W.J. (1982) "Why men resist" in Thorne, B. and M. Yalom, pp.131-150.

Goody, J.R. (1976) *Production and Reproduction: a Comparative Study of the Domestic Domain.* Cambridge University Press.

Goody, J.R. (1983) *The Development of the Family and Marriage in Europe.* Cambridge University Press.

Green, P. (1981) *The Pursuit of Inequality.* Martin Robertson.

Greenstein, F.L. and N.W.Polsby (eds) (1975) *Handbook of Political Science.* Addison-Wesley.

Gunderson, M. (1976) "Work patterns" in Cook, G.C.A. pp. 93-142.

Haavio-Mannila, E. (1970) "Sex role in Politics", *Scandinavian Political Studies,* pp. 209-216, 226-238.

Haavio-Mannila, E. (ed.)(1985) *Unfinished Democracy: Women in Nordic Politics.* Pergamon Press.

Harris, O. (1984) "Households as natural units", in Young, K. et al., pp. 136-155.

Hartmann, H. (1979) "Capitalism, patriarchy and job segregation by sex", in Eisenstein, Z.R., pp. 206-247.

Hartmann, H. (1981a) "The unhappy marriage of marxism and feminism: towards a more progressive union", in Sargent L., pp. 1-41.

Hartmann, H. (1981b) "The family as the locus of gender, class, and political struggle: the example of housework", *Signs,* 6, pp. 366 - 394.

Hatch, L. R. (1986) "A structural analysis of men and women in retirement". *Unpublished Ph.D. dissertation,* University of Washington.

Heitlinger, A. (1979) *Women and State Socialism: Sex Inequality in the Soviet Union and Czechoslovakia.* McGill, Queen's University Press.

Hernes, H.M. (1984) "Le rôle des femmes dans la vie politique en Europe" in Conseil de l'Europe, *La situation des femmes dans la vie politique,* Pt. III.

Herzog, A.R. (1982) "High school students' occupational planes and values: trends in sex differences 1976 through 1980", *Sociology of Education,* pp. 1-13.

Hess, B.B. and M.M. Ferree (eds)(1987) *Analysing Gender, A Handbook of Social Science Research,* Sage Publications.

Holmstrom, N. (1981) "'Women's work', the Family and Capital", *Science and Society,* pp. 186-211.

Humphries, J. (1977) "Working class, class struggle and the persistence of the family", *Cambridge Journal of Economics,* 3, pp. 241-258.

Hunt, P. (1984) "Workers side by side: women and the trade-union movement", in Siltanen J. and M. Stanworth, pp.47-53.

Huntington, S. (1975) "Issues in women's role in economic development: critique and alternatives", *Journal of Marriage and the Family,* 18, pp. 1001-1012.

Iglitzin, L.B. (1974) "The making of the apolitical woman: femininity and sex stereotyping in girls", in Jacquette, J.S., pp. 25-36.

Iglitzin, L.B. and R. Ross (eds) (1976) *Women in the World: a Comparative Study.* Clio Books.

Inglehart, R. (1977) *The Silent Revolution.* Princeton University Press.

Inkeles, A. (1960) "Industrial man: the relations of status to experience, perception and value", *American Journal of Sociology,* pp. 1-31.

Inkeles, A. (1980) "Modernisation and family patterns: a test of convergence theory", *Conspectus of History,* 6, pp. 31-63.

Ishwaran, K. (ed.)(1983) *The Canadian Family.* Gage Publishing.

Israel, J. (1971) *Alienation: From Marx to Modern Sociology.* Beacon Press.

Jacquette, J. S. (ed.) (1974) *Women in Politics.* Wiley.

Jaggar, A. M. (1983) *Feminist Politics and Human Nature.* Rowman and Allenheld.

Jaggar, A.M. and P.S. Rothenberg (1978) *Feminist Frameworks.* McGraw-Hill.

Jancar, B. (1974) "Women under Communism", in Jacquette, J.S., pp. 217-242.

Jasinska, A. and R. Siemienska (1983) "The socialist personality: a case study of Poland", *International Journal of Sociology*, 13, pp. 1-88.

Jennings, M.K. and R.G. Niemi (1971) "The division of political labor between mothers and fathers", *American Political Science Review*, 65, pp. 69-82.

Jennings, M.K. and N. Thomas (1968) "Men and women in party elites: social roles and political resources", *Midwest Journal of Political Science*, 12, pp. 469-492.

Kahn, A. (1984) "The power war: male response to power loss under equality", *Psychology of Women Quarterly*, 8, pp. 234-247.

Kamerman, S.B. (1979) "Work and family in industrialized societies", *Signs*, 4, pp. 632-650.

Kandell, D.B. and G.S. Lesser (1972) "Marital decision-making in American and Danish urban families: a research note", *Journal of Marriage and the Family*, 34, pp. 134-8.

Kanter, R.M. (1976) "Women and the structure of organizations: explorations in theory and behaviour", in Millman, M. and R.M. Kanter, pp. 34-74.

Karchev, A.G. and L.V. Yasmaya (1982) "Changes in the life patterns of families in the USSR after War World II", in *Changes in the Life Patterns of Families in Europe*. European Coordination Centre for Research and Documentation in Social Sciences.

Keller, S. (1983) "The family in the kibbutz: what lesson for us?", in Palzi et al., pp. 227-251.

Kilkpatrick, F., M. Cummings and M. Jennings (1964) *The Image of the Federal Service*. Brookings Institution.

Kirkpatrick, J.J. (1974) *Political Woman*. Basic Books.

Klein, E. (1984) *Gender Politics*. Harvard University Press.

Klein, Y. (1965) *Britain's Married Women Workers*. Routledge and Kegan Paul.

Knowles, K.J.C. (1952) *Strikes. A Study in Industrial Conflict*. Blackwell.

Knychala, K. (1977) *Zatrudnienie kobiet w Polsce Ludowej w latach 1955-1974* (Women's employment in the Polish People's Republic between 1955 and 1974). Panstwowe Wydawnictwo Naukowe

Korabik, K. (1982) "Sex role orientation and leadership style", *International Journal of Women's Studies*, 5, pp. 329-337.

Kuhn, A. and A.M. Wolpe (eds) (1978) *Feminism and Materialism*. Routledge and Kegan Paul.

Kulpinska, J. (1975) "Postawy kobiet wobec pracy" (Women's attitudes toward work), in Dziecielska-Machnikowska (ed.) *Kobieta w rozwijajacym sie spoleczenstwie socjalistycznym*, Wydawnictwo Poznanskiee.

Lamousé, A. (1969) "Family roles of women: a German example", *Journal of Marriage and the Family*, 31, pp. 145-52.

Lampe, P.E. (1981) "Androgyny and religiosity", *International Journal of Women's Studies*, 4, pp. 27-34.

Lapidus, G.W. (1978) *Women in Soviet Society: Equality Development and Social Change*. University of California Press.

Larguia, I. and J. Dumoulin (1976) *Hacia una Ciencia de la Liberacion de la Mujer*. (Towards a Science of the Liberation of Women). Anagrama.

Laslett, P. (1972) "Introduction: the history of the family", in Laslett, P. and R. Wall.

Laslett, P. and R. Wall (eds) (1972) *Household and Family in Past Time*. Cambridge University Press.

Leacock, E. (1975) "Class, commodity and status of women", in Rohrlich-Leavitt, R., pp. 601-16.

Leipoldt, G. (1954) *Die Frau in der antike Welt und in Urchristentum* (The Woman in the Ancient World and in Early Christianity). Koehler and Amelang.

Lenero-Otero, L. (ed.) (1977) *Beyond the Nuclear Family Model*. Sage Publications.

Lesage, M. (1984) "Comparing public institutions, their organisations and procedures: East-West cooperation in East-West comparisons" in Niessen, M. et al., pp. 137-145.

Lipman-Blumen, J. and J. Bernard (eds) (1974) *Sex Roles and Social Policy*. Sage Publications.

Lorber, J. et al. (1981) "On the Reproduction of Mothering: a methodological debate", *Signs*, pp. 482-514.

Lovenduski, J. and J. Hills (eds) (1981) *The Politics of the Second Electorate: Women and Public Participation*. Routledge and Kegan Paul.

Lupri, E. (1965) "Industrialisierung und Strukturhandlungen in der Familie: ein interkultureller Vergleich" (Industrialization and structural performance in the family: an intercultural comparison), *European Journal of Sociology*, 5, pp. 57-76.

Lupri, E. (1969) "Contemporary authority patterns in the West German family: study in cross-national validation", *Journal of Marriage and the Family*, 31, pp. 134-44.

Lupri, E. (1983a) "The changing positions of women and men in comparative perspective", in Lupri, E. (ed.) pp. 3-34.

Lupri, E. (ed.) (1983b) *The Changing Position of Women in Family and Society: A Cross-Cultural Comparison*. E.J.Brill.

Lupri, E. (1990) *Reflections on Marriage and the Family in Canada: A Study in the Dialectics of Family and Work Roles.* Holt, Rinehart and Winston of Canada.

Lupri, E. and G. Luschen (eds) (1972) *Comparative Perspectives on Marriage and the Family,* Special Issue of *The Journal of Comparative Family Studies,* 3, Spring.

Lupri, E. and G. Symons (1982) "The emerging symmetrical family: fact or fiction?", *Comparative Sociology,* pp. 166-189.

Lutte, G., R. de Angelis, L. Giuliano, G. Pantosti, M.L. Solimena, and D. Visca (1984) *I Giovani e le Istituzioni* (Youngsters and Institutions). Editrice Ianna.

Lynn, D. (1974) *The Father. His Role in Child Development.* Wadsworth.

Lynn, N.B. and C.B. Flora (1972) "Societal punishment, amateurism and female political participation". Department of Political Science and Department of Sociology, State University of Kansas (manuscript).

Lynn, N.B. and C.B. Flora (1973) "Motherhood and political participation: the changing sense of self", *Journal of Political and Military Sociology,* 1, pp. 91-103.

Maccoby, E.E. and C. Jacklin (1974) *The Psychology of Sex Differences.* Stanford University Press.

Mayes, S.S. (1979) "Women in positions of authority: a case study of changing sex roles", *Signs,* 4, pp. 556- 568.

McClosky, H. and A. Brill (1983) *Dimensions of Tolerance.* Russell Sage Foundation.

McClosky, H. and J.H. Schaar (1965) "Psychological dimensions of anomy", *American Sociological Review,* pp. 14-40.

McCormack, T. (1976a) "Good theory or just theory? Toward a feminist philosophy of social science", *Women's Studies International Quarterly,* 4, 1-12.

McCormack, T. (1976b) "Towards a nonsexist perspective on social and political change", in Millman, M. and R.M. Kanter, pp. 1-33.

McDonald, G.W. (1980) "Family power: the assessment of a decade of theory and research, 1970-1979", *Journal of Marriage and the Family,* pp. 111-124.

Menschik, J. (1971) *Gleichberechtigung oder Emanzipation?* (Equality or Emancipation?). Fischer Taschenbuch Verlag.

Merkl, P.H. (1976) "The study of women in comparative politics: reflections on a conference", *Signs,* pp. 749-756.

Michel, A. (1967) "Comparative data concerning the interaction in French and American families", *Journal of Marriage and the Family,* 29, pp. 227-244.

Michel, A. (1982) "Changes in the life patterns of families in France" in *Changes in the Life Patterns of Families in Europe.* European Coordination Centre for Research and Documentation in Social Sciences.

Milbrath, L.W. (1965) *Political Participation.* Rand McNally.

Miller J.B. (1976) *Toward a New Psychology of Women.* Beacon Press.

Millman, M. and R.M. Kanter (eds) (1976) *Another Voice: Feminist Perspectives on Social Life and Social Science.* Octagon Books.

Mitchell, J. (1976) "Women and equality", in Mitchell, J. and A.Oakley, pp. 379-399.

Mitchell, J. and A. Oakley (eds) (1976) *The Rights and Wrongs of Women.* Penguin Books.

Molyneux, M. (1979) "The debate on domestic work", *New Left Review,* 116, pp. 3-27.

Molyneux, M. (1984) "Women in socialist societies: problems of theory and practice", in Young, K. et al. pp. 55-90.

Moore, J. W. (1960) "Patterns of women's participation in voluntary associations", *American Journal of Sociology,* 66, pp. 592-598.

Mossuz-Lavau, J., and M. Sineau (1984) "Les femmes dans le personnel politique en Europe" (Women in the European staff policy) in Conseil d'Europe, *La situation des femmes dans la vie politique,* Pt. II.

Mueller, C. (1982) "Nurturance and mastery: competing qualifications for women's access to high public office?" *Working paper No. 94,* Centre for Research on Women, Wellesley College.

Muscott, A. (1983) "Women's place: cookbooks' images of technique and technology in the British kitchen", *Women's Studies International Forum,* pp. 33-39.

Myrdal, A. and V. Klein (1968) *Women's Two Roles.* Routledge and Kegan Paul.

Nash, J. (1965) "The father in contemporary culture and current psychological literature", *Child Development,* 36, pp. 261-297.

Neal, A. and M. Seeman (1964) "Organizations and powerlessness: a test of the mediation hypotheses", *American Sociological Review,* pp. 216-225.

Nie, N.H. and S. Verba (1975) "Political participation", in Greenstein F.I. and N.W. Polsby, Vol. 4, pp.1-74.

Nie, N.H., S. Verba and J.O. Kim (1974) "Participation and the life-cycle", *Comparative Politics,* pp. 319-340.

Niessen, M., J. Peschar, and C. Kourilsky (eds.) (1984) *International Comparative Research: Social Structures and Public Institutions in Eastern and Western Europe*. Pergamon Press.

Nilson, L. B. (1978) "The social structure of marriage and the family", *Journal of Marriage and the Family*, pp. 541-548.

Norris, P. (1987) *Politics and Sexual Equality*, Wheatsheaf Books.

Novarra, V. (1980) *Women's Work, Men's Work: The Ambivalence of Equality*. Marion Boyars.

Occhionero, M. (1978) "Women in Italian political life", *International Journal of Sociology*, 8, pp. 12-37.

Olsen, M.E. (1969) "Political alienation", *Social Forces*, 47, pp. 288-299.

Olsen, M.E. (1972) "Social participation and voting turn-out: a multivariate analysis", *American Sociological Review*, pp. 317-333.

Ortner, S.B. (1974) "Is female to male as nature is to culture?", in Rosaldo, M.Z. and Lamphere, pp. 66-87.

Orum, A.M., R.S. Cohen, S. Grasmuck, and A.W. Orum (1974) "Sex, socialization and politics", *American Sociological Review*, 39, pp. 197 - 209.

Ostrander, S. A. (1980) "Upper-class women: class consciousness as conduct and meaning", in Domhoff, G., pp. 73-96.

Palzi, M. and M.Rosner (eds) (1983) "Equality between the sexes in the kibbutz: regression or changed meaning?", in Palzi, M. et al., pp. 255-296.

Palzi, M., J.R. Blasi, M. Rosner, and M. Safir (eds) (1983) *Sexual Equality: The Israeli Kibbutz Tests the Theories*. Norwood Editions.

Parsons, T. and R. Bales (1955) *Family: Socialization and Interaction Processes*. Free Press.

Pateman, C. (1970) *Participation and Democratic Theory*. Cambridge University Press.

Pateman, C. (1980) "The civic culture: a philosopher critique", in Almond G.A. and S. Verba, pp. 57-102.

Peattie, L. and M. Rein (1983) *Women's Claims: A Study in Political Economy*. Oxford University Press.

Piotrowski, J. (1963) *Praca zawodowa kobiety a rodzina* (Women's work and family). Ksiazka i Wiedza.

Pius XI (1930) *Casti Connubii* (Chaste Marriage).

Pius XI (1937) *Divini Redemptoris* (Divine Redeemer).

Porter, M.C. and C. Venning (1976) "Catholicism and women's role in Italy and Ireland" in Iglitzin, L.B. and R. Ross, pp. 81-104.

Powell, G. (1988) *Women and Men in Management*. Sage Publications.

Przedpelski, M. (1975) *Struktura zatrudnienia kobiet w Polsce Ludowej* (Structure of women's employment in the Polish People's Republic). Panstwowe Wydawnictwo Naukowe.

Purcell, K. (1984) "Militancy and acquiescence among women workers", in Siltanen, J. and M. Stanworth, pp.54-67.

Reeves Sanday, P. (1981) *Female Power and Male Dominance. On the Origins of Sexual Inequality*. Cambridge University Press.

Riesman, D., N. Glazer, R. Denney (1950) *The Lonely Crowd*. Yale University Press.

Robinson, J.P. (1980) "Housework technology and household work", in Berk, S.F., pp.53-67.

Robinson, J.P., J.G.Rusk and K.B.Head (1973) *Measures of Political Attitudes*. University of Michigan Press.

Roby, P. (1976) "Sociology and women in working class jobs", in Millman, M. and R.M. Kanter, pp. 203-239.

Rodman, H. (1967) "Marital power in France, Greece, Yugoslavia and the United States", *Journal of Marriage and the Family*, 29, pp. 320-4.

Rodman, H. (1972) "Marital power and the theory of resources in cultural context", in E.Lupri and G. Luschen.

Rogers, S.C. (1978) "Woman's place: a critical review of anthropological theory", *Comparative Studies in Society and History*, pp. 123-162.

Rohrlich-Leavitt, R. (ed.) (1975) *Women Cross-Culturally: Change and Challenge*. Mouton.

Rosaldo, M.Z. (1980) "The use and abuse of anthropology: reflections on feminism and cross-cultural understanding", *Signs* 5, pp. 389-417.

Rosaldo, M.Z. and L. Lamphere (eds) (1974) *Women, Culture and Society*. Stanford University Press.

Rossi, A. (1969) "Sex equality: the Beginning of Ideology", *The Humanist*, pp. 3-6.

Rossi, A. (1982) *Feminists in Politics: A Panel Analysis of the First National Women's Conference*. Academic Press.

Rossi, G. (1983) *La Famiglia Assistita* (The assisted family). Angeli.

Roszak, B. and T. Roszak (eds) (1969) *Masculine-Feminine. Readings in Sexual Mythology and the Liberation of Women*. Harper and Row.

Rowbotham, S. (1974) *Hidden from History*. Pluto Press.

Rule, W. (1981) "Why women don't run: the critical contestual factors in women's legislative recruitment", *The Western Political Quarterly*, pp. 60-77.

Saarinen, A. (1982) "Towards an 'individuation politics': problems of strategy". *X World Congress of Sociology*, Mexico City, 16-21 August 1982 (manuscript).

Sacks, K. (1974) "Engels revisited: women, the organization of production, and private property", in Rosaldo, M.Z. and L. Lamphere, pp. 207-222.

Safilios-Rothchild, C. (1967), "A comparison of power structure and marital satisfaction in urban Greek and French families", *Journal of Marriage and the Family*, 29, pp. 345-352.

Safilios-Rothchild, C. (1969) "Family sociology or wives' sociology? A cross-cultural examination of decision-making", *Journal of Marriage and the Family*, 31, pp. 290-301.

Safilios-Rothchild, C. (1970) "The Study of family power structure: a review 1960-1969", *Journal of Marriage and the Family*, pp. 339-352.

Safilios-Rothchild, C. (ed.) (1972) *Toward a Sociology of Women*. Xerox College.

Salenson, W. and S. Lipset (eds) (1960) *Labor and Trade Unionism*. Wiley.

Sapiro, V. (1979) "Women's studies and political conflict" in Sherman A.J. and E. Beck, pp. 253-275.

Sapiro, V. (1984) *The Political Integration of Women*. University of Illinois Press.

Saraceno, C. (1984) "Il rapporto famiglia-stato, e i contributi dell'analisi 'on the women's side'" (The family-state relationship and the contributions of the analysis 'on the women's side'), *Inchiesta*, pp. 26-32.

Sarapata, A. (1977) *O zadowoleniu i niezadowoleniu z pracy* (Satisfaction and dissatisfaction related to work). Instytut Wydawniczy Centralney Rady Zwiazkow Zawodowych.

Sargent, L. (ed.) (1981) *Women and Revolution*. South End Press.

Sartin, P. (1967) "La femme, le travail et la politique dans les sociétés modernes" (Women, work and politics in modern society), *Res Publica*, pp. 111-121.

Sas, J. (1982) "Changes in the Life Patterns of Families in Hungary", in *Changes in the Life Patterns of Families in Europe*. European Coordination Centre for Research and Documentation in Social Sciences.

Sauser, W. and C.M. York (1978) "Sex differences in job satisfaction: a re-examination", *Personnel Psychology*, pp. 537-547.

Sayers, J. (1980) "Biological determination, psychology and the division of labour by sex", *International Journal of Women's Studies*, 3, pp. 241-260.

Scarpati, R. (1973) *La Condizione Giovanile in Italia* (The youth condition in Italy). Angeli.

Schelsky, H. (1957) *Die skeptische Generation* (The sceptical generation). Eugen Diederichs Verlag.

Scott, H. (1979) "Women in Eastern Europe", in Lipman-Blumen, J. and J. Bernard, pp.177-197.

Seccombe, W. (1973) "The housewife and her labour under capitalism", *New Left Review*, 83, pp. 3-24.

Seroni, A. (1981) *La Questione Femminile in Italia: 1970-1977* (The woman's question in Italy: 1970-1977). Editori Riuniti.

Sgritta, G.B. (1984) *Emarginazione, Dipendenza e Politica Sociale*. Angeli.

Sgritta, G.B. and A. Saporiti (1982) "Production and reproduction: a research framework for the analysis of the family in Italy", in *Changes in the Life Patterns of Families in Europe*. European Coordination Centre for Research and Documentation in Social Sciences.

Sherman, J.A. and E.T. Beck (eds) (1979) *The Prism of Sex*. Wisconsin University Press.

Siemienska, R. (1983a) "Local party leaders in Poland", *International Political Science Review*, 4, pp. 127-136.

Siemienska, R. (1983b) "Woman and the family in Poland", in Lupri, E., pp. 267-295.

Siemienska, R. (1983c) "Wzkazniki spolecznej i grupowej alienacji dzialaczy" (Indices of social and group alienation of leaders), in Wiatr, J., pp.302-308.

Siemienska, R. (1985a) "Women's work and gender equality in Poland: reality and its social perception", in Wolchik, S. and A. Meyer.

Siemienska, R. (1985b) "Introduction", in Siemienska, R. (ed.), pp. 281- 286.

Siemienska, R. (1985c) "Women's political participation and the 1980 crisis in Poland", in Siemienska R., pp. 332-346.

Siemienska, R. (ed.) (1985d) "Women in politics", *International Journal of Political Science*, 6, p. 3.

Siemienska, R. (1986) "Women and social movements in Poland", *Women and Politics*, 6. pp. 5-35.

Siemienska, R. (1987) "Women in leadership positions in Polish Public Administration". Paper presented at the conference organized by the Friedrich Ebert Stiftung and FGR UNESCO Committee, Bonn.

Siltanen, J. and M. Stanworth (1984a) "The politics of private woman and public man", in Siltanen, J. and M. Stanworth, pp. 185-208.

Siltanen J. and M. Stanworth (eds) (1984b) *Women and the Public Sphere.* Hutchinson.

Simard, C. (1984) "Changement et insertion des femmes dans le système politique" (Change and insertion of women in the political system), *Politique*, 5, pp. 27-49.

Sineau, M. (1986) *Des femmes en politique* (Women in politics). Report for the CNRS, Paris.

Smith, D.E. (1977) "Some implications of a sociology for women", in Glazer N. and H.Y. Waehrer, pp. 15-29.

Smith, D.E. (1979) "A sociology for women", in Sherman, J.A. and E.T. Beck, pp. 153-187.

Smith, L.M. (1974) "Women and the double standard: a feminist re-evaluation of volunteerism". *Annual Meeting of the Midwest Sociological Society* (manuscript).

Sokoloff, N.J. (1978) "Motherwork and working mothers", in Jaggar, A.M. and P.S. Rothenberg, pp. 259-266.

Sokolowska, M. (1981) "Women in decision-making elites: the case of Poland", in Epstein, C.F. and R.L. Coser, pp. 90-114.

Srole, L. (1956) "Social integration and certain corollaries", *American Sociological Review*, pp. 709-716.

Stacey, M. and M. Price (1981) *Women, Power and Politics.* Tavistock Publications.

Stewart, A.J. and D.G. Winter (1977) "The nature and causes of female suppression", *Signs*, 2, pp. 531-553.

Stolcke, V. (1984) "Women's labours: the naturalization of social inequality and women's subordination", in K. Young et al., pp. 159-177.

Sullerot, E. (1968) *Histoire et Sociologie du Travail Feminin* (History and sociology of female work). Denoel.

Sullerot, E. (1970) *La Femme dans le Monde Moderne* (Woman in the modern world). Hachette.

Szalai, A., P. Converse, P. Feldheim, E. Scheuch, and P. Stone (1972) *The Use of Time.* Mouton.

Talmon, Y. (1983) "Sex-Role Differentiation in an Equalitarian Society", in Palzi et al., pp. 8-26.

Tannenbaum, A., B. Kavcic, M.Rosner, M.Vianello, and G. Wieser (1974) *Industrial Hierarchy.* Jossey-Bass.

Thorne, B. and M. Yalom (eds) (1982) *Rethinking the Family*, Longman.

Tiger, M. L. and J. Shepher (1975) *Women in the Kibbutz.* Harcourt, Brace, Jovanovich.

Tilly, L.A. and J.W. Scott (1978) *Women, Work and Family.* Holt, Rinehart, and Winston.

Tresemer, D. (1976) "Assumptions made about gender roles", in M. Millman and R.M. Kanter, pp. 309-339.

Vajda, M. and A. Heller (1971) "Family structure and communism", *Telos*, pp. 99-111.

Verba, S. and N. H. Nie (1972) *Participation in America: Political Democracy and Social Equality.* Harper and Row.

Verba, S., N.H. Nie and J.O. Kim (1971) *The Modes of Political Participation: A Cross National Analysis.* Sage Publications.

Verba, S., N.H. Nie, and J.O. Kim (1978) *Participation and Political Equality: A Seven-Nation Comparison.* Cambridge University Press.

Vianello, M. and L.Caddeo (1985) "Women's political participation in Italy", in Siemienska, R. (ed).

Vroom, V.H. (1964) *Work and Motivation.* Wiley.

Wall, R. (1983) "Introduction", in Wall, R. et al.

Wall, R., J. Robin and P. Laslett (eds) (1983) *Family Forms in Historic Europe.* Cambridge University Press.

Waluk, J. (1965) *Praca i placa kobiet w polsce* (Women's work and wages). Ksiazka i Wiedza.

Watt, J. (1980) "Linkages between industrial radicalism and the domestic role among working women", *Sociological Review*, pp. 55-74.

Watts Powell, L., C.W. Brown and B. Hedges (1981) "Male and female differences in elite political participation: an examination of the effects of socioeconomic and familial variables", *Western Political Quarterly*, pp. 31-45.

Weber, Maria (1981) "Italy", in Lovenduski, J. and J. Hills (eds), pp. 182-207.

Weber, Maria, G. Odorisio Conti and G. Zincone (1984) "Une analyse du comportment politique des femmes en Europe" (An analysis of the European women's political behaviour) in Conseil de l'Europe, *La situation des femmes dans la vie politique.* Pt.I.

Weber, Max (1921) "Wirtschaft und Gesellschaft", in *Grundriss für Sozialökonomie* (Economy and society). Mohr.

Welch, S. (1977) "Women as political animals? A test of some explanations for male-female political participation differences", *American Journal of Political Science*, pp. 711-730.

Welch, S. (1978) "Recruitment of women to public office: a discrimination analysis", *Western Political Quarterly*, pp. 372-380.

Wheaton, R. (1975) "Family and kinship in Western Europe: the problem of the joint family household", *Journal of Interdisciplinary History*, pp. 604-628.
White, R.K. and R. Lippit (1960) *Autocracy and Democracy*. Harper.
Wiatr, J. (ed.) (1983) *Wladza lokalna w przededniu kryzysu* (Local authorities on the eve of crisis). Institute of Sociology, University of Warsaw.
Wieruszewski, R. (1975) *Rownosc kobiet i mezczyzn w Polsce Ludowej* (Equality of women and men in the Polish People's Republic). Wydawnictwo Poznanskie.
Wolchik, S.L. (1981) "Ideology and equality: the status of women in Eastern and Western Europe", *Comparative Political Studies*, pp. 445-476.
Wolchik, S. and A. Meyer (eds) (1985) *Woman, State and Party in Eastern Europe*. Duke University Press.
Wolfe, D.M. (1959) "Power and authority in the family" in Cartwright, D.
Wolk Feinstein, K. (1980) "Kindergartens, feminism and the professionalization of motherhood", *International Journal of Women's Studies*, 3, pp. 28-38.
Wolk Feinstein, K. (ed.)(1979) *Working Women and Families*. Sage Publications.
Women's Studies International Forum (1983) "The domestic ideal and the mobilization of womanpower in World War Two", pp. 401-412.
Young, K., C. Walkowitz and R. McCullogh (eds) (1984) *Of Marriage and the Market*. Routledge and Kegan Paul.
Young, M. and P. Willmott (1973) *The Symmetrical Family*. Routledge and Kegan Paul.

Statistical Literature

Benzecri, J.P. (1973) *Analyse des données*, 2 vols, Dunod.
Diday, E., J. Lemaire and J. Pouget (1982) *Eléments d'analyse des données*. Dunod.
Duncan, O. (1975) *Introduction to Structural Equation Models*. Academy Press.
Greenacre, M. (1984) *Theory and Application of Correspondence Analysis*. Academic Press.
Lebart, L., A. Morineau and A.W. Warwick (1984) *Multivariate Descriptive Statistical Analysis, Correspondence Analysis and Related Techniques for Large Matrices*. Wiley.
Leclerc, A. (1976) "Une étude de la relation entre une variable qualitative et un groupe de variables qualitatives", *International Statistical Review*, 44, pp. 241-248.
Tenenhaus, M. and W. Young (1985) "An analysis and synthesis of MCoA, optimal scaling, dual scaling, homogeneity analysis and other methods for quantifying categorical multivariate data", *Psychometrika*, 50, pp. 91-119.

INDEX OF NAMES

451
291
47
478
18
M
17
134
255
282
65
18